'This is a really splendid addition to the Law in Context series. Agnieszka Kubal has done us all a great service by showing, with meticulous socio-legal methodology, that Russian legality is much more complex than often supposed. In particular, immigration and refugee law, even in this authoritarian state, is not an empty shell, but can make a real difference through the activity of passionate and courageous advocates and activists – and even, on occasion, judges.'

Bill Bowring, Professor of Law, Director LLM/MA Human Rights, Birkbeck College, University of London

'We know too little about how law is experienced by the powerless. Kubal's book shines a welcome light on a corner of the Russian legal system that has been neglected for too long. She succeeds in capturing multiple points of view and weaves these empirical narratives together in a way that is reminiscent of Ewick and Silbey's *Common Place of Law*. Kubal's book does an admirable job of capturing the day-to-day reality of Russian courts and deserves to be read by anyone interested in comparative legal systems.'

Kathryn Hendley, William Voss-Bascom Professor of Law and Political Science, University of Wisconsin–Madison

'In this engaging, insightful and well-crafted ethnography, Kubal sheds light on the critical impact that the scarce resource of access to justice and to dedicated lawyers can make in immigrants' lives – in Russia and elsewhere. Highly recommended for academics and practitioners alike.'

Cecilia Menjívar, Professor and Dorothy L. Meier Social Equities Chair, Department of Sociology, UCLA

'Migration is one of the most pressing challenges that Europe faces now. Kubal produces a methodologically sound and empirically impressive study of contemporary Russian experience in this area. Looking beyond stereotypes and legislative texts, she tells the stories of people affected – above all, migrants and those who try to defend them from the system.'

Dr Sergey Golubok, Human Rights lawyer, member of the St Petersburg Bar Association and the European Criminal Bar Association

'This book – because Russia is one of the major but still under-researched immigration countries – is hugely important in three ways: it addresses a crucial research gap in migration studies, it is an excellent contribution to the study of policy implementation and it is an important case study on Russian politics in general.'

Franck Düvell, Head of Migration Department, German Centre for Integration and Migration Research, Berlin

'A fascinating and nuanced ethnographic account of the legal experiences of migrants in Russia, along with the struggles of their lawyers, migration officials and judges hearing their cases. Many migrants suffered from the application of laws aimed at their control, if only because of the fetishization of legal documents or the quasi-criminalization of minor violations. Yet the noble efforts of the (usually female) lawyers helping migrants and the judges' occasional acceptance of human rights arguments led to happy endings for others. While the regulation of migration in Russia resembled practices found in other countries, its social meaning made the Russian amalgam unique, a conclusion illustrated by vivid personal stories.'

Peter H. Solomon, Jr, Emeritus Professor of Political Science, Law and Criminology, The Munk School of Global Affairs and Public Policy, University of Toronto

'There are two ways to look at the operation of the Russian judiciary. One is to focus on miscarriages of justice in salient and often politically motivated cases. The other is to dismiss such cases and to argue that, in day-to-day enforcement, the rule of law is being maintained. This compelling account demonstrates how the Russian administration and judiciary practise arbitrariness against vulnerable migrants on a daily basis. While the study is limited to immigration, the situation in other fields of public law is no different, so this work should generate a broad interest.'

Krill Koroteev, Legal Director, Human Rights Centre 'Memorial', Moscow, Russia

'This book constitutes a unique resource of immigration and asylum law and its enforcement in Russia; it is empirically rich and analytically nuanced. Kubal reveals who migrants and asylum seekers in Russia are, why they keep coming to the country and how the authorities deal with them. Sometimes, these are stories of life and survival; sometimes, the stories of broken hopes and disappointments on immigration trails. I highly recommend Kubal's work as essential to read for academics and migration policy-makers, but also – given its engaging style – the book should be of interest to a general audience.'

Olga Gulina, Ph.D. in Law, Ph.D. in Migration Studies, founder and CEO of the RUSMPI UG – Institute on Migration Policy

Immigration and Refugee Law in Russia

Immigration and Refugee Law in Russia confronts the issue of access to justice and the realization of human rights for migrants and refugees in Russia. It focuses on everyday experiences of immigration and refugee laws and how they work 'in action' in Russia. This investigation presupposes that the reality is much more complex than is generally assumed, as it is mediated by people's varied positionalities.

Agnieszka Kubal's primary focus is on people, their stories and experiences: migrants, asylum seekers, refugees, immigration lawyers, Russian judges and Federal Migration Service officers. These actors speak with different voices, profess different ideologies and hold opposite worldviews; what they hold in common is their importance to our understanding of how law works in everyday life. By this focus on individual views and opinions, Kubal highlights the complexity and nuance of everyday experiences of the law, breaking away from the portrayal of Russia as a legal and ideological monolith.

Agnieszka Kubal is a lecturer at the Department of Social Sciences, University College London. She is a sociologist and migration studies scholar. She was educated in Kraków, Exeter and Oxford, with a postdoctoral spell at Harvard. Her DPhil looked at Polish migrants' experiences of the British legal environment post-2004 EU Enlargement and was later published. Agnieszka's most recent research projects focused on human rights and access to justice for migrants and refugees in Russia, one of the largest destinations for migrants globally. She is a member of the Socio-Legal Studies Association and author of numerous publications in high-ranking journals, such as *Law and Society Review*, *Law and Social Inquiry* and *Migration Studies*.

The Law in Context Series

Editors: William Twining (*University College London*),
Maksymilian Del Mar (*Queen Mary, University of London*) and
Bronwen Morgan (*University of New South Wales*).

Since 1970 the Law in Context series has been at the forefront of the movement to broaden the study of law. It has been a vehicle for the publication of innovative scholarly books that treat law and legal phenomena critically in their social, political and economic contexts from a variety of perspectives. The series particularly aims to publish scholarly legal writing that brings fresh perspectives to bear on new and existing areas of law taught in universities. A contextual approach involves treating legal subjects broadly, using materials from other social sciences, and from any other discipline that helps to explain the operation in practice of the subject under discussion. It is hoped that this orientation is at once more stimulating and more realistic than the bare exposition of legal rules. The series includes original books that have a different emphasis from traditional legal textbooks, while maintaining the same high standards of scholarship. They are written primarily for undergraduate and graduate students of law and of other disciplines, but will also appeal to a wider readership. In the past, most books in the series have focused on English law, but recent publications include books on European law, globalisation, transnational legal processes, and comparative law.

Books in the Series

Acosta: *The National versus the Foreigner in South America*
Ali: *Modern Challenges to Islamic Law*
Alyagon Darr: *Plausible Crime Stories: The Legal History of Sexual Offences in Mandate Palestine*
Anderson, Schum & Twining: *Analysis of Evidence*
Ashworth: *Sentencing and Criminal Justice*
Barton & Douglas: *Law and Parenthood*
Beecher-Monas: *Evaluating Scientific Evidence: An Interdisciplinary Framework for Intellectual Due Process*
Bell: *French Legal Cultures*
Bercusson: *European Labour Law*
Birkinshaw: *European Public Law*
Birkinshaw: *Freedom of Information: The Law, the Practice and the Ideal*
Brownsword & Goodwin: *Law and the Technologies of the Twenty-First Century: Text and Materials*
Cane & Goudkamp: *Atiyah's Accidents, Compensation and the Law*
Clarke & Kohler: *Property Law: Commentary and Materials*
Collins: *The Law of Contract*
Collins, Ewing & McColgan: *Labour Law*
Cowan: *Housing Law and Policy*
Cranston: *Legal Foundations of the Welfare State*

Darian-Smith: *Laws and Societies in Global Contexts: Contemporary Approaches*
Dauvergne: *Making People Illegal: What Globalisation Means for Immigration and Law*
Davies: *Perspectives on Labour Law*
Dembour: *Who Believes in Human Rights?: Reflections on the European Convention*
de Sousa Santos: *Toward a New Legal Common Sense*
Diduck: *Law's Families*
Estella: *Legal Foundations of EU Economic Governance*
Fortin: *Children's Rights and the Developing Law*
Ghai & Woodman: *Practising Self-Government: A Comparative Study of Autonomous Regions*
Glover-Thomas: *Reconstructing Mental Health Law and Policy*
Gobert & Punch: *Rethinking Corporate Crime*
Goldman: *Globalisation and the Western Legal Tradition: Recurring Patterns of Law and Authority*
Haack: *Evidence Matters: Science, Proof, and Truth in the Law*
Harlow & Rawlings: *Law and Administration*
Harris: *An Introduction to Law*
Harris, Campbell & Halson: *Remedies in Contract and Tort*
Harvey: *Seeking Asylum in the UK: Problems and Prospects*
Hervey & McHale: *European Union Health Law: Themes and Implications*
Hervey & McHale: *Health Law and the European Union*
Holder & Lee: *Environmental Protection, Law and Policy: Text and Materials*
Jackson & Summers: *The Internationalisation of Criminal Evidence: Beyond the Common Law and Civil Law Traditions*
Kostakopoulou: *The Future Governance of Citizenship*
Lewis: *Choice and the Legal Order: Rising above Politics*
Likosky: *Transnational Legal Processes: Globalisation and Power Disparities*
Likosky: *Law, Infrastructure and Human Rights*
Lunney: *A History of Australian Tort Law 1901–1945: England's Obedient Servant?*
Maughan & Webb: *Lawyering Skills and the Legal Process*
McGlynn: *Families and the European Union: Law, Politics and Pluralism*
Moffat: *Trusts Law: Text and Materials*
Monti: *EC Competition Law*
Morgan: *Contract Law Minimalism: A Formalist Restatement of Commercial Contract Law*
Morgan & Yeung: *An Introduction to Law and Regulation: Text and Materials*
Nicola & Davies: *EU Law Stories: Contextual and Critical Histories of European Jurisprudence*
Norrie: *Crime, Reason and History: A Critical Introduction to Criminal Law*
O'Dair: *Legal Ethics: Text and Materials*
Oliver: *Common Values and the Public–Private Divide*
Oliver & Drewry: *The Law and Parliament*
Picciotto: *International Business Taxation*
Probert: *The Changing Legal Regulation of Cohabitation, 1600–2010*
Reed: *Internet Law: Text and Materials*
Richardson: *Law, Process and Custody*
Roberts & Palmer: *Dispute Processes: ADR and the Primary Forms of Decision-Making*

Rowbottom: *Democracy Distorted: Wealth, Influence and Democratic Politics*
Sauter: *Public Services in EU Law*
Scott & Black: *Cranston's Consumers and the Law*
Seneviratne: *Ombudsmen: Public Services and Administrative Justice*
Seppänen: *Ideological Conflict and the Rule of Law in Contemporary China*
Siems: *Comparative Law, 2nd Edition*
Stapleton: *Product Liability*
Stewart: *Gender, Law and Justice in a Global Market*
Tamanaha: *Law as a Means to an End: Threat to the Rule of Law*
Turpin & Tomkins: *British Government and the Constitution: Text and Materials*
Twining: *Globalisation and Legal Theory*
Twining: *Rethinking Evidence: Exploratory Essays*
Twining: *General Jurisprudence: Understanding Law from a Global Perspective*
Twining: *Human Rights, Southern Voices: Francis Deng, Abdullahi An-Na'im, Yash Ghai and Upendra Baxi*
Twining: *Jurist in Context*
Twining & Miers: *How to Do Things with Rules*
Ward: *A Critical Introduction to European Law*
Ward: *Law, Text, Terror*
Ward: *Shakespeare and Legal Imagination*
Wells & Quick: *Lacey, Wells and Quick: Reconstructing Criminal Law*
Zander: *Cases and Materials on the English Legal System*
Zander: *The Law-Making Process*

International Journal of Law in Context: A Global Forum for Interdisciplinary Legal Studies

The *International Journal of Law in Context* is the companion journal to the Law in Context book series and provides a forum for interdisciplinary legal studies and offers intellectual space for ground-breaking critical research. It publishes contextual work about law and its relationship with other disciplines including but not limited to science, literature, humanities, philosophy, sociology, psychology, ethics, history and geography. More information about the journal and how to submit an article can be found at http://journals.cambridge.org/ijc

Immigration and Refugee Law in Russia

Socio-Legal Perspectives

AGNIESZKA KUBAL
University College London

CAMBRIDGE
UNIVERSITY PRESS

CAMBRIDGE
UNIVERSITY PRESS

University Printing House, Cambridge CB2 8BS, United Kingdom

One Liberty Plaza, 20th Floor, New York, NY 10006, USA

477 Williamstown Road, Port Melbourne, VIC 3207, Australia

314–321, 3rd Floor, Plot 3, Splendor Forum, Jasola District Centre, New Delhi – 110025, India

79 Anson Road, #06–04/06, Singapore 079906

Cambridge University Press is part of the University of Cambridge.

It furthers the University's mission by disseminating knowledge in the pursuit of education, learning, and research at the highest international levels of excellence.

www.cambridge.org
Information on this title: www.cambridge.org/9781108417891
DOI: 10.1017/9781108283656

First published 2019

Printed and bound in Great Britain by Clays Ltd, Elcograf S.p.A.

A catalogue record for this publication is available from the British Library.

Library of Congress Cataloging-in-Publication Data
Names: Kubal, Agnieszka, 1983- author.
Title: Immigration and refugee law in Russia : socio-legal perspectives / Agniezka Kubal, University College London.
Description: Cambridge, United Kingdom ; New York, NY, USA : Cambridge University Press, 2019. | Series: The law in context series | Includes bibliographical references and index.
Identifiers: LCCN 2018042758 | ISBN 9781108417891 (hardback : alk. paper)
Subjects: LCSH: Emigration and immigration law–Russia (Federation). | Refugees–Legal status, laws, etc.–Russia (Federation).
Classification: LCC KLB3023 .K83 2019 | DDC 342.4708/2–dc23
LC record available at https://lccn.loc.gov/2018042758

ISBN 978-1-108-41789-1 Hardback

To Ashish, Stefan and Eleanor
With Love

Contents

Figures

Tables

Acknowledgements

First and foremost, I am grateful to Marina Kurkchiyan, my mentor, the most meticulous reader and first critic of the manuscript for this book. I am thankful for her attention to detail, honesty and friendship. This book project hugely benefited from discussions at a seminar in December 2015 at the Centre for Socio-Legal Studies, University of Oxford, and helpful comments by Kathryn Hendley, Peter H. Solomon Jr. and Lauren A. McCarthy. I would like to thank Jeffrey Kahn, who provided detailed and invaluable comments on Chapter 6. Another part of this book was developed during my Visiting Fellowship at Davis Center for Russian and Eurasian Studies, Harvard University in 2016, where I benefited from comments at the Fellows' Seminar by Timothy J. Colton and Kelly O'Neill, as well as informal discussions with colleagues. I am grateful to Dan Healey, Paul Chaisty and Nicolette Makovicky for their encouragement upon presenting this work at a seminar at the Russian and East European Studies Centre at Wolfson College in September 2017, and for their hospitality during my departmental lectureship at the School of Interdisciplinary Area Studies, University of Oxford. My warm and extended thanks go to Margaret O'Brien and Claire Cameron at the Department of Social Science, University College London, for their gentle methodological encouragement of making this book more about people and less about law. Collecting data for this manuscript would not have been possible without the generous funding of the British Academy Post-doctoral Fellowship hosted at the Centre for Socio-Legal Studies, University of Oxford (2013–2017), and the John Fell OUP Fund small awards grant.

My special thanks go to my fieldwork hosts in Moscow and St. Petersburg: Svetlana Alekseevna Gannushkina, the chairwoman of the Civic Assistance Committee and a nine-time nominee to the Nobel Peace Prize, as well as personally one of the most inspiring women I know. I am immensely grateful to the late Elena Ryabinina for her kindness and exemplary sense of duty and for putting me in touch, just before her death in 2014, with her *Three Musketeers* – human rights lawyers, who continue her great work – Daria Trenina, Nadezhda Ermolayeva, Eleonora Davidyan and Kirill Zharinov. I am grateful to all the migrants, asylum seekers and refugees in Moscow who welcomed me into their lives and generously shared their incredible, often painful, sometimes uplifting and hopeful stories of 'dealing with the law'. I am indebted to a number of other human rights, immigration and refugee lawyers: Olga Tseytlina, Natalya Golovanchuk, Roza Magomedova, Irina Biryukova, Kirill Koroteev, Maxim Krupsky, Illarion Vasilyev, Ekaterina Raeva and Sergey Golubok for the interviews and for allowing me to observe their work. My special thanks go to Elena Burtina for her openness and trust, Leila Rogozina, Marina Lexina, Evgeniya Lyozova, Stasya Denisova and Konstantin Troitskiy; the translators: Muiz Aldzhdail, Basel Haj Ismail, Naser Nahim, Fahim Qazizada; and my fellow volunteers: Agnès Blais and Sarah Moode. I would like to thank the anonymous Federal Migration Service lawyers who introduced me to a perspective from 'the other side of the barricade', and to various Russian judges whose cases I could observe. Finally, my profound thanks go to Valentina Chupik, a fearless *pro bono* lawyer with a bottomless heart. May this book be my humble testimony to all your important work.

Note on Transliteration

Transliteration of Russian language follows the Library of Congress system, with the exception of spellings that are common in English-language sources.

Acronyms

AEDPA	Antiterrorism and Effective Death Penalty Act
CAO	Code of Administrative Offences
CIS	Commonwealth of Independent States
ECHR	European Convention of Human Rights
ECtHR	European Court of Human Rights (Strasbourg Court)
FMS	Federal Migration Service (Federal'naya Migratsionnaya Sluzhba)
FSB	Federal Security Service (Federal'naia Sluzhba Bezopasnosti)
GUVM MVD	Main Directorate for Migration of the Ministry of Interior of Russia (Glavnoye Upravleniye po Voprosam Migratsii MVD Rossii)
IIRIRA	Illegal Immigration Reform and Immigrant Responsibility Act
INA	Immigration and Nationality Act
MVD	Ministry of Interior (Ministerstvo Vnutrennikh del)
NGO	non-governmental organization
RF	Russian Federation
Rosstat	Federal State Statistical Service (Federal'naia Sluzhba Gosudarstvennoi Statistiki)
RVP	Temporary Residence Permit (Razresheniye na vremennoye prozhivaniye)
UNHCR	United Nations High Commissioner for Refugees
VnZh	Permanent Residence Permit (Vid na zhitel'stvo)

Table of Laws and Cases

International Conventions

ECtHR Cases

Domestic Laws

Russian Federation

United Kingdom

United States of America

Domestic Cases (USA)

Supreme Court Regulations (Russian Federation)

Constitutional Court Decisions (Russian Federation)

1

Socio-Legal Perspectives on Immigration and Refugee Law in Russia

There were still heaps of snow on the sides of the pavement when I arrived in Moscow for fieldwork. At the NGO where I was to start my observations I was welcomed by Muiz, an asylum seeker from Syria, who was staffing the reception desk. He spoke perfect Russian; he invited me to come in and showed me to the lawyers' office. There was a long queue spanning the adjacent waiting room and the corridor; the lawyers were busy seeing to their clients behind the closed doors. I did not dare enter, so I joined the queue. I did not realize then that standing in line would become the leitmotiv of my field research on the everyday experiences of the law, human rights and access to justice for migrants and refugees in Russia.

'Devushka podozhdite' ('Girl, do wait, please') are some of the first words I heard, later, in the hallways of the Federal Migration Service (FMS) local field offices, where I accompanied migrants to submit asylum claims, applications for work permits or to make enquiries about the outcome of an administrative review against their entry bar. There was always a very high chance of hearing 'Devushka podozhdite' when attempting to enter the office of the clerk of the court, where I joined migrants submitting appeals in their cases, reviewing their case files or enquiring about final judgments. 'Podozhdite v koridore' ('Do wait in the corridor, please') was also part of the unwritten code of conduct ahead of the various court hearings, known to all parties of the legal proceedings: migrants, asylum seekers, their lawyers, court interpreters, even the FMS legal representatives. 'Devushka podozhdite' I would also hear at the entrance to other institutions connected with migration in Moscow, where I attempted to gather data or conduct interviews for my fieldwork. Except, as it turned out, in this NGO.

The news about my arrival must have spread quickly among the staff. At one point, one firm hand of Elena, the vice-chairwoman of the NGO, grabbed my shoulder while the other opened the door to the lawyers' office. Her trusting and kind eyes seemed to say: 'Why are you waiting, silly? Just enter.' She announced me to the lawyers and made me sit on the chair in one corner of the office. The room was fairly small and staffed with three lawyers consulting their clients – asylum seekers from all over the world (mainly East and West Africa, Central Asia, the Middle East and Ukraine) and migrant workers, primarily from Central Asian and other former Soviet Union republics. I had to sit so close to one of the lawyers that even taking out my notebook seemed intrusive to the dynamics of the intimate relations unfolding in front of my eyes in the consultation room. On this first day, I only observed. Later, I managed to make myself less conspicuous, and perhaps even helpful by volunteering at the photocopier, interpreting or running small office errands for the lawyers.

It is therefore with the trust showed to me by the NGO staff that this book adventure began. . .

Socio-Legal Perspectives on Migration

Russia is in the top five migrants receiving countries worldwide (after the United States, Saudi Arabia and Germany), with 11.6 million foreign-born people currently residing in its territory (UNPD 2017). Sergey Abashin supplements this number with another 11 million migrants who live in Russia de facto permanently but do not apply for a residence permit or citizenship (Abashin 2017: 16; see also Schenk 2018: 1). They have come to Russia primarily from the post-Soviet countries in Central Asia (Uzbekistan, Tajikistan, Kyrgyzstan) and other CIS states.[1] Seasonal and undocumented economic migration was part of the Soviet reality, but this reached new levels and took different forms after the break-up of the Soviet Union (Pilkington 1998). Unrestricted cross-border movements between Russia and its 'near-abroad' countries of Central Asia facilitated the migration of desperate people leaving their economically destitute and often politically repressive home countries in search of survival. Migrants account for about 3–4 per cent of the employed population in Russia (if undocumented migrants are included, this share grows to about 7 per cent) (Denisenko and Varshavskaya 2013: 2; Vakulenko and Leukhin 2017: 84). These workers are mostly engaged in the construction industry, agriculture, trade and services. Every large state-funded project, such as building venues and infrastructure necessary for Russia to host the 2014 Winter Olympic Games in Sochi or the 2018 World Cup, is reliant on the extensive employment of migrants. Labour migrants form a group diverse across many variables, including race, ethnicity, religion, legal status and acquisition of Russian citizenship. The migratory movements between Central Asia and Russia have, by now, become intrinsically linked to wider processes of social change and development in the region (Castles 2010; de Haas 2010; 2012). Not only individual families, but whole communities 'left behind' are often dependent on remittances sent by migrants (Buckley and Hofmann 2012). Kyrgyz Republic and Tajikistan in 2016 ranked second and fourth in

[1] Formed in 1991, the CIS – Commonwealth of Independent States – consists of 12 of the former republics of the Soviet Union (Armenia, Azerbaijan, Belarus, Georgia, Kazakhstan, Kyrgyzstan, Moldova, Russia, Tajikistan, Turkmenistan, Ukraine and Uzbekistan).

the list of the main remittance-dependent countries worldwide – with personal money transfers constituting 30.4 and 26.9 per cent of their respective GDPs (World Bank 2016). Remittances sent by migrants constitute an inseparable part of family budgets; this money is primarily used for consumption (daily expenses, house repairs) and small investments, mainly in livestock (Aitieva 2015). Moving to Russia to find work became a culturally ingrained rite of passage towards adulthood for many young Kyrgyz, Tajik and Uzbek migrants (see, e.g. Maier 2014) – a testimony to a specific 'migration culture' developing in the region (Buckley et al. 2008; Bahovadinova 2016). Russia, by virtue of being an important global political player, has also been attracting a steady stream of refugees: from Afghanistan, Iraq, Central Asia and, more recently, Syria, the Middle East, Africa and Eastern Ukraine.

In the area of migration studies, the existing scholarship provides evidence of immigrants' and refugees' incorporation and responses to specific host-country laws and policies, but this is predominantly limited to the North American or Western European experiences (Portes and Bach 1985; Portes and Zhou 1993; Hagan 1994; Alba and Nee 1997; Coutin 1998, 2000, 2002; Hagan 1998; Menjívar 2000, 2006, 2014a, 2014b; Hein and Beger 2001a, 2001b; de Genova 2004; Kubal 2009, 2012, 2013, 2014; Menjívar and Abrego 2012; Salcido and Menjívar 2012). Russia remains, in this respect, a true *terra incognita* (for recent notable exceptions see Reeves (2013, 2015); Davé (2014); Light (2016); Agadjanian et al. (2017); Buckley (2018); Schenk (2018)). Modern Russia (beyond the immediate post-Soviet period) is also largely absent or barely mentioned in global surveys about migration (Cohen 1995; Castles et al. 2014; Hollifield et al. 2014). By situating the Russian case in a comparative perspective with the United States and other major migrant-receiving jurisdictions in Europe, this book demonstrates how the evolution of Russian immigration law in 'the everyday work of producing, defining and precluding both movement and connection' (Coutin et al. 2002: 801) follows a well-established logic of more global trends of migration governance. Russia's fairly unexplored though complex legal environment and visa-free regime with near-abroad countries are also fruitful avenues through which to interrogate broader questions about the growing salience of 'mixed' flows of people (Van Hear 2004; Van Hear et al. 2009) and the persistent separation of the analytical categories of 'migrant workers' and 'refugees', even though the empirical boundaries between them have long been recognized as continuously porous (Kay and Miles 1988; Karatani 2005; Long 2013; Kubal 2016a). Comparing the outcomes of my ethnographic study in Russia with data collected earlier from Western countries and the literature developed there, this book questions whether what happens to migrants and refugees in Russia is as much in contrast with the experiences of migrants and refugees in Europe and America as many observers tend to assume.

Russia's immigration policy and immigration law have recently started attracting increased academic attention (Riazantsev 2007; Ivakhnyuk 2009; Reeves 2013, 2015, 2016; Davé 2014; Ivakhniuk 2014, 2015; Malakhov 2014;

Light 2016; Abashin 2017; Buckley 2018; Schenk 2018). While the immigration controls in the USSR were distinct, in the sense that the state over-ambitiously aimed to fully regularize internal migration by integrating it into a system of administrative controls and localized social policies dependent upon residence registration (Light 2012), modern Russia seems rather to subscribe to a more global trend towards 'irregularization' and deportability, leading to a proliferation of insecure migration statuses (Kubal 2016b; Schenk 2018). At the same time, researchers, reporters and human rights activists have extensively documented the difficult living and working conditions of labour migrants in Russia (Yudina 2005; Greenberg 2007; Doolotkeldieva 2008; Ruget and Usmanalieva 2008, 2010; Round and Kuznetsova 2016; Urinboyev 2016). The list of ways in which their human rights are abused is long: discrimination at work, such as routinely being denied wages; failure to provide required contracts; unsafe working conditions (Human Rights Watch 2009); racial profiling for document checks when using public transport (Open Society Institute 2006); extortion of bribes by the police (Chupik 2015); and other extra-legal strategies aimed at controlling their movements (Light 2010, 2012; Kondakov 2017). Judged by the recent reporting of human rights organizations, in some cases economic migration in Russia is turning into modern slavery (Round and Kuznetsova 2016; Buckley 2018). These accounts intersect with some long-established assumptions about Russia's exceptionalism also in the broader legal sphere: lack of the rule of law, corruption and legal nihilism (Ledeneva 1998, 2006, 2008; Kurkchiyan 2003, 2009; McAulley et al. 2006). Much of the academic literature, analytical reports, mass media and even common wisdom suggest that the justice system in Russia is unreliable. It does not provide equal access to justice, it does not treat its litigants fairly, law enforcement is fortuitous and 'telephone law' still prevail in different court settings (Pastukhov 2002; Solomon 2005; Transparency International 2007; Sakwa 2009, 2010).

But perhaps the full picture is not so uniform and bleak? The main idea behind this book was to find out how the immigration and refugee laws work 'in action' in Russia. How are they experienced in everyday life by the different actors involved in the migration process? Can migrants and refugees access justice and stand for their rights in Russia? How and when? Under what conditions? What is the role of human rights and migration lawyers in mediating access to justice for migrants and refugees? How do Russian judges decide cases involving migrants and asylum seekers, and with what consequences for the litigants involved? Are these experiences so much different to what is happening in other major migrant-receiving countries, mainly the United States and those of Europe?

Researching Immigration and Refugee Laws in Everyday Life

I went to Russia guided by these (and other) questions, with an open mind and an open heart. In my attempted thick description (Geertz, 1975, 1983) of

Russian immigration and refugee legal regimes I wanted to document the different processes, experiences, encounters, pieces of legislation, legal texts, court cases and forms of discourse that make up the lived experiences of the law. In this book, I therefore trace and map the experiences of migrants, immigration lawyers, asylum seekers, refugees, Russian judges and FMS officers. These actors often speak with completely different voices, profess different ideologies and hold diametrically opposite worldviews; however, the thing they share in common is their centrality to understanding migration processes in Russia.

The turn to *everyday life* in the study of immigrants, refugees and state law enforcement officials has long been observed in socio-legal studies in 'Western' academic writing.[2] For example, Roberto de Genova examined extensively the everyday experiences of migrants living under conditions of deportability in the United States (de Genova 2002). Nando Sigona focused on lived experiences of the stigma of illegality in the United Kingdom (Sigona 2012). In my earlier work I looked at how immigrants experience the criminalization of immigration law under different European jurisdictions (Kubal 2014). These pieces of research were founded upon systematic data collection referred to among methodologists as in-depth qualitative and ethnographic fieldwork: first-hand observations supported by intensive, carefully planned interviews with a number of crucial actors. Conversely, much of the analogical research in Russia still suffers from quantitative bias – a conventional approach fixated on quantitative indices and large-scale surveys giving the impression of 'objectivity' but no voice to those whose lives are shaped by the law (see Sarat and Kearns (1995); for a noteworthy and recent exception see Reeves (2013) and Hendley (2017)).

I position this book vis-à-vis much of the scholarship solely referring to legal and social quantitative indices (e.g. the World Bank's Rule of Law index), arguing for an interpretative, in-depth understanding of the various social processes on the ground. Many of the indices, *ceteris paribus*, create an illusion of comparability, as in the process of data collection inconsistent evidence is being used. The 'expert' reports that feed into these indices often, due to the lack of reliable empirical data (how to measure corruption in courts?), operationalize the various indicators on the bases of 'general knowledge' and media coverage. This results in much of the research becoming an unsatisfactory litany of what everybody already knows about Russia, resulting in explanations that strike familiar cords with conspiracies already known to many (Umberto Eco would say this is what makes them believable) – endemic corruption, deeply entrenched patrimonial state, presided over by Putin's steely, unflinching gaze. This description may not be inaccurate, but it is profoundly

[2] I use Western as a heuristic (meaning liberal-democratic) to enable comparison with other main migrant-receiving countries – the United States, United Kingdom and Western European countries – and the scholarship developed there.

incomplete. I think much of the scholarship that reproduces negative myths about Russia is still rooted in the Cold War Sovietology (and its daughter, Kremlinology), which as the 'scientific' study of politics and policies of the Soviet Union, continue to dictate the legitimate ways of 'doing research on Russia'. Russia is orientalized – dark, secretive, sensual and corrupt (for a variation of this argument, see Hendley (2017: 222)).

In order not to reproduce the stereotypes and negative myths about Russia, I conducted my fieldwork in a variety of settings triangulating between different – sometimes conflicting – sources of information. I spent over five months in Russia in 2014, conducted a couple of shorter trips in 2013, and kept in close contact with most of my core informants (both legal professionals and lay people) upon my return.

First, I conducted participatory, long-term observations in a number of Russian NGOs, legal aid clinics and organizations that help immigrants and refugees in Russia with their legal problems regarding status determination, residence and access to the labour market. The lawyers, social workers and members of these organizations also represent immigrants and refugees in courts, in disputes with employers or with the state immigration agencies like the FMS. Over several months, I volunteered in these organizations in a variety of roles. I sometimes worked as an office clerk or an interpreter from English to Russian during the interviews with refugees from the Middle East or Anglophone Africa. On other days, I shadowed the lawyers when they were representing the clients of those NGOs in domestic courts and assisted with writing submissions to the European Court of Human Rights (ECtHR) in more serious cases. Throughout these several months, I observed the interactions between the lawyers, employees of the NGOs and their clients. These daily observations, supplemented by in-depth interviews with a selected number of representatives of the NGOs, migrant organizations, legal professionals and lawyers,[3] were informative about the grass-roots level of implementation of immigration law and its everyday experiences – the 'nuts and bolts' of the refugee status determination procedure in Russia, and its current trends and directions. These observations satisfied my curiosity as to the role the above-mentioned institutions play in mediating immigrants' and refugees' access to justice in Russia and the experiences of handling claims and complaints, their outcomes and consequences.

Second, I often accompanied migrants and refugees – the clients of these NGOs – during their reluctant visits to state immigration agencies like the FMS, to submit an application for a refugee status, renew their temporary asylum, attend an interview as part of the status determination procedure or to clarify the questions regarding one's residence permit in Russia. These were usually whole-day or half-day trips due to the leitmotiv of waiting, which I alluded to in the opening vignette. Waiting in line, sitting in the corridor

[3] Overall, I conducted 50 interviews. For the full list of informants (anonymized), see Appendix 1.

proved, however, conducive to gathering rich empirical data: I could observe the dynamics between the FMS officers and the migrants, asylum seekers and other FMS officers, as well as ancillary staff – clerks and interpreters. Migrants, whom I accompanied, were usually my guides to these different interactions; they painstakingly explained to me who was who, who was important, with whom we should talk, and whom we should ideally avoid. During these hours in the corridors of the FMS offices, I also met with other migrants and asylum seekers, learned about their stories, migratory journeys, families and plans for the future. They often shared with me the intricate details of their individual petitions to the FMS. Upon entering the concrete FMS offices, I could observe the interactions between the FMS officers and their clients, the modes of assessment of their cases, the type of advice given and potential outcomes. Sometimes I was told I was not welcome, but more often than not the FMS officers treated me as a curious distraction to their daily business, and were largely willing to engage and talk with me.

Third, I conducted a three-month ethnographic study in a sample of low-level courts and courts of appeal in Moscow (district courts, Moscow City court and Greater Moscow *oblast* court). This was informative about the nature of cases when migrants, refugees or their representatives mobilized the law – either in challenging the alleged immigration law violations resulting in administrative removal (expulsion) orders, appealing the decisions of the FMS regarding their refugee status or complaining about unauthorized issuance of the entry bar by the specific FMS territorial unit. The observations of the interactions in the courtroom gave first-hand information on the type and volume of immigration law cases, how the migrants and refugees were treated in court and about their ability to defend themselves. The actual observations of the different cases were closely linked to the hours spent in the halls of justice awaiting the hearings. That again provided an opportunity to engage and build rapport with the different actors of the legal process – immigration lawyers, migrant-defendants and FMS legal representatives – who were also waiting in line for the hearings to commence. Through informal conversations with judges, I have learned how the system views migrant-litigants and how it responds to their grievances.

Fourth, I analysed a number of judgments from the Russian domestic courts at different levels of jurisdiction in immigration and refugee cases. I have obtained the written texts in a number of ways: mainly I received copies of the judgments from the immigration lawyers; sometimes I accessed the judgments directly as they were available on the courts' websites. They originate not only from the five months of 2014 when I was actually in Russia, but cover the years 2014–2018, when I continued to maintain electronic or telephone contact with the lawyers. The analysis of the different judgments provided the crucial empirical material to support my argument about the 'case file' versus the 'human rights' logics that asymmetrically unfold in immigration and refugee cases in Russia (see Kubal 2018). Out of a collection of around 100 judgments,

35 refer to human rights.[4] While this picture is therefore by no means generalizable, it nevertheless offers important qualitative and discursive insights into the use (and absence) of human rights arguments in immigration and refugee law cases. I accompanied the textual analysis of domestic court judgments with collecting and reading a number of ECtHR judgments against Russia in immigration and refugee law cases. These judgments mainly stem from the *Garabayev* group of cases,[5] which spans more than 80 cases decided by the Strasbourg Court between 2007 and 2018.

Finally, my regular observations in the NGOs, FMS offices, courts and the analyses of written court judgments were supported by in-depth interviews with migrants themselves, sometimes in more formal settings, sometimes less structured and less formal (e.g. at social gatherings or at homes). This book thereby also strives to give a voice to those whose lives are shaped by the law, and discusses immigrants' and refugees' everyday life experiences of immigration and/or refugee law, the intricate strategies of living under its shadow, but also the practices of challenging it. The interviews included in this book reach beyond the straightforward evidence and legal argumentation of a case and inquire into the background of the problem at hand, the various assumptions and expectations of the parties involved, and the personal hopes and fears of each respondent. This is not to say that I discard the quantitative evidence; I rely on the statistical and macro-trends as the first step of the enquiry, with each of the chapters extending it with in-depth qualitative, ethnographic explanations and analysis.

In the pages of this book, the reader will get to know the story of a Kurdish-Syrian family from Iraq with four young children, who spent nearly two months in the transit zone of Sheremetyevo Airport as the Russian authorities decided to prioritize criminal prosecution of their alleged illegal entry over processing their asylum claims. The intervention of the charismatic chairwoman of the legal NGO and the work of her lawyers led to the family being ultimately allowed into Russia and granted temporary asylum. The reader will learn the story of Akmal, a taxi driver turned construction manager from Uzbekistan, who despite residing in Moscow for over ten years found himself deportable with a three-year entry bar due to minor traffic violations. I share the story of Bahrom, an asylum seeker from Uzbekistan, whom the FMS refused to recognize as a refugee and insisted he should legalize his stay in Russia as a migrant worker. Discussing the use of human rights law in Russian domestic courts, I weave in the narratives of two Syrian refugees and one

[4] As I was interested in the arguments around human rights, I have removed from the text all information that could identify the defendant, their legal representative, the judge or the geographical area where the court was located. For analytical reasons, however, I still present the facts of the case, and mention the level of the court that rendered a particular judgment. This information, if cited, was anonymized in the text.

[5] For the description and analysis of the *Garabayev* group of cases before the ECtHR, see Chapter 7.

Palestinian, whose claims to international protection were initially denied by Russian domestic courts until the decision of the ECtHR.[6] The Strasbourg Court found their planned administrative removal to Syria to be in breach of their right to life, and the men were ultimately granted temporary asylum in Russia. Finally, the narratives of Myriam and her husband, refugees from Tajikistan and applicants before the ECtHR accused of membership in a banned Muslim allegedly 'extremist' organization – Hizb ut-Tahrir[7] – guide the reader through myriad questions that cannot usually be answered with reference to the written court judgments. Their personal, often intimate, experiences contained in these narratives cast more light on the meanings, ideas and understandings behind those legal cases. They transcend the narrow legal parameters of the case and provide a window to the broader social context within which the immigration and refugee laws are firmly embedded. These and other stories contained in this book show how important it is to complement the observations of cases and reading of the judgments with the voices and experiences of people themselves in order to arrive at a bigger picture as to whether human rights are for migrants. In order to protect the anonymity of my respondents I have changed their names, and sometimes details of their stories by weaving through them some of the recurring themes and experiences appearing within other interviewees' personal narratives. All this was done so that my respondents could not be identified in real life.

What Is this Book About?

This book offers an ethnography of access to justice and the realization of human rights for migrants and refugees in Russia. It focuses on the everyday experiences of immigration and refugee laws and how these different legal frameworks work 'in action' in Russia (Pound 1910). This investigation is sociological, starting from a premise that the situation on the ground is much more complex than the law 'in the books' assumes, as it is mediated by people's varied positionalities within the justice system. The legal experiences of every kind of person – whether an immigration, refugee or human rights lawyer (Chapter 3); an immigrant or a refugee (Chapters 4 and 7); an FMS official (Chapters 4 and 5); a Russian domestic judge or a judge at the ECtHR (Chapters 5–7) – is informed by a multiplicity of structural variables such as age, gender, education and ethnicity. Their experiences of the legal system are mediated by various contexts, personal histories, beliefs and ideologies that influence social dynamics (sometimes leading to social conflicts). All these

[6] *L.M. and Others* v. *Russia* (nos. 40081/14, 40088/14 and 40127/14, judgment of 15 October 2015) – concerning the removal of Syrian nationals for ordinary immigration offences in the midst of the civil war in Syria (2011–ongoing), the first such case in Europe (see also Kubal 2016a).

[7] For an explanation of Hizb ut-Tahrir as an organization, see Chapter 7.

factors and different positionalities intersect, so they need to be dissected with care (McCall 2005).

My primary focus in gathering material for this book was on people, their stories and experiences. Researching something as complex, intricate and ever-changing as immigration and refugee legislation in Russia, especially given the long tradition of Russian legal formalism (Kurkchiyan 2009; Kahn 2010; Hendley 2017), one could easily get distracted by the legal changes, amendments and different interpretation of written rules, and lose sight of the people who operate within (and outside) this system. I did not go to Russia with a pre-determined list of legal acts, paragraphs and ordinances that I wanted to trace 'in action'. My socio-legal approach was rather informed by the 'bottom-up' logic of ethnography. I observed the everyday experiences of immigration law as they unfolded in the lives of the different actors to see what issues come to the fore as most relevant and analytically significant for defining access to justice and the realization of human rights for migrants and refugees in Russia. It is only after collecting the empirical material that I went back to the law in its textual, black-letter sense. Even though this book starts with an overview of the legal environment to provide the context, clarify certain legal points and equip the reader with the necessary legal background to comfortably approach the subsequent chapters, it is important to mention that this legal overview was compiled at the end of the writing process.

Chapters 3–7 constitute the main body of this book. Each of these is a self-contained ethnographic case study of an aspect, element or constituent part of how the immigration and refugee laws are experienced in everyday life in Russia.

I begin Chapter 3 by introducing some of the main actors responsible for access to justice for migrants and refugees. There are many conceptualizations of access to justice in the socio-legal literature. The broader understanding combines 'the complexity of procedural rules, the transparency of the law, and the overall efficiency of the court system' (Hendley 2017: 182) alongside the availability of legal expertise. While Russia is considered to have fairly straightforward access to civil justice as far as Russian litigants are concerned (Hendley 2017: 182), this might not necessarily be true for migrants or refugees. Their access to justice or the status determination procedure in Russia (as elsewhere in the world) is complicated by a number of barriers, including linguistic ones (Burtina et al. 2015). Therefore, the figure of a legal representative – an immigration, refugee or human rights lawyer – is crucial to interrogate the full picture of access to justice. Given that my fieldwork commenced in the legal NGO, I first focus on the immigration, refugee and human rights lawyers in Russia and position them analytically within the broader socio-legal debates on cause-lawyering in the United States, Western Europe, Israel–Palestine and South Africa (Bisharat 1998; Menkel-Meadow 1998; Sarat and Scheingold 1998a, 1998b, 2001a, 2006; Appelqvist 2000; Coutin 2001; Hilbink 2004; Scheingold and Sarat 2004; Krishnan 2006;

Boukalas 2013). I argue that Russian cause-lawyering in the areas of migration and refugee law has certain specific features that distinguish it from 'mainstream' cause-lawyering – the latter focusing on impact and strategic litigation, changing laws and reforming the legal system. Russian immigration and human rights lawyers have something different 'to believe in' (Scheingold and Sarat 2004) that characterizes their specific style of cause-lawyering: humanism and care for the individual client. They would often abandon important legal victories or setting legal precedents for the sake of saving individual clients, attending to the specific needs of a refugee or asylum seeker in front of them. Some scholars question whether this style of lawyering – without transforming the status quo or prevailing arrangements of power but 'accepting a detrimental precedent or rule if the client can be made to "fit" within its parameters' (Hilbink 2004: 687) – should even be considered as part of the cause-lawyering movement (Bisharat 1998; Shamir and Chinski 1998; Sterett 1998; Hajjar 2001). I argue that it should, given the change in the status quo in the lives of the represented individuals (Porter 1998) and strong connection between law and morality (Sarat and Scheingold 1998a) exhibited by the lawyers. In this book, I conceptualize this as cause-lawyering *with the grain*.

Having introduced the lawyers in Chapter 3, I next focus on their clients and examine migrants' perspectives on the everyday grass-roots level of implementation of immigration law through the case study of the recent entry bar legislation (Chapter 4). From 2013, a three-year entry bar (*zapret na v'ezd*) has been issued in Russia to migrants with a record of two or more administrative offences. What counts as an administrative offence may be a simple traffic offence such as driving without a seatbelt or crossing the street in the wrong place. I introduce the everyday experiences of living with an entry bar through the story of Akmal, a migrant worker from Uzbekistan, who has been residing in Moscow for many years with his young family only to find himself deportable (and without much possibility of regularizing his status) due to these new legal changes. This chapter further analytically positions the socio-legal characteristics of *zapret na v'ezd* in a more global, comparative perspective, vis-à-vis the legal developments in the areas of deportation and removal in the United States and the United Kingdom. The entry bar in Russia follows a well-established logic of an increased reliance on deportability as a form of post-entry control of the migrant population (Morawetz 1998; Kanstroom 2000). The comparative analysis also invites a deeper reflection about the consequences of the civil/criminal labels in migration law. Although formally within the remit of administrative law, *zapret na v'ezd*, if analysed from the perspective of severity and impact on migrants' lives, actually constitutes a quasi-criminal sanction, a form of punishment. Ultimately, I argue that the entry bar could best be understood as a form of deportation, exclusion from legality, albeit a surreptitious one: demonstrating the possibility of deportation, the possibility of being removed which constitutes a specific form of contemporary migration governance (de Genova 2002; de Genova and Peutz 2010).

The inspiration behind the following two chapters was born in the Moscow courtrooms while observing cases involving migrant-litigants. These cases pertained to common administrative violations of the immigration regime expressed by two specific articles of the Code of Administrative Offences: art. 18.8 (Part 3) and art. 18.10 (Part 2) – lack of a residence registration or a valid work permit, respectively. The defendants in these cases were migrant workers from Central Asia (Tajikistan, Uzbekistan and Kyrgyzstan) and other post-Soviet republics (Ukraine, Azerbaijan and Georgia). My observations revealed that the great majority of these cases were adjudicated according to the so-called *paper* or case file model (see Kubal 2018). Judges arrived at their decisions on the bases of the written evidence presented in front of them and contained in the case file. During the trial, they did not engage in questioning the defendants about the circumstances or their version of the events to build up a full picture of the facts of the case. Instead, they relied on the seemingly unquestionable formal evidence produced by the FMS: protocols from immigration raids, affidavits by the defendants and reports and photographic evidence taken by FMS officers. Ultimately, the case file – not the defendants, the witnesses or even the judges – occupied centre-stage in these immigration proceedings. These observations made me further interrogate the role of the case file in the everyday life of immigration law: How was it put together? By whom? Under what circumstances? At what stage of the process did the case file acquire the epistemological function of translating the empirical reality for the purpose of the legal proceedings? What was the role of the different documents contained in the case file (dated envelopes, official stamps and handwritten signatures)?

Addressing these questions, tracing the genesis and the life of the case file in Chapter 5, took me back to the immigration and refugee lawyers' offices and to the offices of the FMS. There, I met lawyers who had meticulous case law libraries and categorized their clients through the thickness of their individual case files. I met with FMS officers who had it in their power to decide which case files were strong in documentary evidence to warrant further attention. I also consulted broader comparative, socio-legal and anthropological literature on the documentary practices and culture of materiality in legal proceedings (Riles 1999; Tuitt 2005; Scheffer 2007; Levi and Valverde 2008; Latour 2009; van Oorschot 2014; van Oorschot and Schinkel 2015), especially the capacity of the case file 'to make things come into being' (Frohmann 2008: 166; Vismann 2008; Hull 2012). Ultimately, this chapter contends that while all legal case files have the epistemic capacity to mediate the empirical reality for the purpose of the trial – 'to mediate between the laws and specific oral utterances' (Vismann 2008: 9) – under some jurisdictions the paper files construct reality more actively than in others, beyond a mere legal translation. This active production of reality – or hyperbolic epistemic function – folding of complex, interrupted and messy events into a linear narrative, happens in Russia in response to legal formalism and literal reading of the law. 'Quod non est in actis, non est in mundo' – What is not kept in the case file does not exist (see also Kahn 2010). The truth or falsity of documentary claims is often beside the point to the different individuals involved in the legal proceedings, and the formal-looking documents serve as grounds for official actions and decisions even when they can be shown to be ultimately fake.

While case file logic dominates most of the decision-making in immigration and refugee cases in Russian domestic courts, it does not mean that its rule is supreme. In certain exceptional circumstances, the judges rely on and invoke different sets of arguments – referring to Russian obligations under human rights law. Russia became a member of the Council of Europe in 1996 and ratified the European Convention of Human Rights (ECHR) in 1998. While it is a matter of open debate whether the human rights safeguards contained in the ECHR and the Strasbourg Court jurisprudence are suitably specific to effectively protect the rights of migrants (Dembour and Kelly 2011; Dembour 2015; Costello 2016), certain provisions of the ECHR are directly relied upon by domestic courts in Russia in immigration, asylum and refugee law cases. This is when consideration is given to the fact that migrants or asylum seekers cannot be deported to a place where they might find themselves at risk of torture, inhuman and degrading treatment (art. 3 ECHR) or when the return may mean a grave risk to their lives (art. 2 ECHR). Along the same lines, the judge may give due recognition to the fact that a deportable migrant has close family members in Russia, and that the imminent deportation would violate their right to private and family life (art. 8 ECHR). Other human rights arguments were invoked when setting the time limits of detention pending administrative removal (or detention pending extradition) in order to protect the human right to liberty (art. 5 ECHR).

In order to develop my argument about the human rights logic in Chapter 6, I turned to specific court judgments from various domestic courts of general jurisdiction: low-level district courts, regional (and city) courts, the Supreme Court of Russia, and supreme courts of the different republics (subjects) of the Russian Federation. I also consulted certain judgments of the Russian Constitutional Court in St. Petersburg. My sampling of judgments for this chapter was purposeful; I selected judgments that made *some* reference to human rights to discern the broader practices and understandings: if Russian domestic judges did invoke human rights, how exactly did they do it? Working with the various textual documents helped me construct a typology of how the different human rights arguments were raised and invoked. The application of the human rights logic by the domestic judges was not straightforward, and there was a significant variation in how the courts ultimately relied on it. It ranged from: (1) an explicit application and recognition of specific human rights claims (with reference to the ECHR and other international human rights instruments); (2) implicit reliance on human rights claims (with reference to domestic legal provisions, e.g. the Russian Constitution); (3) affirmation of the ECtHR jurisprudence; and, finally (4) outright rejection of human rights arguments (if and when these were raised by the defence during the proceedings).

The picture of the human rights application in immigration and refugee cases in Russia that emerges from the written judgments is, however, incomplete. The formal court judgments do not allow the reader to get to know the applicants before the court, as their personal experiences are often reduced to a few words under the heading 'facts of the case'. Who are the humans *behind* these and other migration cases in Russia? What are *their* stories and *their* experiences?

The last substantive chapter, Chapter 7, therefore gives voice to the migrants, asylum seekers and refugees themselves, and serves as a platform to let them assert their side of the story (Delgado 1996; Natapoff 2005; Levit 2010; Di Donato 2011; Fielding 2013). These narratives, aside from their purely expressive role, also serve broader analytical functions. First, they demonstrate the epistemological limits of the different courts – both at domestic and international levels – in capturing and defining the various human rights violations. Addressing this question cannot really take place without bringing to light *migrants'* lived experiences of inhuman and degrading treatment, *migrants'* experiences of detention as deprivation of liberty, *migrants'* understandings of family life. Second, these stories act as 'sites of resistance' (Ewick and Silbey 2003) by demonstrating how resistance to formal law can also be achieved through telling an alternative story that disrupts and exceeds the textual confinement of the facts of the case before the court. Telling a story 'on their own terms', telling 'what really happened' constitutes a challenge to the legally affirmed facts and sequences of events. Finally, these narratives are important as they offer a rich, contextual and ethnographic illustration to an intricate dialogue between Russian immigration authorities, domestic courts and the Strasbourg Court. They supply a number of clues that help to trace the adaptability of Russian immigration law to the ECtHR jurisprudence, and interrogate the broader relationship between Russia and the ECtHR.

2

Immigration and Refugee Law in Russia

An Overview of the Legal Environment

Introduction

This chapter focuses on the migration and refugee legal environment in Russia – the laws, their major changes and amendments – alongside certain policy and institutional developments. The overview of the legal environment 'on the books' helps to contextualize the varied experiences of the law 'in action' for a plethora of different actors that I talk about in this book: immigration and human rights lawyers, migrants and refugees, Federal Migration Service officials and Russian domestic judges hearing immigration law cases. The legal background and evolution of the migration and refugee legislation in Russia sets the important context in which to understand how these different actors experience laws and legal changes in everyday life.

Russia, like every modern migration regime, governs its migration flows through myriad administrative (civil) and criminal laws. The refugee law is a complex hybrid of international conventions to which Russia is a party (1951 Convention on the Status of Refugees and its 1967 Protocol, hereafter the Geneva Convention)[1] and domestic legislation: the Law on Refugees (Law No. 4528-I from 19 February 1993, with amendments) and the Law on Forcibly Displaced Persons (Law No. 4530-I from 19 February 1993). By virtue of Russia being party to the European Convention on Human Rights (from 1996), the Convention Against Torture (from 1987) and the International Covenant on Civil and Political Rights (from 1973), international human rights law – especially its regional dimension via the European Court of Human Rights and its jurisprudence – strongly intersects with various domestic legal developments in the area of refugee protection. The migration law, in turn, primarily relies on the following domestic legislation (with their respective changes and amendments):

- On the Attraction and Use of Foreign Labour in the Russian Federation (Decree of the President of the Russian Federation No. 2146 of 16 December 1993);
- On the Order of Exit and Entry from the Territory of the Russian Federation (Federal Law No. 114 of 15 August 1996);

[1] Russia ratified the convention on 13 November 1992.

- On Citizenship (Federal Law No. 62 of 31 May 2002);
- On the Legal Status of Foreign Citizens (Federal Law No. 115 of 25 July 2002);
- On Migration Registration (Federal Law No. 109 of 18 July 2006).

These different laws interact, to different degrees, with the Code of Administrative Offences (Federal Law No. 195 of 30 December 2001), Code of Administrative Procedure (Federal Law No. 21 of 8 March 2015), Labour Code (Federal Law No. 197 of 30 December 2001) and the Criminal Code (Federal Law No. 63 of 13 June 1996). This complex legal architecture is also supplemented by the decisions of the Russian Constitutional Court or the Russian Supreme Court that clarify the interpretation of the various domestic and international normative acts and together shape the 'law of the land'. Different 'soft law' policy documents – speeches and newspaper editorials by the president or the prime minister of Russia[2] or formal policy documents[3] – provide the necessary contextual background and are helpful in analysing (and sometimes predicting) the direction of forthcoming legal changes.

This chapter highlights the major phases in the sphere of Russian migration and refugee laws, focusing particularly on those deemed most relevant to people's everyday experiences. This is by no means an exhaustive survey of Russian immigration and refugee legal developments. Instead, the logic of this legal chapter is subsumed under the broader logic of the book. My socio-legal approach was informed by observing the everyday lives of immigration legal professionals, their clients, Federal Migration Service officers and domestic courts adjudicating migration cases to see what issues come to the fore as most pertinent and analytically significant for defining access to justice and the realization of human rights for migrants and refugees in Russia. It is only after collecting my 'live' ethnographic material that I went back to the law in its textual, black-letter sense, and started linking these experiences with concrete legislative initiatives, policy directions and legal changes.

The legal overview contained in this chapter rests on two analytical pillars. With regard to the refugee regime, I discuss the bifurcated (dual) logic in accommodating refugees in Russia following the dissolution of the Soviet Union in 1991.[4] This dual approach was later replaced by a less discriminatory

[2] For example, the speech by President Vladimir Putin at the ad hoc meeting of the Russian Federation National Security Council on 17 March 2005 or the editorial by Prime Minister Vladimir Putin, 'Russia: the National Question' in *Nezavisimaya Gazeta* on 23 January 2012.

[3] For example, the Conceptual Foundation for Regulating Migration Process in the Russian Federation (developed by the Ministry of Interior in 2003), the Conceptual Foundation of the State Migration Policy for the Russian Federation until 2025 (adopted by the President of the Russian Federation on 12 June 2012).

[4] Oxana Shevel made this distinction earlier in her excellent analysis of Russia's refugee policy, when writing about Russian state being preoccupied with 'protecting only compatriot refugees' (2011b: 98). Sergey Abashin (2017) referred to this as 'us versus them' conceptualization of refugees in Russia for policy purposes.

and more unified policy characterized, however, by a high degree of restrictionism (Pilkington 1998; Buckley et al. 2008; Shevel 2011a; Abashin 2017). As a result, the rate of refugee recognition at present in Russia is one of the lowest in the world; in 2016, it stood at 3 per cent (Matusevich 2018).

With regard to the migration regime, I argue that in contrast to the rather linear development of 'Western' (inclusive of the United States) migration laws, characterized by a downward spiral towards increased criminalization of the migrant (and asylum seeker) populations (De Genova 2004; Stumpf 2006; Bosworth and Guild 2008; De Genova and Peutz 2010; Aas 2011; Bosworth and Kaufman 2011; Aliverti 2012), there is no clear pattern of such developments in Russia. In Russia, the majority of immigration law is still governed by the civil, administrative legislation. To my knowledge, only the amendments following from the relatively recent legal changes related to fictitious residence registration (a legacy of the Soviet *propiska* system) found their well-publicized conclusion in the Criminal Code (changes from 21 December 2013). Part of the explanation behind this type of legal arrangement is clearly linked to the nature of migration flows into Russia. As a majority of migrants come from former Commonwealth of Independent States (CIS) visa-free countries of 'near-abroad' (Nikiforova and Brednikova 2018), criminal charges of illegal border crossing (as contained in the Criminal Code) are barely relevant here. They are more likely to be invoked in the cases of asylum seekers who have been found trying to enter Russia without the 'correct' documents.[5] Another explanation lies in the already highly *punitive* nature of the Russian administrative law as entrenched in Russia's legal tradition (Chapters 4 and 5). Perhaps, therefore, there was no need to criminalize Russian immigration law, as its repressive functions could be equally accommodated within the existing framework of historically punitive administrative law (see Kubal 2017).

Russia's broader migration policy balances therefore between criminalization and liberalization. In the recent history, there were a number of visible swings and turns in migration policy along these two ends of the spectrum. This demonstrates how, to a certain extent, the state tries to remain responsive to a number of (conflicting) pressures, lobbyist groups (Abashin 2017) and commitments: economic, demographic, political and populist – what Caress Schenk conceptualizes as a multi-level balancing act (Schenk 2018: 41). This chapter documents these legal changes, placing them in the broader context of state migration policy and the immigration debate.

The Refugee Regime: Bifurcated Logic of the 1990s

Russia and the Soviet Union experienced several different forms of migration and migratory regimes in the twentieth century: resettlement (colonization of

[5] See the history of the Kurdish-Syrian family from Erbil, Iraq, and on the broader implications for art. 31 of the 1951 Geneva Convention, in Chapter 3.

Russia's hinterland), migration to the city, deportation and evacuation, career and military migrations and labour and seasonal migration (Siegelbaum and Moch 2014). These different movements were significantly transformed and reached new levels after the dissolution of the Soviet Union, when almost overnight former administrative and internal province borders between the different republics of the USSR became state and international borders, and crossing them in the 1990s was made subject to a special regulation (Buckley et al. 2008; Ivakhnyuk 2009: 11–12). Throughout the 1990s, millions of people in the post-Soviet space became forcibly displaced, escaping ethnic tensions, deep economic crisis, civil wars, and deterioration of living standards (Pilkington 1998). They all experienced forced or voluntary 'repatriation': 'ethnic Tajiks were moving to Tajikistan, ethnic Armenians – to Armenia . . . Russians were moving back to Russia' (Ivakhnyuk 2009: 16). According to Irina Ivakhnyuk, in the first half of the 1990s as many as five million people were forced to leave their places of residence; about 2.4 million left for other CIS states (of these over one million received a refugee or a forced migrant status), and 2.2 million became internally displaced (Ivakhnyuk 2009: 27).

Not surprisingly, therefore, the first federal laws that regulated migration in post-Soviet Russia were the Law on Refugees and the Law on Forcibly Displaced Persons (Abashin 2017: 17)[6] – both adopted in February 1993. These laws introduced important distinctions between 'foreign' (developing world) refugees and forcibly displaced persons ('compatriots' or 'forced migrants' from within the post-Soviet space) (Shevel 2011b: 73). The latter term was reserved for former Soviet citizens navigating different national and regional boundaries of the post-Soviet republics. Between 1991 and 1998 as many as three million ethnic Russians sought to return to Russia (Ivakhnyuk 2009: 16).[7] Oxana Shevel (2011b), in her seminal study of early Russian refugee policy, observes that the legal status of forcibly displaced persons (or 'forced migrants') in Russia was without precedent in international law. It embraced two categories of people seeking humanitarian protection: refugees (those who crossed international borders, e.g. came from former Soviet republics) and internally displaced persons (IDPs – those fleeing from one part of Russia to another) (Shevel 2011b: 98).

While the Law on Refugees was a direct response to the ratification by Russia of the 1951 Geneva Convention, the Law on Forcibly Displaced Persons was a specific Russia-only legal instrument. On many levels, it was a very liberal law that responded to true social needs following the geo-political chaos initiated by the dissolution of the Soviet Union. In order to seek protection under this law, there was no need to prove individual persecution (persecution against family members was deemed sufficient by Russian migration

[6] Also known as the Law on Forced Migrants (see Shevel 2011b).

[7] Caress Schenk talks about 3.6 million ethnic Russians who ultimately 'returned' to Russia (Schenk 2018: 3).

authorities). Furthermore, the status of 'a forcibly displaced person' was also granted to persons fleeing a situation of general public disorder or violation of human rights (Shevel 2011b: 98), without the need to demonstrate individualized risks of persecution or undergoing the individual status determination procedure (Shevel 2011b: 100).[8] While both laws were more generous than the 1951 Geneva Convention in terms of social and economic rights (at least on paper), the forced migrant status carried with it 'greater socio-economic benefits that were to be guaranteed by the state, such as compensation for lost property ... and free housing in refugee accommodation centres' (Shevel 2011b: 98–99). Shevel observes that this distinction between refugees (from the developing world) and forcibly displaced persons (from post-Soviet space) in black-letter law had clear repercussions for the differential treatment of these two groups 'in practice' and their access to status determination procedure throughout the 1990s:

> [While] a citizen of Uzbekistan and a citizen of Somalia, for example, were to be treated equally under the law ... in practice, however, applications from the developing-world asylum seekers were simply not accepted ... whereas compatriot refugees from the former Soviet states received status virtually automatically. (Shevel 2011b: 99)

The large-scale cross-border movements within the post-Soviet space accompanied by the chaos and crisis of the 1990s, with their 'extremist politics, volatile economics and bewildering legislation' (Kurkchiyan 2003: 26), have clearly led to prioritization by Russian authorities of forced migrants from the post-Soviet space. The consequence of that policy was low-level recognition rates of international (developing world) refugees in Russia throughout the early 1990s. In 1994, Russia had given refugee status to 33 persons from beyond the post-Soviet space (out of 26,500 asylum seekers registered by the office of the United Nations High Commissioner for Refugees (UNHCR)); in 1996 the status was granted to 78 persons from developing countries (out of 30,600 asylum seekers registered by the UNHCR) (Shevel 2011b: 100, 106).

The institutional developments in Russia at that time also reflected this bifurcated logic of refugees versus forcibly displaced persons as established in law. In July 1992, the Federal Migration Service (FMS) was established in Moscow 'to oversee the development and implementation of migration policy, and was primarily occupied with protecting the rights of migrants and refugees' (Schenk 2018: 3). The main focus of the FMS was the large-scale population movements from the former post-Soviet republics (Pilkington 1998; Abashin 2017). The different regional FMS branches placed priorities on regional issues – some were more open to accommodating forced migrants (especially in regions that experienced demographic decline) than others, which were already

[8] The latter was true for people fleeing Moldova, Azerbaijan, Georgia and Tajikistan (Shevel 2011b: 100).

saturated as a result of large-scale displacements (Schenk 2018) and had infrastructure that could not cope with new 'temporary accommodation' camps (Ivakhnyuk 2009: 30). Three months later, in October 1992, the UNHCR opened its first office in Moscow (Shevel 2011b: 107). The UNHCR, as the UN Refugee Agency, derived its mandate directly from international law, and its role was to provide 'international protection, under the auspices of the United Nations, to refugees who fall within the scope of the present Statute and of seeking permanent solutions for the problem of refugees' (UNHCR, n.d.). Given the UNHCR's close association with the 1951 Geneva Convention, the organization was primarily occupied with assisting international refugees in Russia (i.e. from the developing world). It initially had no interest in assisting the forced migrants from the former post-Soviet space (Shevel 2011b: 108). Shevel brilliantly documents how Russian authorities invited the UNHCR into Russia with the idea of receiving assistance in managing the large-scale displacements in the post-Soviet space, only to have their hopes quashed by UNHCR's initial sole focus on the refugees from the developing world (Shevel 2011b: 107–110). Vyacheslav Bakhmin, then head of the Foreign Ministry's Directorate of International Humanitarian and Cultural Cooperation, and a staunch supporter of the 1951 Convention, poignantly captured this sentiment:

> We signed [the 1951 Refugee Convention] so that the international community would actively help with refugees – but international help has been very weak. Our position is that the Russian refugees in Russia are refugees in the international sense, and we want the same kind of help that other states get . . . It is a strategic mistake on the part of international organizations to deal only with non-CIS [Commonwealth of Independent States] refugees.
>
> (Cienski 1994)

While the UNHCR tried to refute this criticism, pointing to some joint programmes with the FMS, such as assisting forced migrants in Krasnodar (Cienski 1994), it had to acknowledge that its programme for operations in Russia included instructions whereby the UNHCR's 'assistance to the former Soviet citizens in Russia should not be encouraged on a large scale' (Shevel 2011b: 114). As a result, the gap between the FMS and UNHCR widened in the early 1990s and was further exacerbated by politically heated statements against the UNHCR by Russian politicians and civil servants (for details, see Shevel 2011b: 110). This complex and tense relationship between the UNHCR and Russian local migration authorities was somewhat indicative of the global position of this UN agency and its high degree of independence. The UNHCR, although formally constrained by states' policies, has developed its own agenda and operational practice in ways 'not expected nor necessarily sanctioned by states' (Loescher 2001).

The situation changed in the second half of the 1990s, when the UNHCR got more involved in the situation of forced migrants and refugees in the local context. The UNHCR's initial inflexibility in response to post-Soviet population displacement (as not within its direct prerogatives) was followed by its partial adaptation to the local conditions but only to the extent that these conditions fitted the international legal mandate of this organization. For example, following the aftermath of the first (1994–1996) and second (1999–2009) Chechen wars, the UNHCR extended its assistance to Chechen IDPs in Russia (given the General Assembly authorization to conduct operations under certain circumstances; see also Shevel 2011b: 112). The UNHCR further adjusted its strategy following the 'Regional Conference to Address the Problems of Refugees, Displaced Persons, Other Forms of Involuntary Displacement and Returnees in the Countries of the Commonwealth of Independent States and Relevant Neighbouring States' (30–31 May 1996, Geneva). It extended its mandate to assist forced migrants from the former Soviet republics, stateless and internally displaced persons within the post-Soviet space, and post-Soviet refugees (e.g. Georgians and North Ossetians) (Messina and Shamshur 1997).

In the 2000s, the bifurcated logic with regard to the developing world refugees and forcibly displaced persons was replaced by two different trends. On the one hand, refugee status started being granted in a less discriminatory manner – the distinctions between post-Soviet and developing world refugees became blurred. On the other hand, this turn to equality was associated with extremely low recognition rates (see Figure 2.1). While in 1997 Russian authorities gave refugee status to 7,116 people (Shevel 2011b: 106), in the early 2000s the number of recognized refugees have consistently dropped to double-/triple-digit figures per year, and continue to remain so today (Troitskiy 2017; Rosstat – Federal State Statistics Service 2018). In other words, the equality between developing

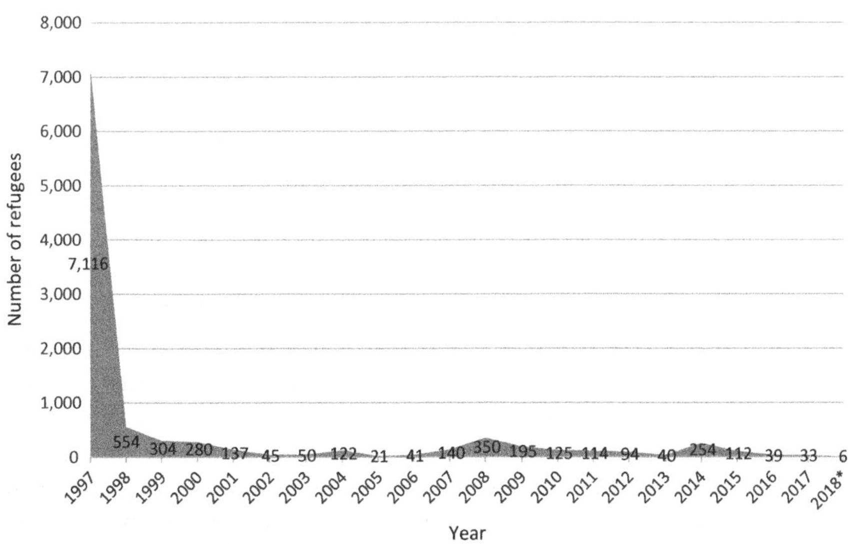

Figure 2.1 Refugees recognized in Russia each year under the Law on Refugees, 1997–2018. The figures for 2018 cover the first four months of 2018 (personal communication from Elena Burtina and Konstantin Troitskiy, Civic Assistance Committee).

world and post-Soviet refugees was achieved in Russia by extending the logic of low recognition rates to all asylum seekers, regardless of their origin.

Contemporary Refugee Legal Architecture

In the Russian legislation, aside from the already discussed specific 'forcibly displaced person' status (regulated by the Law on Forcibly Displaced Persons from 1993) reserved for people of (usually) Russian ethnic origin coming from the post-Soviet space, there are three other legal statuses that are in operation for people seeking international protection.

Refugee status, introduced by the Law on Refugees in 1993, was a direct consequence of Russia's accession to the 1951 Refugee Convention and its 1967 Protocol. According to the analysis of the primary sources, the application procedure for a refugee status is formalistic. One has to apply for asylum in person within the shortest possible time following arrival in the Russian Federation, by submitting a brief, written petition in Russian (art. 4.1 of the Law on Refugees) in one of the field offices of the FMS. The petition is followed by a personal interview (with a right to an interpreter) conducted by an FMS officer on duty, and a decision (upon the examination of the application on its merits) is issued within three months (art. 7.1 of the Law on Refugees) (Silvestri and Tchernishova 1998; Afshar 2005). It is important to stress that in practice the refugee status determination procedure is far from simple and is fraught with bureaucratic and linguistic barriers – starting from the initial difficulty of accessing the refugee status determination procedure through to the realization of the right to court appeal against refusals (Troitskiy 2017).[9] The available statistics (see Table 2.1) demonstrate that this is not a popular status according to Russian refugee policy; in April 2018 there were 'only' 585 recognized refugees in Russia, the majority of them from Afghanistan (52 per cent) and Ukraine (27 per cent). For comparison, there were only two recognized refugees from Syria (0.3 per cent), despite the UNHCR's estimates of around 10,000 Syrians in Russia designated as 'persons of concern' fleeing the Syrian civil war (ongoing since 2011) (Kubal 2016a).

Russian legislation also offers a special form of protection under the status of political asylum, introduced by the Order of the President of the Russian Federation No. 746 of 21 July 1997. This status functions in black-letter law as a domestic legal alternative to refugee status – the latter derived from the 1951 Refugee Convention. According to refugee law practitioners, this special status has a double life: 'in the books' and 'in practice'. In the books (or *na bumage*), this status forms an inseparable part of the Russian refugee legal architecture; it has also been a matter of 'vibrant academic discussions: there were numerous conferences organized, articles written and PhD theses

[9] For the detailed analysis of refugee status determination in Russia, see Burtina et al. (2015).

Table 2.1. Refugees, forcibly displaced persons, and persons with temporary asylum in Russia by country of origin (as of April 2018)

	Refugees	Forcibly displaced persons	Persons with temporary asylum
Azerbaijan	7	135	6
Afghanistan	307	–	377
Georgia	29	5,590	156
Kazakhstan	1	2,746	4
Kyrgyz Republic	3	169	17
Russian Federation	–	2,225	–
Syria	2	58	1,047
Tajikistan	6	600	21
Turkmenistan	–	69	5
Uzbekistan	19	1,285	53
Ukraine	157	177	113,926
Other countries	54	238	253
Total	**585**	**13,292**	**115,865**

Source: Rosstat – Federal State Statistics Service (2018).

defended on the right to political asylum in Russia' (Troitskiy 2017). Moreover, there were important legal changes introduced to this status in 2012 (Troitskiy 2018). In practice, however, the political asylum status is much more elusive – in 2008, the head of the FMS press service (quoted by Troitskiy 2017) acknowledged that it has not yet been awarded to anyone. In light of there being no available statistical information – the status, as a separate legal category, does not even feature in the yearly demographic reports of the Federal State Statistics Service (ROSSTAT) – it is difficult to believe that the situation has changed since then.[10] I find it, however, important to mention this status as part of the legal review, not only to present a comprehensive list of the different forms of legal protection available in Russia. It also has important repercussions for the discussion of cause-lawyering strategy by immigration and refugee lawyers, which I develop in Chapter 3.

The most popular, and thereby important, form of international protection in Russia is the institution of 'temporary asylum'. It was incorporated into the 1993 Law on Refugees (art. 12) as a subsidiary form of protection by government degree No. 274 of 9 April 2001. According to the law, the status of temporary asylum can be issued to foreign nationals and stateless persons who are entitled to a 1951 Convention-derived refugee status but 'wish only for a temporary protection or residence in Russia' (art. 12.2(1) of the Law on

[10] According to the data by the Civic Assistance Committee, there is one person in Russia with recognized political asylum (Troitskiy 2018).

Refugees). In practice, however, this form of protection is given to foreign nationals who have been denied refugee status (failed asylum seekers), and who cannot be deported from Russia due to humanitarian considerations (and the principle of non-refoulement) (art. 12.2(2) of the Law on Refugees). A person seeking international protection under the institution of temporary asylum has to apply in writing to the field office of an FMS; the temporary asylum is initially given for one year and has to be renewed. From the outset of its operation the temporary asylum status proved to be a particularly important step towards greater recognition rates (and thereby protection) of asylum seekers hailing from the developing world. Between 2001 and 2004, 1,849 people received status under the decree, 93 per cent of whom were from Afghanistan (Shevel 2011b: 118). In recent years, Russian authorities have relied on this subsidiary form of protection to accommodate the large numbers of Ukrainian refugees from Donbas and Luhansk oblasts fleeing the armed conflict in Eastern Ukraine (ongoing since 2014) (see Table 2.1). Out of the 115,865 holders of temporary asylum as of April 2018, 98 per cent were Ukrainian. For comparison, in April 2018 there were 1,047 Syrians in Russia with temporary asylum (0.9 per cent). The legal category of temporary asylum also has important political consequences for the administration and institutional unification of the refugee status determination procedure in Russia. As of January 2008, the UNHCR stopped conducting its own parallel refugee status determination, having concluded that 'all asylum seekers in Russia now have unimpeded access to the national asylum procedure' (Shevel 2011b: 118).

Migration Regime: Main Phases of Development

The main academic narrative around the directions of Russia's modern migration policy distinguishes 'four periods … characterised as the stages of confusion, indifference, restrictions and liberalisation' (Malakhov 2014: 1065). This diagnosis by Vladimir Malakhov has been repeated numerous times (e.g. Buckley 2018a: 219), but I find it rather analytically confusing and not conducive towards capturing the nuanced nature of the changes in Russian migration policy. Malakhov's periodization casts the net of arguable 'confusion or indifference' far too wide, also without acknowledging that some arguably restrictionist phases in migration policy were accompanied by parallel liberal trends (and vice versa). In the following review, I therefore rely on a different analytical lens and examine the changes in Russian domestic legislation along their position on the spectrum between restrictionism (criminalization) and liberalization (civil/administrative migration management).

2002: Restrictionism with Elements of Liberalization

In 2002, major migration legal changes were introduced 'in an attempt to create a more cohesive (albeit more restrictive) overall strategy for migration' (Schenk

2018: 4). These changes were defined by a major piece of migration legislation: 'On the Legal Status of Foreign Citizens in the Russian Federation' (Federal Law No. 115 of 25 July 2002). This law introduced two important mechanisms that – to different extents – defined the shape of Russia's migration policy in the following decade. These were the obligation to register one's residence in Russia (legacy of the famous *propiska*), and the introduction of work permits for all foreign workers. All foreign nationals (the majority of whom were labour migrants from the post-Soviet republics exercising visa-free movement with Russia) now had to fill in a migration card upon their arrival in Russia at the border control point, and register their residence within three days of arrival. Upon registering, they could legally reside in Russia for up to three months (90 days). In order to prolong their legal residence, many would chose to formally leave Russia, returning on the same day (the practice of the so-called *zayezd – vyyezd*). Upon arriving and obtaining a new residence registration, migrants from post-Soviet republics automatically acquired another 'grace period' of 90 days of lawful residence in Russia. A way to avoid the three-monthly interruption and the hassle of *zayezd – vyyezd* was to apply for a temporary residence permit (*razresheniye na vremennoye prozhivaniye* (RVP)) and later permanent residence permit (*vid na zhitel'stvo* (VnZh)). However, access to these has since 2002 been regulated by strict quotas tied to geographical location, thereby making them unavailable to many migrants. These legal changes reinforced the temporality of migrants' residence in Russia, and encouraged circular movements with Central Asian countries. Furthermore, the initial three-day deadline for residence registration was difficult to maintain for many migrants, such as those who had to travel long distances to their final destinations in Russia or whose landlords were unresponsive or away, and also due to regular backlogs and delays at FMS field offices.

With regard to the work authorizations, all migrants now had to be in possession of a valid work permit (*razresheniye na rabotu*). However, the institution of a work permit occurred much earlier, in 1993 (Decree of the President of the Russian Federation No. 2146 of 16 December 1993, 'On the Attraction and Use of Foreign Labour in the Russian Federation'). According to Sergey Riazantsev's impressive historical analysis of the Russian migrant worker legislation, the decree was the first instrument regulating the employment of migrant workers, and as such it came with a number of shortcomings (Riazantsev 2007). For example, the 1993 decree did not cover all categories of migrant workers; it clearly spelled out the rules and regulations pertaining to the employment of foreigners (i.e. under labour contracts), but left out others providing services under civil law contracts (flat repairs, childminding, and housekeeping) or working as self-employed persons (Riazantsev 2007: 513). The latter two groups of de facto migrant workers were unaccounted for in the previous law. The 2002 law, 'On the Legal Status', extended the work permit as a precondition for legal employment to all migrant workers in Russia; it also changed its form from a paper to a modern 'plastic card' version (Riazantsev 2007: 514). The 2002 law, therefore, despite its restrictionist and security-based rhetoric (Ivakhnyuk 2009), could also be seen as enabling regularization of those migrant workers who previously were left outside the purview (and protection) of the law. While the procedure for issuing work permits was very bureaucratic (something to be expected, given the long history of red tape in Russia), it also tied the migrant worker to a specific employer. It was the latter who was applying for and ultimately issued with a work permit for a particular foreign worker (Riazantsev 2007: 517). Not surprisingly, therefore, this system reinforced and reproduced the unequal bargaining power between employers and foreign workers, and was often sidestepped in practice. It thereby inadvertently resulted in an increased number of undocumented migrant workers, deteriorating labour conditions (Riazantsev 2007) and increased xenophobia (Ivakhnyuk 2009; Buckley 2018a). Experts estimated the number of undocumented migrants to be 3–5 million for the years 2002–2005 (Ivakhnyuk 2009: 42; Schenk 2018: 5).

2005: Liberal Turn towards Migration Management

The year 2005 was a turning point for re-imagining Russia's immigration policy, from migration control towards migration management. President Putin's highly publicized speech at the impromptu meeting of the Russian National Security Council on 17 March 2005 outlined a new strategy towards migrant workers, recognizing the bureaucratic burdens and administrative barriers to legalizing migrant workers' residence and employment:

> Our primary task today is to encourage immigration … Of course, what we are talking about is legal and, especially important, regulated immigration. The main reason for [undocumented migration] are the notorious administrative barriers that create an insurmountable obstacle for people who would like to legally establish their presence in Russia or their right to work here. Immigrants are especially hard hit by many of our chronic bureaucratic ailments. That is not to mention the absence of any comprehensive social protection system for them. This is also an important factor because by simply ignoring these millions of people who are living in our country, we are pushing them into a criminal environment.
>
> (Putin 2005)

A direct result of this policy-discursive turn were major changes introduced into the domestic immigration legislation – 'On Migration Registration' (Federal Law No. 109 of 18 July 2006) and 'On the Legal Status' – on 16 January 2007.[11] First, the initial deadline for residence registration was extended from three to seven days, and allowed foreigners to register either at the place they lived or worked,[12] making the law 'On Migration Registration' more flexible

[11] An excellent study by Caress Schenk (2018) demonstrates how these legal changes were implemented in domestic migration governance practice by law enforcement bodies (FMS) in various regions of Russia (Moscow, Sverdlovsk and Krasnodar).

[12] To understand the distinction between being registered at the place of living versus at the place of working, see Kubal (2016b).

(Schenk 2018: 19). Second, with regard to work authorizations, the new procedures allowed individual migrant workers to apply for a work permit without the oversight of their employer and to move freely between different employers. These changes thereby made the whole process more liberal also for those workers who were previously forced by unscrupulous employers to work in an undocumented way (reducing the phenomenon of bonded labour). The migration policy experts noted also the more restrictive elements of the new law, i.e. introduction of work permit quotas for all migrant workers, including those from the CIS countries (Schenk 2018). In other words, not all labour migrants who applied for a work permit could easily get one; they had to make sure they were accommodated within the quota system first. However, given the fact that the quota in the first year of its operation (2007) was set at six million (Riazantsev 2007: 517), perhaps it would rather be more appropriate to interpret this move as a silent regularization, enabling the previously estimated five million undocumented migrant workers to come out of the shadows and apply for a work permit.[13]

The quota system was further reformed in 2010, under what came to be known as another wave of liberalizing changes in immigration legislation. A certain type of labour relations (i.e. working for individuals and private households based on civil law contracts) was removed from the quota administration system. This type of labour relations was made subject to a different, quota-free (i.e. regulated by market demand) type of work permit called 'patent', or labour licence. These labour licences were introduced by the changes to the law 'On the Legal Status' on 19 May 2010 (Federal Law No. 86). This significantly simplified the procedures by which migrant workers could regularize their residence and employment: the validity of the initial patent (issued for one month) could be extended by simply paying a fee (known as a 'tax' among migrant workers), and keeping the receipt as proof of payment in an event of random document inspection. The work licence functioned as a document certifying both legal work and residence in Russia (upon the expiry of the 90-day temporary registration).

2013: Restrictionist Turn with Elements of Criminalization

It is impossible, however, to defend the position that Russia by its 2007 legislation has firmly entered the liberalization phase as far as migration legislation is concerned. The alleged regularization and liberalization have been countered by other legislative initiatives in 2013 and 2014. Amendments to the law 'On the Order of Exit and Entry' and Criminal Code from 21 December 2013

[13] Schenk's (2018) study demonstrates how work permit quotas were subsequently and strategically reduced (reaching 1.6 million in 2014, their final year of operation) to create a publicly acceptable number of legal migrants, while allowing increasing numbers of undocumented migrants to meet labour demands.

positioned fictitious registration within the realm of criminal law responsibility, introducing fines of 100,000–500,000 roubles for 'submitting deliberately false information for registration, or registering at a place with no intention to stay there' (Schenk 2018: 19). Furthermore, the amendments to the law 'On the Legal Status' from 1 January 2014 limited the stay in Russia on the basis of (solely) the registration to three months within every six-month period (90 days out of every 180 days) for citizens from the visa-free countries. This move was to eliminate shadow employment among Central Asian migrants (without work permits or patent) and terminate the practice of *zayezd – vyyezd* as a mean of extending one's legal residence in Russia.

The entry bar (*zapret na v"yezd*) legislation in turn locked a number of migrants into a situation of deportability – an uncertain socio-legal condition marked by the possibility of deportation (De Genova 2002). Initially, a three-year entry bar was to be issued to anyone who had not left the territory of Russia within a 30-day grace period following the expiry of their residence registration (Federal Law No. 321 of 30 December 2012, 'On the Order of Exit and Entry'). In July 2013, stricter amendments followed – the three-year entry bar was to be issued to foreign citizens who, within a period of three years, had committed two or more administrative offences (Federal Law No. 224 of 23 July 2013, 'On the Order of Exit and Entry'). Administrative offences include speeding or parking tickets, or being caught crossing the street in the wrong place. Two of those offences forbade a person's entry into the Russian Federation for three years, or – if issued within the country – rendered a person effectively deportable. The number of people against whom the entry bar was issued increased over eightfold between 2013 and 2014, peaking at 1.7 million in February 2016, demonstrating that this has become a popular tool for migration management. Given the gravity of these changes, Chapter 4 of this book is fully devoted to the discussion of the phenomenon of entry bar and its everyday impacts on migrants from Central Asia.

An important set of changes was also introduced to the Code of Administrative Offences (CAO) in the sphere of penalties for immigration violations, demonstrating the socially punitive face of Russian administrative law. The great majority of the immigration violation cases that take place in Russian courts are, respectively, offences against articles 18.8 (part 3) and 18.10 (part 2) of the CAO – lack of residence registration and working without a work permit/or work licence (patent). Until 2013, the sanction for both of these offences, according to the CAO, was a fine of up to 5,000 roubles (approximately £60), together with a discretionary expulsion order. These terms of sentencing prevailed in the majority of jurisdictions (subjects) of the Russian Federation; however, following amendments to the CAO of 23 July 2013 (Federal Law No. 207), in Moscow, Moscow Oblast, St Petersburg and Leningrad Oblast, the expulsion (administrative removal) now follows automatically and is included in the 'minimum' sentence. Making the sanction of administrative removal non-discretionary in the places of greatest concentration of

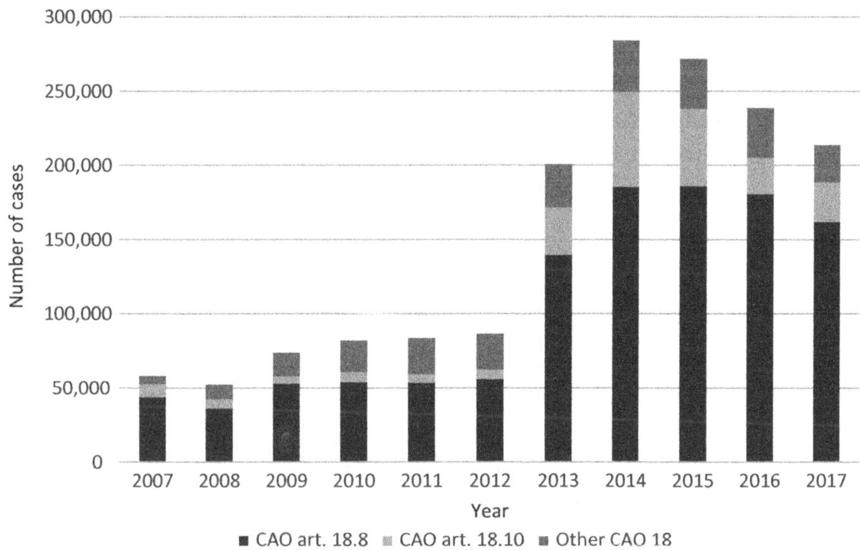

Figure 2.2 Immigration law cases in district courts in Russia, 2007–2017.

migrant workers, like Moscow or St Petersburg, suggests that the judges and courts have been called upon to be important enforcers of Russian immigration law because of their special role in the immigration management and control system. Court statistics demonstrate that, as a result of this new law, the number of immigration administrative cases increased by 100 per cent between 2012 and 2013. The record year thus far was 2014, with 249,303 art. 18.8 and art. 18.10 CAO cases. This translates into nearly 250,000 foreigners being brought to trial, with potential expulsion orders issued against their names (Figure 2.2). Furthermore, a five-year entry bar was extended to all those foreigners who were administratively removed (expelled) from Russia following the court order (Federal Law No. 224 of 23 July 2013, 'On the Order of Exit and Entry'). These legal changes in the CAO set the important legal context for the broader arguments and analysis contained in Chapters 3, 5 and 7.

2015: Liberal Turn Belied by Law Enforcement?

The dual system of regular work permits and simplified patents existed until January 2015, when work permits were abolished for all migrant workers from the former Soviet Union. The system of patents was subsequently extended to all forms of migrant employment in Russia (Federal Law No. 357 of 24 November 2014), resulting in extensive de jure liberalization of the migrant worker regime. The system of patents allowed migrant workers to work legally in all kinds of commercial enterprises and private households, in exchange for a monthly fee ('tax') payable to the local and federal budgets. The representative of the Russian Federation at the 13th Coordination Meeting on International

Migration argued that 'this new system will promote legal migration, reduce illegal migratory flows and allow many migrant workers to come out of the tax shadow' (Permanent Mission of the Russian Federation to the United Nations 2015).

Indeed, in many aspects this reform could also be viewed as another attempt towards a 'silent' regularization of many migrant workers from Central Asia, who had previously accessed the labour market semi-legally (Kubal 2013): they possessed the administratively and formally easier-to-obtain patents, but were working outside the conditions specified in those permits (working for business establishments, companies and so on). The apparent simplicity of these legal measures belied the way in which they were bureaucratically administered, however. The confusing duality of the work permit versus patent category was actually implicitly prolonged under the new 'patent-only' system. Despite the rhetoric of unification, two types of permits continued to be issued, authorizing work for an individual (*fizicheskiye litso*) or a business establishment (*yuridicheskiye litso*) (Polyanina 2015). And while under the 'old' system the application for a patent followed a fairly easy administrative procedure, after January 2015 the new patent application had to be accompanied by a number of attachments: a medical insurance policy (valid for the duration of the employment contract) and certificates of passing a set of state exams on the Russian language, history and 'basic' knowledge of the legal system of the Russian Federation (Polyanina 2015; Abashin 2017). In practice, it was difficult to fulfil these conditions, particularly obtaining the requested certificates and documents, within the prescribed timeframe of 30 days from arrival in the Russian Federation (Polyanina 2015). This gave rise to a proliferation of various legally fictitious spaces (Reeves 2015), where, under the veneer of formal legality, medical insurance policies were purchased, 'certification centres' were established, exam certificates issued and money exchanged hands as migrants tried not to miss the 30-day deadline for legalization (Chupik 2015). These and various other 'grey schemes' ultimately exposed migrants to inconsistent and socially punitive law enforcement. These teething problems were particularly associated with the initial phase of eliminating work permits and rolling out the new and comprehensive patent-only scheme. How this system works in practice in the long term remains to be seen (Abashin 2017; Buckley 2018a; Schenk 2018).

Federal Migration Service: Between Law Enforcement and Migration Management Agency

The institutional arrangement of immigration law enforcement is a good case in point to interrogate the relationship between formal migration policy and the law in action. In many continental European jurisdictions, immigration law still lies within the formal domain of administrative justice. However, immigration law enforcement officers have been – either historically or more recently – equipped with criminal law-like prerogatives (e.g. for the Netherlands see van der Woude (2016) and Brouwer et al. 2018). The institutional history of the Russian FMS since its establishment in 1992 up to the present day also speaks to these broader developments at the crossroads of administrative and criminal law systems.

The FMS (Federal'naya Migratsionnaya Sluzhba) was created in 1992, primarily to deal with the mass displacement of the population following the dissolution of the Soviet Union (Abashin 2017), though it was also equipped with wider prerogatives in the areas of implementation of migration law and policy and protection of rights of migrants and refugees (Schenk 2018). Back then, it was an independent agency with a modest number of civil servants founded 'on the basis of the Soviet Committee for Migration Affairs at the Ministry of Labour and Employment' (Abashin 2017: 20). By 1996, the FMS had branches in all the subjects of the Russian Federation, which reported directly to FMS Russia in Moscow (Pilkington 1998). However, in the wave of the changes in immigration law and regulations in 2002 the FMS was disbanded and its functions incorporated into the Ministry of Interior (Ministerstvo Vnutrennikh Del (MVD)) (Abashin 2017: 20). The MVD had a historical supervisory role over the police and secret police in Russia, therefore placing immigration enforcement within the MVD was a clear sign of aligning immigration enforcement – at least institutionally – more closely with the criminal law domain. Indeed, the priorities of immigration enforcement, as demonstrated by the rather restrictive policy changes of 2002, shifted from managing migration flows and humanitarian assistance to forcibly displaced persons towards immigration control in order to demonstrate 'a strong will of the state' and 'a solid law and order in the area of migration' (Abashin 2017: 20). These new priorities were developed within the historically punitive functions of the MVD and conceptually captured in the 2003 policy document 'Conceptual Foundation for Regulating Migration Processes in the Russian Federation'.

The institutional annihilation of the FMS did not last long, however. In 2004, it was recreated under the organizational framework of the MVD and attributed new responsibilities for passport and visa procedures. With time, the FMS became more and more independent: it was awarded a separate financing stream within the MVD (its budget increased tenfold from 3.5 billion roubles to 36.1 billion roubles between 2005 and 2014), and in 2005 it was given a new, charismatic head, Konstantin Romodanovsky (Abashin 2017: 21). In 2004, the FMS as a sub-agency within the MVD employed 20,000 staff; in 2014 this number doubled to 40,000 (Abashin 2017: 21). Migration experts within the rapidly expanding FMS were central to introducing some of the most liberal changes in Russian immigration policy: the 'silent regularization' of 2007 (with the record six million quota allocation for work permits) and the system of out-of-quota work permits (patents or labour licences) in 2010, which significantly increased the local and federal revenues from the labour licence fees. Sergey Abashin goes so far as to say that the FMS, still formally within the institutional framework of the MVD, became 'a monopolist in the formulation of migration policy *independently* of repressive institutions' within which it was actually embedded (Abashin 2017: 22, my emphasis).

In 2012 the FMS was formally released from subordination to the MVD, and was made a civil agency under direct supervision of the Russian government. The period between 2012 and 2016 marked the 'golden years' of the agency's independence and authority, as well as a broader turn in its institutional priorities from immigration law enforcement towards migration management. This style of migration management was still, however, embedded within the rather punitive nature of Russian administrative immigration law (as demonstrated by the policy changes in 2013–2014, discussed earlier in this chapter, especially the rise in administrative removals (expulsions) in Moscow and St Petersburg and record numbers of entry bars for migrants (primarily Central Asians) for minor administrative infringements). The FMS created and had at its disposal some of the most impressive electronic migration databases – de facto tools of migration administration, management and governance (Bahovadinova 2016). These databases were a pertinent metaphor for the technocratic, arguably corruption-proof, approach to migration management that characterized the ethos of the 'independent years' of the FMS. As part of the broader bureaucratic infrastructure, these specific migration administration mechanisms were also, however, highly inflexible and often lost sight of the 'human face' of migratory processes: migrant personal records in these databases could easily become misplaced, and some entry bars were issued in an automated fashion without the necessary human supervision. Appealing the decision of a faceless database proved very difficult in practice (see Chapter 4). Sergey Abashin eloquently captured the organizational nature, broad mandate and international links of the civil and independent FMS as a migration management agency:

> A rather powerful bureaucratic structure was created, with its own hierarchies, centre, and regional offices, daily routine activities and a number of services . . . This institution could actively interact not only with the president's administration and the government, but also with regional governments via the regional offices of the FMS. The FMS also received the possibility and right to cooperate with other countries on issues of migration, as well as with international organisations dealing with this issue.
>
> (Abashin 2017: 21)

Has this relative success of the FMS led to its subsequent demise? The FMS ceased to exist as an independent organization in 2016, and by Presidential Decree No. 156 of 5 April 2016 it was incorporated back into the MVD. On many levels, the organization was disbanded once again – its position fell beyond the semi-autonomous status it held within the MVD between 2004 and 2012. The implementation of migration policy – and more importantly the enforcement of immigration law – became the prerogative of the Main Directorate for Migration of the Ministry of Interior of Russia (Glavnoye Upravleniye po Voprosam Migratsii MVD Rossii). This internal agency of the MVD is headed by a senior police officer of the rank of major general. This institutional re-alignment, despite the alleged liberalization trend of the wider migration policy 'on the books' since 2015, demonstrates that immigration enforcement in contemporary Russia is clearly focused on migration policing and control. This gives a special hybrid identity to migration law in Russia: while formally within the domain of administrative regulation, the migration law is now (and once again) enforced by an agency with long-standing punishment and repression functions, and a history and affinity with criminal law.

* * *

While Russian refugee and migration law and policy are complex pieces of legislation that have undergone a number of significant changes, these developments are not just random 'amendments ... followed by amendments to the previous amendments and also further laws' (Buckley 2018a: 219), but exhibit a certain logic. With regard to the refugee law, the bifurcated system that existed historically in the 1990s – dividing refugees into forced migrants (hailing from the former post-Soviet space) and developing world refugees – was unified in the 2000s. The two policy approaches, one fairly liberal and one fairly restrictive, became aligned towards the restrictive end of the spectrum, resulting in extremely low refugee recognition rates in contemporary Russia.

The immigration law – one of the most prolific and dynamic pieces of legislation in present-day Russia – also escapes easy categorization. In order to better understand the logic of changes behind the immigration law, I heuristically divided these developments into a number of different phases, placing each of them on the spectrum between restrictionism (with elements of criminalization) and liberal (administrative) migration management.

Finally, the evolution of Russian immigration law and the different legal developments cannot be separated from the institutional history of the FMS. The FMS throughout the 1990s and 2000s experienced a number of re-alignments, moving its identity between that of a criminal and administrative law institution. Its responsibilities shifted between strict law enforcement and more creative migration management. The most recent institutional changes in 2016 placed it (once again) within the punitive and restrictive migration control domain of the MVD.

3

Immigration and Refugee Lawyers as Cause-Lawyers

Cause-Lawyering with the Grain?

Introduction

'Yest' takaya professiya – ot rodiny zashchishchat.' 'There is such a profession – to protect one from their fatherland.' This saying is very popular among many of the immigration and refugee lawyers in Russia who I encountered during my fieldwork. Some of the lawyers had it always displayed as their 'status message' on Skype, WhatsApp or other communication app. Others invoked it rather liberally when sending each other greetings on the occasion of 'Lawyer's Day' (*Den' yurysta*) on 3 December.

This statement seems to be an important identity marker for many immigration and refugee lawyers – the idea of a cause that unites them and a commitment that they share – to protect individuals from the overly expansive purview of the state. In their everyday professional practice, these lawyers help migrants stand for their rights in Russia and assist asylum seekers making refugee status applications; they defend both groups against extradition, unlawful administrative removal, expulsion or deportation to a country where they may find themselves at risk of torture and inhuman and degrading treatment. They fight for migrants' and refugees' right to legal stay in Russia, drawing on national legal instruments and international protection frameworks (the 1951 Refugee Convention, the European Convention of Human Rights) in courts and beyond. As individuals, they have 'chosen legal careers which express their commitment to social change and helping' (Menkel-Meadow 1998: 48).

In this chapter, I introduce the work and the daily struggles of the real heroes of this book – and some of my most important informants in the field – the immigration and refugee lawyers in Moscow. I conceptualize these immigration and refugee lawyers as cause-lawyers, and I place them on the spectrum of the different types of cause-lawyering that could be found in the established legal professional and academic literature. The most popular type of cause-lawyering in Russia seems to be represented by the strong commitment to and care for an individual *case*, which does not necessarily lead to transformative or systemic legal changes.

In the second part of the chapter, drawing on a case study of a Kurdish-Syrian family stranded in the transit zone of Sheremetyevo Airport,

I introduce an additional and rather specific type of cause-lawyering that somewhat surpasses all the references to cause-lawyering found in the literature (Sarat and Scheingold 1998, 2001a, 2006; Coutin 2001, 2006; Boon 2004; Krishnan 2006). I conceptualize it as cause-lawyering 'with the grain'. This specific type and commitment to cause-lawyering goes beyond the statement that the cause is never more important than the individual case. Behind each legal case is an individual client; the exhaustion of legal remedies that impedes the advancement of a particular case only means that the individual client *becomes the cause*. The responsibility to care and protect the individual takes priority over not only the legislative amendments or international legal precedents that could change the broader structural conditions and the interpretation of the law in Russia. The responsibility to protect the individual goes also beyond the law itself and available legal remedies. It exceeds the formal confines of a legal case. The immigration and refugee lawyers who subscribe to this type of lawyering readily recognize the limits of the law in Russia, or the possibility to achieve immediate change through law for a particular individual. These lawyers share the broader societal cynicism and scepticism about the law (see Kurkchiyan 2009); as a result, they are willing to pursue their clients' interests within established legal means, but do not hesitate to bypass or sidestep the law or even lose important legal battles altogether if that is to ultimately help their client.

With the grain refers therefore to a specific type of cause-lawyering in which the lawyers do not always challenge legal systems by bringing impact or strategic litigation but rather work *within* the parameters and confines of specific legal systems (and their respective flaws and pitfalls): formal and informal rules, power structures, legal mores and customs, vested interests and incentives. I borrowed the 'with the grain' metaphor from the wider developmental literature on good governance in Africa (Kelsall 2008; Booth and Cammack 2013). It was originally coined to account for alternative approaches to introducing meaningful change in African societies, an alternative to simply 'transplanting' Western institutions and practices that on many occasions sat poorly with local traditions, beliefs and values. The idea behind 'going with the grain in African development' was to work *with* various cultural and pre-colonial systemic legacies, not *against* them (Kelsall 2008: 627). 'Going with the grain' for Russian cause-lawyering means working with the broader legal system (with its various and well-documented ills), not against it, even if it ultimately means sidestepping the law in order to help the client. There are scholars who openly question whether this type of 'with the grain' cause-lawyering in Russia – without transforming the status quo or prevailing arrangements of power but working very much within their parameters and making the client's case directly adapt to these broader structures – should even be considered as part of the cause-lawyering movement (Bisharat 1998; Shamir and Chinski 1998; Sterett 1998; Hajjar 2001). I argue that it should, given the change in the status quo in the lives of the represented individuals (Porter 1998) and strong connection between law and morality (Sarat and Scheingold 1998a) exhibited by the immigration and refugee lawyers.

Caring about Individual Cases: A Portrait

Varvara[1] is a *pro bono* immigration lawyer in Moscow, and a refugee herself. Her identity document based on which she can travel in and out of Russia, but also enter the courts to represent her clients, is a Convention Travel Document (in accordance with art. 28 of the 1951 Refugee Convention). Her family migrated to Central Asia when it was still part of the Soviet Union back in the twentieth century. Back home, Varvara received university education and became interested in human rights. She started a non-governmental organization (NGO) and was rather successful at receiving grants for her activities from various US and European institutions that were interested in making headway for human rights in Central Asia. The local authorities saw this as threatening. They applied a variety of pressures on her – for a couple of weeks Varvara was being taken to the police department every evening, and kept there until the following morning without food or water. Ultimately, she decided to flee to Russia. She enrolled as a graduate student at St Petersburg University, where she obtained a PhD in law. She returned to Moscow, where for some time she collaborated with different human rights NGOs. However, her 'special' character – feistiness, impatience, determination and individualism – finally led her to work on her own. She has good professional relationships with many migration NGOs, activists and scholars in Russia and abroad, but more as a consultant than an employee or a project worker. Her lawyering work is solely supported by grants – from both international (e.g. Red Cross) and Russian national donors.

Varvara is very busy. Her main mission is to work directly with migrants, particularly migrant workers from Central Asia. When I first met Varvara for an interview, we could not talk properly. Nearly every question was interrupted by a phone call Varvara received. And she picked up each and every one of them, devoting 5–15 minutes to every call. I thought this was not going to work. I adopted a different data-collection strategy, and instead of interviewing her, I decided to shadow Varvara. She has no office, and she is always on the move – either to a police station, to court, for a seminar or meeting with migrant-clients. And the mobile phone accompanies Varvara everywhere.

Varvara has a 'hotline' that migrants can call at any time of the day or night with their legal problems. Usually she receives around 45 phone calls per day – on quiet days it will be around 30, and on particularly busy days it can reach 80 calls. The phone usually starts ringing before 6 a.m. (when migrants

[1] The name has been changed to protect the anonymity of the respondent.

become subject to document checks by the police on their way to work), and does not stop until 2–3 a.m. the following day. The hotline number is usually used by migrants who are about to found themselves in police custody and require immediate help or advice. Varvara's response needs to be immediate – the longer a person spends at the police station, the more difficult it is to 'win them back' (see Kubal 2016b). What does Varvara mean by this?

> When you are in police's custody, do not speak good Russian and the police officer will tell you "sign these papers, and you will be let free" – what would you do? You sign them obviously. And many of my clients do sign documents without understanding what is in them. These are usually affidavits and police protocols, which are later included in the case file, when migrants are taken to court. Quite often, my defendants by signing these documents also do sign away their rights to an interpreter or legal help. So when I come to the police station, the police officer shows these papers to me. What am I to do? It then just gets all the more difficult to defend these migrants in courts.

Varvara then has to act quickly. In her large black bag, which she always carries, aside from papers, grant proposals, court judgments and appeals, she also has a small notebook computer. On that notebook, she has a spreadsheet with phone numbers of all the district police offices in Moscow and the greater Moscow area.

On Easter Monday, when I accompanied her on a field trip outside of Moscow to a monastery with a group of friends, she received a particularly worrying phone call. A group of Tajik men had their documents checked near the metro entrance by police officers from OMON.[2] One of these men had been subsequently detained. His colleagues called Varvara and explained that the Tajik migrant had a work licence (a patent) that was nearing its expiry date, but he still had two more days to prolong it by paying the monthly fee. The document expiry date was 23 April. The man normally paid the required fee on the twentieth of every month, but as 20 April fell on Easter Sunday he planned to pay the fee the following day. The OMON officers disagreed with this explanation and accused him of breaking Russian immigration law on account of an expired work licence. According to the Tajik men on the phone, they also requested a bribe. Their colleague, now in OMON custody, refused the bribe and asserted that he was 'perfectly legal in Russia'. He was taken to a nearby van and the men thought he was being beaten up at the time of the phone call. The Tajik men on the phone were distressed, and the legality of the work licence was obviously a grey area. I asked Varvara if there was anything she could do. We were a good hour and a half drive from Moscow.

Varvara was calm. This obviously was not the first time she had dealt with a situation of this sort. She took all the details of the detained Tajik man, his

[2] OMON is the *Otryad Militsii Osobogo Naznacheniya*, the Special Purpose Police Unit. The OMON officers could be likened to riot police, or a gendarmerie-like paramilitary force.

name, surname, as well as the licence plate number of the OMON van and the time and exact location of the document check and encounter with the OMON officers. She then called the chief police officer responsible for that particular area and explained to him in detail what his subordinates were doing. She was adamant that a man, a citizen of Tajikistan, was illegally apprehended by the OMON police, and demanded his immediate release. Otherwise she was about to press charges and complain against the police's illegal abduction of a foreign citizen legally residing in the territory of the Russian Federation. After this firm, but polite, phone call to the police she then called back the Tajik men and suggested they all phone 112 (a toll-free number for emergency services in Moscow) and report exactly what happened to the police. The men were reluctant to follow this advice. The phone went silent. After half an hour the Tajik men called again – their friend had been released after a phone call from a superior police officer. He looked a little scruffy but otherwise he was safe. Varvara advised the men to escort their colleague to the nearest first-aid post (*medpunkt* or *punkt meditsinskoy pomoshchi*) for a medical examination. She would use the written result of the examination to file a complaint for compensation against this particular OMON unit. The Tajik men never called again. I would not be surprised if instead of a first-aid post they went looking for the nearest bank to pay the fee to extend the problematic work licence.

When I congratulated Varvara on possibly one of the most quickly solved cases and migrant release, she said it was not the fastest. Her absolute record was when she called a chief of a police station, introduced herself and . . . the police officer interrupted and 'asked for the names'. When she repeated her name and that she worked as a *pro bono* lawyer for migrants, the police officer allegedly had said:

> Yes, I know who you are. Just tell me the names of the people you want released.

Varvara was happy; she obviously was also in a bragging mood. She took every case extremely personally. All these phone calls, which to an external observer looked like part of her daily routine – behind each of them was a human being, with their own life. 'Every other person is basically you', she used to say. Varvara did not always win, of course. And the victories were not always easy. Therefore, it was important to talk about the small, everyday successes; it was important for Varvara to blow her own trumpet sometimes to recharge her batteries for future challenges.

Varvara was also a legal professional. She had one important advantage over other immigration and refugee cause-lawyers in Moscow. She actively used the phone calls from the hotline to pre-screen her clients and their cases. She paid attention to legally and formally significant details: names, sequences of events, licence plate numbers, expiry dates on documents, receipts and reference letters (*spravkas*). If, during a phone call, she concluded that there was enough substance in the case, that it was possible to win justice for a particular client, she would take that case. Alternatively, if she found out that the case was hopeless, she would tell her caller: 'Zaychik,[3] you are illegally in Russia, you know that?' With this, she would decline to take the client's case via the legal channels. I would often hear her say the following on the phone:

> In Russia you are illegally. There is nothing I can do. But you can leave this country, go back home, enjoy some holidays and time with your family, and return in three months' time. When you are back in Moscow call me, but do not wait as long as you waited now. Call me immediately. I will help you navigate the law and obtain work licence.

Varvara carefully selected her cases based on her experiences of 'winning the clients back' from police custody or representing their interests in domestic courts. This important strategy informed Varvara's broader attitudes about the Russian justice system and the possibility of defending migrants' rights. Varvara was, of course, critical of the immigration enforcement system; she considered the police apprehensions of migrant workers illegal and racially motivated (Open Society Institute 2006; Nikiforova and Brednikova 2018). At the same time, she knew how to navigate the system and use it to her clients' advantage. She was adamant that it was possible to achieve justice through law. Her response to a question about the 'on the ground' effects of a specific and rather complex immigration policy change in 2015 particularly highlighted Varvara's ideas about championing her clients' cases before domestic courts:

> I go to courts to represent migrants. But I mainly go to court to win. In the past I won around 85 per cent of cases for migrants with work licences [patents] accused of false or no registration.[4]

This strategy of cause-lawyering, focused on individual cases, required Varvara to strictly filter the different grievances at the beginning of her relationship with the clients. She could not afford to take every case. She needed to be selective in order to be efficient in pursing her clients' interests within the boundaries of formal law.

A Spectrum of Cause-Lawyering Types

Varvara's style of lawyering could be placed firmly at one end of the spectrum of the many different cause-lawyering types. I constructed this spectrum from the different definitions and conceptualizations of 'the cause' in cause-lawyering, reviewing the vast and ever-growing literature

[3] Zaychik literally means 'a bunny'. It is a very informal (if not a tad patronizing) way of referring to one's interlocutors.

[4] These charge referred to art. 18.8 Code of Administrative Offences. See Chapter 2 for the specific legal context.

on cause-lawyering in different parts of the world: the United States, United Kingdom, Israel–Palestine and South Africa (Sarat and Scheingold 1998b, 2001a, 2006; Scheingold and Bloom 1998; Appelqvist 2000; Hilbink 2004; Scheingold and Sarat 2004; Perelman 2005; Krishnan 2006; Tam 2010; Munger 2015; McEvoy 2017). The 'cause' in cause-lawyering is not just an objective fact; to borrow from Ronen Shamir and Sara Chinski, it is a socially constructed concept that evolves with 'experiences, circumstances, memories and aspirations' (Shamir and Chinski 1998: 231) of the lawyers and their clients.

At one end of the spectrum, quite distant from Varvara's pursuits, the cause symbolizes broader transformative changes in the law and social structure, undoing the patterns of privilege, power, inequality and domination (Scheingold and Bloom 1998: 214); challenging the prevailing distributions of political, social, economic and/or legal values and resources (Sarat and Scheingold 2001b: 13). Achieving these goals meant pursuing and winning 'high-profile' precedent cases that would result in tangible changes in the law, at national or international level. These types of legal and political transformations could also be championed outside the courtroom, though political lobbying, human rights activism and social movements. The representative causes under this type of cause-lawyering range from equal pay rights, women rights (Trubek and Kransberger 1998), anti-racism and civil rights movements, fighting broader discrimination (Davis 1993; Bagenstos 2009), through to

> seeking to energize grassroots political activism, promoting reform of corporate capitalism, and in general, pursuing a broadly eclectic policy agenda with systemic implications.
>
> (Scheingold and Bloom 1998: 214)

Within this type of cause-lawyering, 'individual clients are accepted, indeed recruited, not in relationship to a personal injury but in accordance with how well their injuries embody a cause' (Scheingold and Bloom 1998: 214). Under this type of cause-lawyering, success is defined 'not primarily in terms of the impact on the individual client, but on the system or the larger population' (Hilbink 2004: 677). Some scholars have gone so far as to suggest that cause-lawyers sometimes have to stay true to political aims of their entire constituency and 'must keep an eye on the interests of future generations ... even at the price of wronging individual clients' (Luban 1988: xxv) and sacrificing their individual cases. Under this conception of a cause as advancing a broad legal or political principle, changing the rules of the game and unsettling the broader status quo, the individual client often faded into the background (Hilbink 2004: 680).

At the other end of the spectrum, the cause is defined as 'caring for individual cases' (Sterett 1998), bringing about the change gradually through representing the interests of those whose legal needs remain unmet (Scheingold and Bloom 1998: 214). The goal is to pursue small-scale, allegedly 'low-profile' struggles at micro-sites of power: the workplace, the family, the community (Laclau and Mouffe 1985). The lawyers caring about individual cases encourage resistance not necessarily within the centre of power and decision-making but fight inequality within the capillaries of power (Foucault 1982; de Certeau 1984), and put themselves directly at the service of the most marginalized. Litigation in immigration, more than in other areas of law, is more likely to help individual claimants than change the rules. The excellent research by Susan Sterett (1998) on immigration lawyers in the UK revealed how in Britain lawyering first for a cause often meant 'lawyering first for individual clients rather than focusing primarily on rule change' (Sterett 1998: 307). Even if the government later did change the immigration rules in response to a victory of specific claimants (more often than not by closing a specific legal loophole or making the overall immigration law stricter), the lawyers would have won for their particular clients, and Parliament could not change rules retroactively (Sterett 1998: 305).

The type of cause-lawyering presented by Varvara very much fits within this 'low-profile' end of the spectrum. In her daily work of representing her clients, she does not lose of sight the individual cases. She carefully pre-screens the cases, not by their prospects of bringing about transformative legal changes, but rather by which cases have a chance of winning in court, given the current state of the legal rules and their interpretation. She attends to the needs of one of the most marginalized groups within Russian society, and she does that completely *pro bono*. When I asked her whether she encourages her clients to take part in some form of social protest or activism to improve the rights for migrants in Russia more generally, she was adamant in her response:

> God no! Do you know the Latin phrase *primum non nocere*?[5] Why would I want to expose my migrants to even a greater attention from the law enforcement authorities? In a group, they become very vulnerable; they can easily be targeted. Why would I land them in trouble and get myself even more work?

To those familiar with immigration law cause-lawyering in other jurisdictions, such as the United States (Coutin 2000, 2001, 2006) and the role of migrant organizations in campaigning for change in law (Abrego 2008), Varvara's response may sound extremely conservative, if not outright outside the perimeters of cause-lawyering. Instead of challenging the broader status quo, she rather tailors her practices to accommodate or benefit her

[5] In Latin, this means: 'first, to do no harm'.

legal cases within the prevailing arrangements of power (Hajjar 2001: 68). However, Varvara's style of lawyering cannot be detached from the conditions of migrant Moscow, where many migrants simply stay behind or fall through the cracks of the ever-changing immigration rules through no fault of their own (Reeves 2013, 2015, 2016; Kubal 2016b, 2017). Varvara's preferred choice of cause-lawyering is to pursue the cases of individual migrant-clients without calling additional and unnecessary attention to them or her work. The cause, delineated by this type of cause-lawyering, aims not to challenge the system but to 'help individuals get the best outcome they can working within that system' (Hilbink 2004: 669). Varvara works strictly within the limits of the formal law and legal rules; her potential to challenge the status quo comes not in structural, broader legislative changes but in the lives of the individuals she represents and defends in courts in discrete cases (Hilbink 2004: 669).

Why does this type of cause-lawyering seems to predominate in Russia in immigration and refugee law cases? Varvara' choice of style of representing migrants, when put in comparative perspective, highlights the specificities of cause-lawyering in immigration and refugee law cases more globally. I put forward an observation that the immigration and refugee cause-lawyers in Russia – and elsewhere in the world – suffer from a double marginalization both in terms of their position within the broader legal profession and in terms of the position of immigration and refugee law against other strands of state law. Austin Sarat and Stuart Scheingold, the most profound writers and researchers of cause-lawyering, whose work over the years has placed this concept firmly within the socio-legal scholarship (Sarat and Scheingold 1998b, 2001a, 2006), argue that cause-lawyering everywhere in the world is 'a deviant strain of legal profession' (Sarat and Scheingold 1998a: 3). What distinguishes cause-lawyers is

> the moral posture ... beyond a crude instrumentalism in which lawyers sell their services without regard to the ends to which those services are put.
>
> (Sarat and Scheingold 1998a: 3)

The cause-lawyers in Russia in a similar vein distinguish themselves from the many ordinary immigration lawyers whom I observed in the courtrooms or 'corridors of justice' ahead of hearings. The latter seemed to take cases simply for the fees and with little concern for how good the case actually was. As an example, I once observed an immigration lawyer representing a group of Uzbek and Tajik migrant workers, who argued that his defendants, captured in photographs by the Federal Migration Service (FMS) working on a building site as bricklayers with work permits issued for the profession of 'a process technologist', should be acquitted by the court. After all, they were in possession of valid, non-expired work permits. Another ordinary Russian immigration lawyer insisted the clients paid her ahead of the hearing (the money did change hands), upon which her only line of defence against charges of lack of residence registration was that her clients 'only visited' the raided apartment rather than actually lived there. This, admittedly, was a believable version of the facts; however, the lawyer had nothing to prove this. The judge had to weigh her arguments against the arguments and evidence provided by the FMS, which consisted of pictures of the men in the raided apartment, their belongings, and protocols from the raid as well as personal affidavits by the defendants confirming that this indeed was where they lived. This lawyer not only appeared unprofessional before the judge, she also neglected to familiarize herself with the evidence and materials of the case file ahead of the trial. Not surprisingly, therefore, immigration law has earned itself a particular reputation in Russia (and elsewhere in the world – see Sterett (1998) for the United Kingdom). The prevalent idea seems to be that immigration cases mainly consist of 'bad lawyers arguing badly for dishonest clients' (Sterett 1998: 299). The clients seem desperate, and some lawyers will take any case that comes their way.

In that sense, immigration and refugee cause-lawyers distinguish and distance themselves from the infamous immigration lawyers 'mainstream' in Russia and threaten the profession by 'destabilizing the dominant understanding of lawyering' (Sarat and Scheingold 1998a: 3). Through their commitment to the cause of their clients they cannot escape, however, identification with rather unpopular groups within the broader Russian society (and elsewhere in the world) – undocumented migrants, failed asylum seekers or refugees – whose reputation often rubs off onto the cause-lawyers themselves (Sarat and Scheingold 1998a: 213). Furthermore, immigration and refugee cause-lawyers in Russia operate within an area of the law that not only seems to suffer from 'bad reputation' and abundance of 'bad lawyers', but they also 'embroil the profession with potential conflicts with the state' (Sarat and Scheingold 1998a: 4). Challenging the authorities' decisions in immigration and refugee law cases – as embedded in their mission statement: 'there is such a profession – to protect one from their fatherland' – seems to directly question the modern Westphalian order of nation states. It challenges the values of the political mainstream: that a certain degree of restrictionism in immigration and refugee policy is necessary to protect the institutions and values of the state (Gibney 2004: 83). The states may have an obligation to assist migrants, asylum seekers or refugees when 'the costs of doing so are low' (Gibney 2004: 231), but definitely not in every case. Therefore, the overall restrictiveness and politicized character of immigration and refugee laws globally, combined with professional marginalization and limited opportunities for pursuing strategic impact litigation within the Russian legal system (Burkov 2017), means that quite often immigration and refugee cause-lawyers resort to the rather low-profile cause-lawyering through caring about the individual cases.

Coming to Terms with the Limits of the Law: Introducing Cause-Lawyering 'with the Grain'

The spectrum of 'high-profile' to 'low-profile' cause-lawyers, and the different conceptualizations of the causes that accompany them, have all been constructed with reference to law, legal tools, legal procedures and legal actions. However, what to do when the law does not seem to be the best avenue to pursue clients' interests? What if 'I fought the law and the law won' (see Halliday and Morgan 2013)? What if the formal, legal avenues had been exhausted, but this did not bring relief to the client? Many lawyers around the world, especially cause-lawyers, sometimes on a daily basis come to terms with the limits of the law (Menkel-Meadow 2002; Fu and Cullen 2008; Munger 2015). After all, law is but one place where battles for social change can be fought (Hilbink 2004: 682). The limits of the law often expose the limits of a particular legal case. But it does not mean that the cause-lawyering ends here: the individual client is still very much in need of representation, in need of help. What do Russian cause-lawyers do in these circumstances?

Some of the immigration and refugee lawyers drop their cases at this point. Others, however, pursue them regardless of the means, quite often resorting to practices outside the formal law but 'with the grain' of mainstream politics and the dominant legal culture. What does it mean? I introduce this term to capture a unique approach to cause-lawyering in Russia – when the lawyers do not reject legal action in favour of social movement activism, civil disobedience or throwing 'sand in the machine' (Sarat 1998: 334). For Russian lawyers, the cause surpasses the legal case and puts the individual at the centre. *The individual becomes the cause.* The responsibility to protect the vulnerable client – a refugee, an asylum seeker, a deportable migrant – goes beyond the law and available legal remedies themselves. What follows is that the individual's interests should be pursued by all means, both legal and a-legal. Russian lawyers engaged in cause-lawyering 'with the grain' may look as if they have abandoned any sense of a cause simply by trying to save their client going *with* rather than *against* disadvantageous legal precedents or rules if their client can be made to 'fit' within their narrow or discriminating parameters (Bisharat 1998; Hajjar 2001). The empirical case study that follows casts more flesh on this argument and introduces the main point of cause-lawyering with the grain in Russia – saving people's livelihoods, working *with and within* the prevailing legal system, often at the cost of losing important legal battles.

Before I move on to the case study, however, I have to clarify two points. First, the 'with the grain' type of lawyering does not reflect the work of all the immigration and refugee cause-lawyers in Russia with whom I spoke, who could more readily be characterized by the traditional types of cause-lawyering found in the established literature (Hilbink 2004; Scheingold and Sarat 2004). These cause-lawyers adopt formal legal strategies to seek justice for their individual clients at the domestic level (like Varvara). There is also a small and elite group of cause-lawyers, who pursue legal challenges addressing legal limitations beyond the domestic level, advancing individual cases that lead to precedent judgments before the European Court of Human Rights, or other international legal fora (the United Nations). I decided to distinguish the 'with the grain' lawyering as a special type of cause-lawyering upon conducting fieldwork in one particular NGO in Moscow. This NGO is staffed by both professional and lay lawyers (*advokaty i yuristy*) and headed by a truly charismatic leader, who devoted nearly all her life to championing humanitarian work among migrants, refugees and internally displaced persons (IDPs) in Russia. This NGO is widely known in the professional world (Malakhov 2014), has an impressive record of national and international cases, and helped numerous migrants and refugees to secure their livelihoods within and outside of Russia.

The second point I need to stress is that whenever I refer to cause-lawyering 'with the grain', I mean *a type* of cause-lawyering, and not an attribute of individual lawyers. In other words, the lawyers from the above-mentioned NGO cannot be solely identified with this type of cause-lawyering. In their everyday immigration and refugee cases they often employ different techniques of cause-lawyering. Both the more traditional and 'with the grain' types surfaced at different times and under different circumstances in their professional legal work, depending on the particular cases and the limits of the law. The lawyers would move in and out of the different strategies, depending on which served the cause and their clients better at a particular point in time.

Kurdish-Syrian Refugee Family Case Study

In early September 2015, a large Kurdish family – mother, father and four children aged between twelve and three – boarded a flight from Istanbul to the international airport in Sheremetyevo, Russia. Although immediately prior to their arrival in Russia they lived in Erbil, Iraq, as Kurds they held double Iraqi–Syrian citizenship. Their Russian visas were in their Syrian passports. They were escaping the advances of the army of Islamic State (ISIS) that controlled many territories in northern Iraq with Kurdish presence. The father, Ahmed,[6] was born in Afrin, a town in northern Syria, part of the Aleppo Governorate. Elif, the mother, was born in Azerbaijan, but lived most of her life in Iraq with her husband and four children – three boys, and the youngest, a girl, Adan, only three years old. I suppose their complex ethnicity and the multicultural nature of their family escaped the narrow boundaries of the nationalistic premise that 'ethnic boundaries should not cut across political ones' (Gellner 2008: 1).

[6] The names of all the family members have been changed.

The family was stopped at passport control in Sheremetyevo Airport. The border guard officers questioned the authenticity of their Syrian passports. Elif and Ahmed were charged with attempting an illegal border crossing by presenting counterfeit documents – a criminal offence in Russia.[7] The Kurdish family was detained. Elif and the children were separated from their husband and father for the duration of the pre-trial proceedings.

Through their family members in Russia, they managed to get in touch with the chairwoman of the legal aid NGO; their case also became known to the United Nations High Commissioner for Refugees (UNHCR). The chairwoman of the NGO gave their case to one of the most experienced lawyers at the NGO; however, she and everyone else in the NGO and its wider networks kept a close eye on the developments in the case.

Two weeks later, the family was brought under escort to the K. District Court, which considered the question of the measure of restraint in the pending criminal proceedings. The NGO lawyer represented the family in these proceedings. The judge agreed to the release of the family and ordered bail of 50,000 roubles. The bail was paid; however, the family was not released into mainland Russia, but taken to the transit zone of Sheremetyevo Airport.

This was the beginning of over two months of de facto detention in Sheremetyevo Airport. The material conditions that prevailed in the transit zone were not fit to accommodate a family of six, with four minor children. The family lived in the former smoking room at the airport – the room had no walls, but glass panels, so there was not even a hope for a little bit of privacy. The family spent their first days in Russia 'in the panopticon of Sheremetyevo' in the public gaze. The children had no opportunity to take a shower; they used the airport toilets for personal hygiene and the family slept on the floor on two inflatable mattresses. In the Moscow weather conditions of early winter, they suffered from cold, as the heaters in the former smoking room were either not working, or regardless of their condition they were switched off at night. For food, they ate whatever was available in the few airport fast-food restaurants – the children had their life share of burgers and fries! A month and a half into 'airport life', the Elif's health significantly deteriorated. She was taken to hospital in K. District of Moscow, where she spent ten days, only to be released back to the transit zone of Sheremetyevo Airport.

Mobilizing Public Support

The NGO chairwoman, the lawyers and the family members called upon public support – and the response was overwhelming. People delivered mattresses, bed linen, warm clothes and food for the children to the NGO headquarters. A special bank account was opened for financial donations for the family. Freelance journalists from the non-state media bought plane tickets

[7] Pursuant to art. 30.3 and art. 322.1 of the Criminal Code of the Russian Federation.

to specific European destinations just to enter the transit zone, pass these donations to the family and make their story known to the wider public. The family even featured in a short report for the BBC that highlighted the echoes of the 'European refugee crisis' in Russia (Rainsford 2015).

With the help of the NGO lawyers, Elif and Ahmed applied for refugee status for their family in Russia. The FMS refused the applications on account of the pending criminal proceedings against the family.[8] This is when the UNHCR became more actively involved in the case. The NGO chairwoman started a very successful online media campaign to highlight the fact that art. 31 of the 1951 Refugee Convention – to which Russia is a party – does not require refugees to be in possession of a valid travel or identity document. The refugees are escaping war, escaping the risk of torture or persecution – in this case the advances of ISIS – and they should be granted the right to apply for asylum in Russia. The main idea was to symbolically re-focus the story and reshape the identity of the Kurdish family from alleged criminal offenders to lawful refugees. The campaign centred on their right to claim asylum and humanitarian protection and provided an alternative narrative to the legal proceedings against Ahmed and Elif for attempting purportedly illegal entry to Russia. For a couple of weeks and news cycles the case was very prominent in the public sphere, widely discussed in human rights circles and on social media. This campaign definitely raised the public profile of this case.

Losing the Legal Battle before the European Court of Human Rights

The NGO lawyer, in addition to representing the family in the criminal proceedings before the domestic courts, also applied to the European Court of Human Rights (ECtHR), complaining that the forcible return of the Kurdish family would violate articles 2 and 3 of the European Convention (right to life, prohibition of inhuman and degrading treatment). She also applied for Rule 39 of the Rules of the Court (interim measures) – to prevent the family's removal from Russia – for as long as their case was being examined before the ECtHR. The Court grants such requests only on an exceptional basis, when the applicants would otherwise face a real risk of serious and irreversible harm (Press Unit ECtHR 2018).

The government, in its response to the request for interim measures, indicated that there was no real danger of returning the applicants to Syria, given that 'they were Iraqi nationals and arrived from Iraq'. The state lawyers insisted that the family were not Syrians, but rather 'used forged passports of Syrian nationals', a statement which was communicated to the ECtHR before the conclusion of the domestic criminal proceedings against the Kurdish family. Furthermore, the government insisted that the applicants had not exhausted domestic remedies in their appeals of the refugee status proceedings; therefore,

[8] Art. 5, para. 1.1 of the Federal Law 'On Refugees'.

the request for interim measures was premature. The state lawyers pointed out that the ECtHR was perhaps exceeding its authority by

> violating the principle of subsidiary [sic]; acting as a domestic law enforcement or investigative body rather than an international tribunal, the Court has initiated proceedings and requested information from the parties, essentially conducting its own investigation of the circumstance of the case and collecting evidence instead of the applicants and their representative.
>
> (Para. 15 Government submission to ECtHR, 10 November 2015)

Finally, the government complained that the application for interim measures had no authority form (*doverennost'*) signed by the applicants (Elif and Ahmed). The government alleged that the request originated from the lawyer herself, rather than from the applicants, and therefore should be rejected on procedural grounds.

In this particular case the ECtHR agreed with the government's observations and refused to apply the interim measures 'owing to the lack of substantiation of the request' and on procedural grounds. The ECtHR did not, however, reject the application under articles 2 and 3 as manifestly ill-founded, and advised that the lawyer prepare a full application.

The NGO community and the lawyers were understandably hugely disappointed with the ECtHR's decision. In conversation, they stressed the profound misunderstanding by the Court of the 'on the ground' situation in Russia. Indeed, the NGO lawyer had not attached to the application the authority form signed by her clients. She was a *pro bono* lawyer and the NGO, with limited resources, could not afford to buy a plane ticket for her just to see her clients in the transit zone to obtain signatures. Indeed, the application for interim measures was perhaps premature – Ahmed and Elif had not exhausted all domestic legal remedies and rights to appeal with regard to refugee status – however, the family was in limbo, stranded in Sheremetyevo transit zone, in 'no man's land'. Who could guarantee that they would not be deported before they exhausted all rights to appeal in Russia?[9]

Finding Alternative Solutions

The lawyers and the NGO community perhaps misjudged the ECtHR's possibility to act in this particular case. Given the past successful experiences of obtaining Rule 39 of the Rules of the Court (see Kubal 2016a; Chapter 7), they had high hopes for immediate justice. However, the 'transit zone' situation and complex questions of jurisdiction, in combination with alleged non-exhaustion of domestic remedies and the principle of subsidiarity,

[9] The ECtHR has an established jurisprudence of systemic violation of principle of non-refoulement by Russian national authorities in cases where interim measures were not applied – e.g. in *Dalimov* v. *Russia* (app. 77339/11) the applicant was extradited to Uzbekistan, disregarding pending asylum proceedings. This takes place despite the enshrinement of the non-refoulement principle in Ruling of the Supreme Court no. 11 of 14 June 2012.

demonstrated that the ECtHR, at least at this point, could not fulfil these expectations. The legal logic of ECtHR proceedings did not meet the NGO lawyers' needs to move the case forward; neither could it deliver a symbolic upper hand in further negotiations with the government.

The first legal battle might have been lost, but it did not mean the case was over. The NGO lawyers were, however, not prepared at this point to wage a full-scale legal 'war' – a long, complex and protracted dispute before the ECtHR. It could have been won eventually, but this route of legal action would not provide immediate relief to the stranded family and their minor children. The ECtHR application clearly exposed the limits of the law in this particular case, and its ability to bring about real change to the livelihoods of people stranded at the airport.

Not surprisingly, therefore, this legal avenue was abandoned by the NGO lawyers as ultimately ineffective. It has to be stressed, however, that the ECtHR route was renounced not because of the initial loss *per se*, but because the initial loss pointed to a structural feature of the ECtHR's limited ability to influence the domestic jurisdiction and bring about immediate change. Any potential change through law was located in a rather distant future, whereas time was a very important factor here. Time was an element that mobilized the NGO lawyers' resources away from the ECtHR case, towards the search for other, immediate solutions. Something had to be done to remove the Kurdish-Syrian family from the transit zone, get the children washed, fed and comforted, and provide them with the opportunity to attend school.

Having exhausted the legal means of helping the family, and having come to terms with their ineffectiveness, the lawyers and the NGO chairwoman turned to a different set of tools at their disposal. These are illustrative of some of the 'with the grain' cause-lawyering strategies in immigration and refugee law cases in Russia.

The NGO, where the lawyers were located, holds seminars for its immigration and refugee professional community from all over Russia twice each year. The aim of these seminars is to review the changes in Russian immigration and refugee law, both at the level of legislation and 'in action'. The lawyers share best practices for enforcing the rights of migrants and refugees, their experiences under different domestic jurisdictions (Moscow, St Petersburg and the regions), and the developments in their cases before the ECtHR. These seminars are always well attended, and the speakers are invited to present include experienced ECtHR lawyers, human rights activists, legal experts and FMS representatives. These seminars are therefore a unique opportunity for a meaningful dialogue between the different stakeholders in migration and refugee law. The guest speakers, especially the FMS representatives, are often invited to attend personally by the NGO chairwoman. These seminars also provide a rare chance for closed, 'behind the scenes' negotiations of the most complex cases – to informally lobby the FMS for action in the most pressing instances. It is through the opportunity structures provided by the seminar environment, and the invaluable personal contacts of the NGO chairwoman, her charisma and the great respect she commands among the state legal and human rights circles, that the Kurdish-Syrian family case was added to the agenda.

The subsequent developments demonstrate that during the seminar's informal discussions the lawyers appealed successfully to the FMS to exercise its discretion. Some form of a compromise must have been reached, and for those readers who find this strategy suspicious, let me explain that compromise was a tactic highly favoured by activists and lawyers in the southern civil rights movement in the 1960s United States (Hilbink 2004: 685).

In mid-November 2015, the Kurdish family again appeared before the domestic court for their appeal in the criminal proceedings for the attempted illegal border crossing. The prosecutor demanded a 30,000-rouble fine. The NGO lawyer maintained her line of defence that both Elif and Ahmed were refugees. There was, however, a significant shift in her argument relating to from where the right to asylum should be derived. The NGO lawyer no longer relied on the 1951 Refugee Convention, but appealed to the political asylum institution as inscribed in the Russian domestic legislation and the Constitution.[10] The lawyer insisted that her clients should be released from criminal liability according to art. 322 of the Criminal Code of the Russian Federation. This article indicates that the Constitution exempts individuals from liability for illegal border crossing if the alleged perpetrator openly declares that they did so to obtain political asylum in Russia (and had not committed other criminal or administrative offences).[11]

Although both Elif and Ahmed were found guilty of the 'attempted illegal entry' charges, the judge proved sympathetic to the arguments raised by the defence and accommodated them in the final decision: the fine for the criminal offence was reduced to 5,000 roubles. The judge also ordered that the bail of 50,000 roubles be returned to the family. Through this action, the judge ensured that the family had the resources to pay the fine, and that the criminal case against them could be considered concluded (and put behind them). Upon the completion of the criminal proceedings, Elif and Ahmed were taken back to the transit zone of Sheremetyevo Airport. Acting on the advice of the NGO lawyer, they formally applied for political asylum in Russia. The chairwoman of the NGO summarized these developments as follows:

> Today a miracle happened. At our seminar spoke Mr. R. – the Head of Department of Asylum FMS Russia. We brought up the situation of the family in Sheremetyevo. [. . .] He said that in his opinion 'our Syrians' should now reapply for asylum [. . .] During our meeting Mr. R. called one of his subordinates in the FMS. An hour later Elif called us, said that the FMS officers had arrived at the airport, and were ready to accept their refugee application. The family was asked to get ready to leave Sheremetyevo [. . .] What we could not manage in two months was achieved in half a day.
>
> (NGO chairwoman, via Facebook, 20 November 2015)

[10] See the legal overview in Chapter 2 for the explanation of the difference between the refugee status as derived from the 1951 Refugee Convention and the political asylum status in Russia.

[11] For the full report from the hearing, see Fomina (2015a).

Three days later, the whole family was released from the transit zone and placed in the temporary accommodation centre of the FMS.[12] In February 2016, the family was granted temporary asylum in Russia; they left the FMS centre and joined Elif's family members.

The Practice of Cause-Lawyering 'with the Grain'

This case study illustrates a number of characteristic features of the specific type of cause-lawyering adopted by the NGO lawyers to represent the Kurdish family. The narrative is quite long and full of details, but this stylistic form was chosen intentionally – to provide an ethnographically rich description of the 'with the grain' type of cause-lawyering in Russia. I wanted to convey the story of the Kurdish family with the same attention to detail, care and emotional charge with which it was originally told to me by the NGO refugee and immigration lawyers. This case study highlights three main features of the practice of cause-lawyering 'with the grain' in Russia: (1) determination to act despite the limits of the law; (2) care towards individual clients; and (3) working with the existing system, often at the cost of losing important legal battles.

The NGO immigration and refugee lawyers too often in their professional practice come up against the limits of the law. They find it impossible to achieve justice for their clients solely with reference to legal means. It is not necessarily because of corruption or telephone justice that has been referred to in much analysis of the Russian system, but due to specific logics according to which the system operates (Kurchiyan and Kubal 2018a, 2018b). The same could be said to be true for the ECtHR – the interim measures were not applied, which constituted a huge blow to the NGO lawyers and activists. No one would venture to speculate that the European judges were unsympathetic to the case, or acted on behalf of political orders; however, their inaction clearly exposed the limits of international human rights law in this case. With regard to domestic law, elsewhere I have presented the Russian justice system in the immigration and refugee sphere as focused on the *po zakonu* – very literal, formal and legalistic – interpretation of the law (Kurkchiyan 2009; Kubal 2016a). Chapter 5 of this book provides an in-depth analysis of the role of case files and documentary evidence in administrative immigration cases, which could be seen as an extension of that logic.

This structural rigidity of the system does not inspire much confidence in more creative interpretation of the law, beyond the purely 'black letter', textual reference. For example, we learn from the case study that the initial refusal of refugee status to Elif and Ahmed was motivated by their pending criminal proceedings, with clear reference to specific paragraphs of the domestic Russian law 'On Refugees'. This conservative strategy, very close to the black-letter law meant the authorities were 'playing it safe' (see McCarthy 2018). The

[12] For a full report from the release, see Fomina (2015b).

alternative interpretation, as derived from the spirit of art. 31 of the 1951 Refugee Convention (a refugee or asylum seeker should not be prosecuted for an alleged illegal entry), and which the chairwoman of the NGO highlighted many times in interviews and public speeches, was not initially considered by the authorities. The 1951 Convention is integrated within the Russian legal framework, and yet repeatedly it can be seen – as with other countries – that domestic law takes precedence in many legal status determination decisions. It is only when a new strategy was consensually worked out between the FMS and the NGO lawyers with reference to the institution of political asylum (as ingrained in Russian domestic law and the Constitution) that the FMS became more sympathetic to the cause. This agreement did not develop in a vacuum. It would not have been reached without the widespread public campaign, the personal involvement of the activists, the pressure from public opinion (which displayed massive support for the Kurdish-Syrian family), the online media campaign and the support of the UNHCR. All these actions resulted in a more conducive environment that pushed against the limits of the law towards a broader and creative legal interpretation.

Following from this, the next important element of 'with the grain' cause-lawyering is the focus on the individual client. As we can see in the Kurdish-Syrian family case study, the main idea behind all the steps taken both by the NGO lawyers, the chairwoman and the activists was to have the family released from the transit zone in Sheremetyevo Airport, so that they could regularize their status, join their family members in Russia and together somewhat resume their normal lives. This is why the ECtHR as an option for fighting for the family's interests was ultimately abandoned. No interim measures were applied, and all the subsequent correspondence from the Court led to a single conclusion: if any change in the actual day-to-day living conditions of the family were to be brought by the ECtHR ruling, this would be until some point in a quite distant future. More pressing humanitarian considerations were at stake, especially due to the welfare concerns of the four minor children.

The NGO lawyer went beyond the legal representation to ensure that the family was safe. For the lawyer, her mission was not legal, but humanitarian. Once the Kurdish-Syrian family was released from the transit zone, she visited them on numerous occasions in the temporary accommodation centre of the FMS. Aside from giving legal advice, representing them in the ongoing temporary asylum proceedings and bringing documents to sign, she delivered gifts and donations from the different members of the public that were dropped off at the NGO's main headquarters. She popularized their case in social media. Critics could say that these practices do not fit squarely with the classic definition of cause-lawyering, but I would argue that they are important characteristics of cause-lawyering in Russia. The legal representation becomes an important undertaking that extends well beyond the courtroom. The NGO lawyers indeed do care for their individual clients, their wellbeing and welfare, and consider them as their utmost priority. Sergey Golubok, a prominent Russian lawyer, has argued recently that the role of a defence lawyer in Russia

Figure 3.1 Lawyer speaking to Russian and international media about the Kurdish-Syrian family case after a court hearing.
Source: R. Magomedova Facebook archives, 2015

does not begin and end with legal representation. A good lawyer is often a psychologist, offering care and alleviating the emotional suffering of the defendant. At different times, the lawyer has to be a succinct storyteller, whose main audience is not the judge before them, but international media, human rights groups and global civic society (see Figure 3.1). The lawyer uses different available channels to tell a story of their defendant with the idea to 'win' the case in the hearts of the public and thereby exert pressure on domestic legal institutions or 'push them into compliance' (Golubok 2018).

What also distinguishes cause-lawyering 'with the grain' in Russia is the readiness to abandon – sometimes even lose – important legal battles if that is ultimately to help the clients. The NGO immigration lawyers in the Kurdish-Syrian case study preferred to work out a compromise with the FMS within the prevailing arrangements of power and not to pursue the legal route before the ECtHR on behalf of their clients. It does not mean, however, that litigation was impossible. For example, analogous to the Kurdish-Syrian family case was the case of an Iraqi, Syrian, Palestinian and Somali nationals (*Z.A. and Others* v. *Russia*, no. 61411/15, 61420/15, 61427/15, 3028/16, judgment of 28 March 2017) stranded in the transit zone of Sheremetyevo Airport. The case of *Z.A. and Others* v. *Russia* had a successful conclusion in the ECtHR. In this particular case, the ECtHR found violations of art. 5 (right to liberty) and art. 3 (prohibition of inhuman and degrading treatment), stating that the confinement of the applicants to the transit zone of Sheremetyevo Airport:

> amounted to the deprivation of liberty.
>
> (Para. 90)

> The Court has little doubt that a public space such as the transit zone of an airport, lacking such basic amenities as beds, showers, and areas designated for cooking, is by definition ill-equipped to serve as a long-term residence.
>
> (Para 107)

> [The Court] considers it unacceptable that anyone might be detained in conditions in which there is a complete failure to take care of his or her essential needs.
> (Para. 108, all from Z.A. and Others v. Russia 2017)

The ECtHR awarded the men in *Z.A. and Others* v. *Russia* significant financial compensation: between 15,000 and 26,000 euros. These four (adult) men were stranded in the transit zone of Sheremetyevo Airport for 6–23 months (no interim measures were applied here by the ECtHR either). None of the four men received refugee status or temporary asylum in Russia. Two of the applicants were ultimately resettled by the UNHCR to a third country (Denmark and Sweden) after approximately eight months of confinement in the transit zone. Two of the men returned to Gaza in Israel–Palestine and Somalia after 6 and 23 months of confinement, respectively. Their cases were brought before the ECtHR over the course of December 2015 and January 2016 (at the point of the men's detention at Sheremetyevo Airport), and decided in March 2017, 13 months later. At the time of writing, the decision in *Z.A. and Others* v. *Russia* is not yet final, as upon the Russian government's appeal the case was referred to the Grand Chamber.[13]

The ECtHR decision in *Z.A. and Others* v. *Russia* has the potential to become a landmark case and bring about important systemic and structural changes in how Russia balances the prevention of:

> unlawful immigration while complying with [its] international obligations, in particular under the 1951 Convention relating to the Status of Refugees and the European Convention on Human Rights. States' legitimate concern to foil the increasingly frequent attempts to circumvent immigration restrictions *must not deprive* asylum-seekers of the protection afforded by these conventions.
> (Para 104, Z.A. and Others v. Russia 2017, my emphasis).

This legal route, although formally available, was not necessarily the best option for the Kurdish-Syrian family from the case study. It becomes clear especially if we balance this decision against the time frame of the proceedings before the Strasbourg Court, the broader welfare of the family (especially the four minor children) and the fact that none of the men from *Z.A. and Others* v. *Russia* were ultimately allowed into Russia, nor given a protected status there. On balance, therefore, the NGO lawyers had all the reasons to resort to 'with the grain' cause-lawyering as the best avenue to protect the Kurdish-Syrian family's interests at the cost of bringing an important legal case to the ECtHR. Focusing their actions and resources on bringing about immediate change to the situation of the family instead, the lawyers ensured that the family was allowed to enter Russia and their welfare needs were responded to.

[13] This case has a very interesting dissenting opinion by Judge Dmitry Dedov, representing the Russian Federation in the panel of judges. I analyse this dissent separately in Chapter 6 of this book, which is devoted to tracing the human rights logic in various court judgments in immigration and refugee law cases.

Who Engages in Cause-Lawyering 'with the Grain'?

Earlier in this chapter, I introduced cause-lawyering 'with the grain' as a *type* of cause-lawyering. I cautioned that as a type it should not be attached to particular individual lawyers as defining their entire professional practice. Different legal professionals adopt this type of lawyering depending on the limits of the law and the individual circumstances of the case. There are certain characteristics, however, that make some lawyers resort to this style more often than others. In the final substantive section of this chapter, I therefore introduce Violet, a composite character of a cause-lawyer, who highlights the conditions and reasons why some lawyers resort to cause-lawyering 'with the grain' more frequently or might find it more effective for their professional practice. The story of Violet is based on more than one individual; it is a compilation of the various interviews I conducted with different immigration and refugee lawyers in Moscow, including their experiences of when, why and under what conditions they resorted to cause-lawyering 'with the grain'. After all, how lawyers think about the legal system shapes how they conceive of the cause and their role in it as a lawyer (Hilbink 2004: 663).

Violet has worked for the NGO for many years; she is one of the core lawyers, but also a vibrant and colourful personality. It was not her first choice to come to Moscow to work with migrants and refugees. She had a life, family, job and successful career in a different part of Russia. In her 'previous life', as she now refers to her time back in the region, she was a primary school head teacher; she liked her job and her students. But then the war came, and Violet, like many others, had to flee the region to save her life and escape violence. She became internally displaced.

I often observed Violet's work. She allowed me to accompany her to court, and it was after one of these hearings in court that I learned her story and her motivation to join the NGO and become a lawyer, a committed cause-lawyer. The court case was not particularly interesting, and the whole morning was a bit of an anti-climax: we waited for about 40 minutes for the case to start, but when we finally entered the courtroom, the judge adjourned the hearing at the request of the FMS. When we left the court, Violet loudly and heartily greeted a man who was selling newspapers on the pavement in front of the court building. I wondered how she knew him. Violet saw my surprise and said:

> Not so long ago I was selling newspapers on the street myself. I had my stand next to this man: a folding bed with different journals and magazines. We were colleagues. I somehow managed to move on... He was less lucky.

The image of Violet selling newspapers on the street was so far removed from her current identity as a powerful lawyer that I found this story difficult to believe. At the NGO or in court she was always immaculately dressed and wore perfect make up. She was a feisty woman. Violet was strident towards her opponents, ambitious, sometimes outright rude (especially in relation to the state authorities). She often verbally challenged court officers checking identity documents at the entrance to the court if she felt they were taking too much time:

> I am in this court at least three times a week, every week; do you really see my passport for the first time?

In her relations with clients, at first sight she might have appeared rather restrained, laconic and sometimes short-tempered. Once, one of her clients brought a group of supporters from Amnesty International to the court to sit in on his case and had not informed Violet about this earlier. She warned him in a stern voice she would leave the courthouse now and he would need to be represented by 'his friends'.

However, those who were close to Violet knew that deep down she was very caring and compassionate. Whenever she was brisk with her clients, it was because she did not want anything to jeopardize their cases – seeing public interest and Amnesty International support in this particular case could potentially raise suspicions from the judge. Violet did not need this; she already felt the cards were stacked against her.

Violet held the wellbeing of her clients as her main priority. Not necessarily the success of their legal cases, as she did not have much faith in the Russian system of justice, but the personal and physical wellbeing of her clients mattered most. She would make sure they were safe; often she would go the extra mile to ensure they were not in any physical or psychological danger. Depending on the details and circumstances of the case, she would spend long hours in front of police stations (if the police officers did not want to let her in) waiting for clients against whom charges had been pressed in connection with the lack of valid residence or work permit. In cases involving extradition of asylum seekers to Central Asia, she waited long hours in the corridors of the General Prosecutor's building to make sure the clients were not secretly transferred out of the country. Sometimes she would urge her clients not to leave the detention centre until she arrived, to ensure they were not apprehended by the police in 'random' document check on their way to the metro, giving rise to a new set of administrative immigration-related charges. At other times, she would accompany her clients to the FMS local field offices to apply for asylum, again to make sure the FMS officers did not charge her clients with fresh administrative immigration-related offences instead of processing their asylum applications. She was visibly distressed when, due to her own oversight in the application, the ECtHR did not award her clients compensation for prolonged detention pending expulsion. I heard her complaining:

> Why there is no compensation? These men [the clients] have been in detention for nearly two years. When they are released now, they will be dog-poor (*golyye kak sokoly*).

This quote was very characteristic of Violet. She would not challenge the Strasbourg Court, seeing the decision as one of the many limits of justice she encountered daily in her professional practice. She did not know how to appeal this judgment to correct this oversight – after all, the judgment was very much in her favour: the Court forbade Russia extraditing or deporting these men back to Uzbekistan, as that would be a violation of art. 3 (prohibition of torture, inhuman and degrading treatment). However, in every discussion of the case she was preoccupied that her clients would leave the detention centre in a very vulnerable state, both mentally and economically.

Violet's broader attitude to law was ambiguous – drawing on her professional practice she was highly sceptical about whether justice could ever be achieved by legal means. I think it is fair to say she was cynical about law's potential to save her clients. She would not hesitate to adopt cause-lawyering 'with the grain', bypassing the formal law altogether, sometimes at the cost of losing important legal battles at the international level, only to save her clients. One of her cases was struck from the ECtHR register after her client – an asylum seeker facing the danger of deportation to Uzbekistan – found himself safely in one of the Schengen countries. When Violet learned about the result of this case, she wrote to me a one-line email:

> We need to explain [to the Strasbourg Court] that we feared for his life and therefore sent him [away from Russia].

Her professional reputation of losing a case before the ECtHR, of potentially being seen as not very effective in the wider circle of immigration and refugee lawyers in Moscow, was of secondary importance. What mattered was the safety and physical security of her client. Violet, perhaps naively, believed that the ECtHR would see her argument and her side of the story – the commonsense part of the story – that awaiting the Court's decision meant personal risk to her client, an asylum seeker with no legal status in Russia.

Back on the street next to the newspaper stand, and seeing my surprise at her sudden testimony, Violet continued her story of what motivated her to become an immigration lawyer:

> When the war broke in our region, normal life was not possible. It was just constant fear, stagnation or deterioration of everything I knew and held dear. I left. I came to Moscow. Of course it was difficult. No one wanted to hire us, as we were the terrorists. No one wanted to give us residence permits, as we were the bombers. I found shelter at the NGO. Initially I was just volunteering a couple of days a week so that my life here would not feel so futile. I had to make ends meet so I was also selling the newspapers.
>
> Why I stayed at the NGO?
>
> One day there was a terrorist attack in Moscow. Everybody, all the papers, all the media, everyone – they were saying it was one of us, that the attacker was from our region. Someone also came to the NGO and said 'the rebels from the region set up a bomb in Moscow'. Then Elena, the vice chair, turned away from her desk and asked: 'Are you sure it was the rebels? Do you have proof?' I felt like giving her a big hug. Everyone was saying the bomb was because one of us. And she, they, the NGO . . . they were different. From that moment, I knew I wanted to work for them.

Violet started assisting the lawyers and jurists at the NGO, photocopying documents, composing the case files, accompanying the clients to the FMS when they applied for asylum. At some point, the chairwoman of the organization received a grant that paid for Violet's formal juridical education. A former primary school head teacher in her early forties, she went back to university, this time with the goal of becoming a lawyer. She received her degree, became a professional lawyer (*advocate*) and from then onwards she started formally working for the NGO.

Most of the immigration and refugee lawyers with whom I spoke were women: strong, feisty, often single women. Their personal stories, when coupled with strong commitment to cause-lawyering seem to confirm the highly idiosyncratic conclusion found in the broader literature that women seem more likely to 'personalize and humanize' their tales of commitment to cause-lawyering (Menkel-Meadow 1998: 47). For Violet, the journey to become an immigration cause-lawyer was also very personal, motivated by the injustice she experienced as an underdog – 'a migrant-rebel in Moscow'.

The lawyers who most often resort to cause-lawyering 'with the grain', by the nature of their position within the various NGOs and their organizational alliance with the UNHCR, work primarily within the logic of the responsibility to protect. The NGOs do not pre-screen or pre-select their clients, taking 'whoever came in the door' during office hours. Their clients range across Kyrgyz, Tajik and Uzbek migrants with pending extradition cases on politically motivated or religious (Muslim) extremism charges; Syrians, Ukrainians, Iraqis, Afghans or Africans (Eritreans, Somalis, Congolese, Senegalese, Malians) with pending asylum applications; and victims of racially motivated hate crime. People who come to consult the lawyers range from former citizens of the USSR who arrived in Russia back in the 1990s, but never regularized their stay and are now stateless; IDPs who, due to conflict in different republics in Russia, arrived in Moscow; Chechen and Dagestani deportees from different parts of the European Union (e.g. Poland). The type of help these people need and require varies a lot – quite often it cannot be limited to legal representation, but also includes financial, humanitarian assistance or petitioning the authorities. The role of the charismatic chairwoman of the NGO is indispensable for the majority of these cases to find a satisfactory conclusion, often due to the inability of the law to effectively deal with them.

* * *

In this chapter, I conceptualized a specific group of Russian immigration and refugee lawyers as cause-lawyers. Through the portrait of Varvara, I defined the characteristic features of cause-lawyering in Russia as corresponding with one particular model of cause-lawyering that could be found in the broader literature, namely 'caring for individual cases'. This model stresses commitment to defending vulnerable clients based on the formal parameters of the law, at the cost of pursuing precedents leading to transformative changes in the broader legal system. In the second part of the chapter, drawing on the case study of the Kurdish-Syrian family stranded in the transit zone of Sheremetyevo Airport, I introduced a new type of cause-lawyering, arguably unique to Russia, which I termed cause-lawyering 'with the grain'. This illustrates that cause-lawyering does not stop even when the limits of the law often expose the limits of a particular legal case. Behind each case is an individual, often a very vulnerable individual – an asylum seeker, a refugee, a deportable migrant – who requires support and protection regardless of the limitations of the law. Lawyers who engage in this type of cause-lawyering prioritize the livelihoods and welfare of individual clients, often at the cost of losing important legal battles.

4

Everyday Experiences of Russian Immigration Law

The Entry Bar Case Study[1]

Introduction

Having introduced access to justice in Russia as mediated through the figure of the immigration, refugee and human rights lawyer, this chapter turns to immigrants' everyday experiences of the law at the grass-roots level. During my fieldwork in Moscow in 2014, it was the legislative changes of 2012 and 2013 – showing the punitive and restrictionist face of administrative (immigration) law regulations – that became most prominent in people's everyday lives. Entry bar or *zapret na v'ezd* is an immigration law sanction that came into force in Russia gradually in 2012 and 2013. Initially, a three-year entry bar was to be issued to anyone who had not left the territory of the Russian Federation (RF) within the 30-day grace period after the expiry of their residence permit. In July 2013, new, stricter amendments followed – the three-year entry bar was issued to foreign citizens who committed two or more administrative offences within a three-year period – a category that included, for example, a speeding or parking ticket. In practice, this new law applied to past offences (Gannushkina 2014). If issued from within the country, the entry bar rendered a person effectively deportable.[2]

The issuance of this form of entry bar did not result from a judicial decision, but lay within the discretion of staff members of the Federal Migration Service (FMS) or – since 2016 – the Ministry of Internal Affairs (MVD).[3] In the

[1] An earlier version of this chapter has been published as Kubal, A. (2017). "Entry Bar as Surreptitious Deportation? Zapret na v'ezd in Russian Immigration Law and Practice: A Comparative Perspective." *Law & Social Inquiry* **42**(3): 744–768. *Law and Social Inquiry* is a quarterly peer-reviewed academic journal published by Wiley-Blackwell on behalf of the American Bar Foundation.

[2] According to the Law on the Order of Entry and Exit (1996), an entry bar can be issued for two categories of offences: not possessing a valid residence registration or working without a valid work permit (art. 27; attracts a five-year entry bar) or petty administrative offences (art. 26; attracts a three-year entry bar). Here I focus on the second category.

[3] As described in Chapter 2, the FMS has been disbanded by the Presidential Decree of 5 April 2016 No. 156. The functions of the FMS have been transferred to the Main Directorate for Migration Affairs of the MVD, which currently issues the entry bars. In principle, a number of other Russian state institutions can issue the entry bar: the Federal Security Service, Ministry of Defence, Russian Financial Monitoring, External Intelligence Service, Ministry of Justice,

majority of cases, an FMS or MVD officer issues *zapret na v'ezd* after cross-referencing the police databases of petty administrative (e.g. traffic) offences (the Central Database of the State Inspection of Road Safety) with the database that holds information about foreign citizens' residence status in Russia (the Central Database of the Registration of Foreign Citizens, also known as the Automated System of the Central Database of Foreign Citizens). If two offences are registered against a foreign national's name, the entry bar is issued (see Bahovadinova 2016).

Among migration scholars and human rights lawyers in Russia, this is called *popast' v bazu*, meaning to 'fall into the database' or to 'get caught into the database' – language that captures the lack of agency on the part of the migrants against whom a bar has been issued. This language intuitively points to the haphazard law enforcement and a negative image of law – a reflection of the all-too-familiar traits of Russian legal culture – legal nihilism and cynicism about the law (Kurkchiyan 2005: 263–264) that the legal scholars inexorably share with the wider society. After all, tripping and falling into something does not inspire much confidence in how the law in general is applied among citizens and non-citizens alike, but brings to mind the rather well-known and well-rehearsed arguments about how the law does not really work in Russia.

But is this the full story? How does one come to understand the evolution and enforcement of the entry bar legislation in Russia? Should it be explained solely from the perspective of Russia's lack of the rule of law (Kahn 2002; McAulley et al. 2006; Kahn 2008), the country's historical and political otherness (Ledeneva 2006, 2013) or obscure and notorious bureaucratic caveats (Kononenko and Moshes 2011) giving rise to massive abuses? While I acknowledge the importance of these explanations, I argue that the clue to understanding the entry bar legislation and enforcement in Russia also lies elsewhere.

This chapter attempts to understand the *zapret na v'ezd* by bringing to light the experiences of those it affected most – the migrants. To this effect I argue that capturing the distinctive nuances and subtleties of Russian immigration law requires a comparative perspective (Nelken 2004), drawing on similarities and differences with immigration law developments in other migrant-receiving jurisdictions. Taking a step back, and looking at the entry bar from an analytical and comparative perspective, I trace how the evolution of the entry bar legislation in Russia reflects the global trends and directions of immigration law in the United States and Western Europe (Aranda et al. 2014; Menjívar 2014a) of an increased reliance on deportation and *deportability* (de Genova and Peutz 2010) as a form of post-entry control of the

Drug Control Federal Service, Federal Service on Surveillance for Consumer Rights Protection and Human Well Being, and Federal Medical Agency. I am grateful to Malika Bahovadinova for pointing this out.

migrant population (Kanstroom 2000).[4] Situating *zapret na v'ezd* in a more global, comparative perspective clearly demonstrates how the evolution of the Russian immigration law follows this logic, well-established in other major migration-receiving jurisdictions, which although formally different, in practice share similar modes of operation and have analogous consequences. The comparative perspective adopted here acknowledges the specificity of Russia, while (hopefully) avoiding the intellectual trap of treating Russia as exceptional or deviant. My comparative analogy demonstrates that the entry bar could best be understood as *a form of* deportation, exclusion from legality very much resembling the conditions of deportability: the possibility of deportation, the possibility of being removed (de Genova 2002: 439), which constitutes a specific form of contemporary migration governance. I ultimately contend that this practice, despite its name of entry bar, is actually very much akin to deportation – albeit a silent or surreptitious one. The predicament in which many migrants in Russia with entry bars find themselves is similar to that of a legal *limbo* under the conditions of deportability: migrants are prevented from regularizing their stay, and are subject to administrative removal (expulsion or deportation) in the event of an immigration raid or an ad hoc control.

Looking at the entry bar from a migrant's perspective, I analyse the proportionality of this sanction relative to the offence (minor administrative violation). Russia – in contrast to the United Kingdom or the United States – has not formally criminalized its migration law (see Chapter 2). The violations of migration law are of an administrative nature and follow administrative processes. Yet, with the introduction of the entry bar for minor administrative offences, such as speeding or parking tickets, the migration law appears disproportionally harsh, leading towards increasingly punitive administrative processes aimed at non-citizens.[5] While much of the discussion on deportation or administrative removal in the United States and the United Kingdom takes place in the context of criminalization of migration (Aliverti 2012; Kubal 2014), overcriminalization (Chacón 2012) or – blatantly – 'crimmigration' (Stumpf 2006; Romero 2010), the analysis of the entry bar in Russia invites a deeper reflection about the nature and the consequences of the civil/criminal labels in migration law (Steiker 1997; Sarat et al. 2011a). I contend that *zapret na v'ezd*, although formally within the remit of the administrative law, if analysed from the perspective of the impact on migrants' lives, actually constitutes a quasi-criminal sanction, a form of punishment.

[4] For the explanation of how the adjective Western, as a heuristic, is used throughout this book, see Chapter 1.

[5] By contrast, deportation in the United States or the United Kingdom, however harsh and inflexible, is nevertheless primarily attached to a criminal conviction (Legomsky 2007; Chacón 2009, 2012).

This chapter proceeds as follows. The next section presents the legal evolution of the entry bar legislation, followed by an empirical case study based on the story of Akmal (a migrant worker from Uzbekistan) on how the entry bar operates in Central Asian migrants' everyday lives in Moscow. The following sections, in turn, adopt a comparative perspective and analyse the similarities and differences between the entry bar and deportation practices in Russia and in the United Kingdom and United States. The similarities focus on the increased reliance on entry bar and deportation to specifically control the post-entry conduct of migrants amid retroactive application of immigration law. The differences concern the appeal structures available for entry bar in Russia and deportation in Western jurisdictions, and the proportionality (severity) of these sanctions in relation to the alleged transgressions of the law.

Evolution of the Entry Bar Legislation in Russia

Prior to 2012, the *zapret na v'ezd* was solely tied to extradition, administrative removal (expulsion) or deportation proceedings. Once a court determined a person to be eligible for administrative removal, that person would be physically removed from the territory of RF and a *zapret na v'ezd* would be issued against their name for a particular period of time. It was an auxiliary mechanism, similar to how re-entry bars are administered currently in the United States or the United Kingdom (Aleinikoff et al. 2015).

On 30 December 2012, Russian lawmakers decoupled the entry bar from the deportation/expulsion proceedings. The entry bar was made a stand-alone sanction issued to foreign citizens who have not left the territory of RF within the 30-day period since the expiry of their residence permits (Law on the Order of Entry and Exit, amendments introduced to art. 26, para. 8). This first stage in the evolution of *zapret na v'ezd* was an element of Russia's wider migration governance policy and practice. As with every immigration policy, a number of different factors could have inspired the introduction of the entry bar as a stand-alone sanction. In my earlier analysis I focused on two of them. First, there was a (true or perceived) realization of a large number of Central Asian migrants living and working in Russia, as a consequence of the strategically pursued liberalization of migration policy since 2005. The second factor was related to the economic crisis that hit Russia severely in 2009 (Kubal 2017, a consequence of the 2007–2008 global financial crisis) which, in turn, fed political populism about undocumented migration (see also Abashin 2017; Kondakov 2017; Schenk 2018).

And yet, understanding the first stage of the evolution of the *zapret na v'ezd* legislation solely in the context of Russian government's response to the growing number of allegedly undocumented (or 'illegal') migrants from Central Asia tells only part of the story. Migrants with perfectly legitimate immigration documents (both in terms of residence and work permits) face, in Russia, haphazard law enforcement on the side of the different state organs,

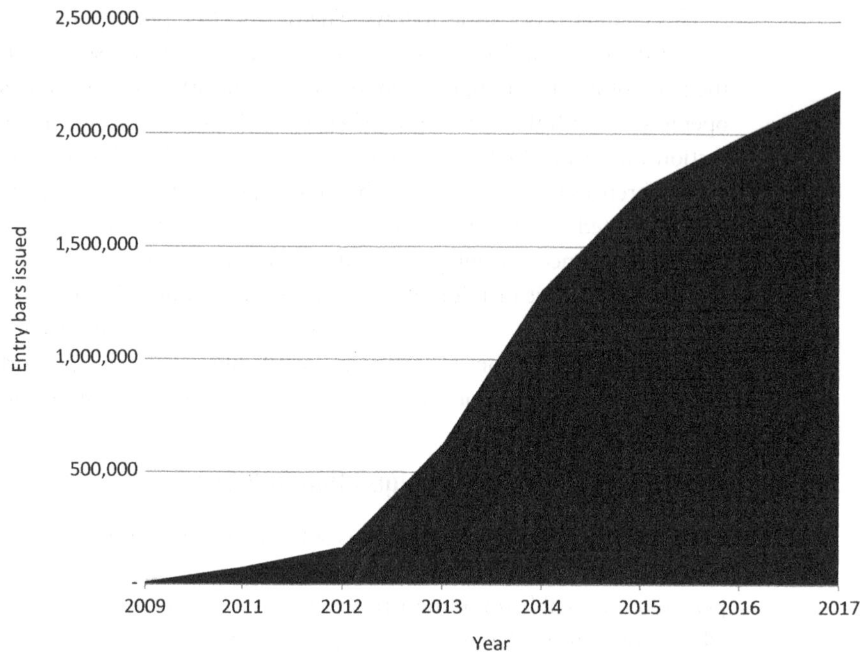

Figure 4.1 Entry bars issued in Russia to foreign nationals between 2009 and 2017 (cumulative).

mainly police officers (Davé 2014). The enforcement of the immigration rules and practices is focused on disciplining and punishing migrants who fail to obey the law, rather than facilitating general compliance. In other words, migrants are often caught in the net of potential immigration fraud that is cast far too wide, with discretion given to law enforcement agents but not enough accountability or safeguards in the system to protect those 'facing the law' (Kubal 2016b). This demonstrates that the introduction of the entry bar in Russia in response to alleged migrant illegality was in fact a response to a phenomenon constructed by the state law and its oppressive law enforcement.

The second stage in the evolution of the entry bar legislation began on 23 July 2013, when the law was amended so that any foreign citizen who, within a period of three years, had committed two or more administrative offences received a three-year entry bar (Law on the Order of Exit and Entry, art. 26, para. 4). This amendment shifted *zapret na v'ezd* from purely immigration law convictions (overstaying one's leave to remain) to more general administrative law offences. As a result, a single traffic offence that leads to no prison time now falls within the reach of the new entry bar grounds. This significantly increased the possibility and likelihood of *zapret na v'ezd*: administrative offences that previously would have had no possible immigration law consequences now mandate *surreptitious deportation* (Kubal 2017) – a three-year (re-)entry bar making it effectively impossible for a migrant to regularize his or her stay in Russia. This new legislation has also created a complicated regulatory structure with regard to past offences. Entry bars have been enforced ex post facto, for traffic offences that have already been settled in law (with the fines paid). The retroactive application of this new law makes deportable migrants who were charged with offences that at the time of conviction would not have had any immigration law-related consequences.

When the law introducing *zapret na v'ezd* for administrative offences entered into legal force, the number of people against whom re-entry bars were issued increased over sevenfold between 2013 and 2014, reaching two million in 2017 (see Figure 4.1).

Controlling Whom? An Entry Bar Case Study

To add some empirical flesh to this legal information and illustrate whom the entry bar affects and with what consequences, I present the case study of Akmal. Migrants like Akmal, as legal residents, work, often marry in Russia, raise children who then go to school, and lead lives in many respects similar to those of Russian citizens. When lawful residents face charges in a court of law, the formal qualities of the process largely resemble those encountered by a citizen. Migrants have the same procedural protections and face the same system of trial and sentencing with the same right to appeal. According to the Russian Constitution, they cannot be charged with a crime that was not a crime at the time it occurred; they cannot receive a sentence that exceeds that authorized at the time the crime was committed. And yet, despite these procedural safeguards in place, the legal residents face one big difference in the legal process – with the changes in the entry bar legislation over 2012 and 2013, two or more simple administrative offences, such as parking or speeding tickets, now make them effectively deportable, since these offences lead to a three-year entry bar and the impossibility of further legalization.

Akmal is 31, Muslim and comes from Fergana in Uzbekistan. He arrived in Moscow nearly 11 years ago and initially stayed with one of his extended family members, an uncle. He was working for his uncle on one of Moscow's many construction sites. When he drove me in his car around the city, he would point to buildings that he helped to construct or to restore, or where he offered a consultation. With time, Akmal moved to work for himself. He bought a car and in his spare time, mostly at night, he worked as a taxi driver – mainly for people he knew and extended family members who were coming from Uzbekistan to Moscow and needed to be picked up from the airport.

Akmal, now an experienced builder, rose through the career ranks in the construction industry and started working as a team leader for one of the building companies. That company was an example of the complex and intricate pyramid of intermediaries, where, until the crisis of 2009, Akmal controlled who would be hired on the different construction projects, making sure to fill the available vacancies with the network of his kinsmen from Fergana. At one point, he was managing a team of 15 people on a large construction project outside Moscow. Akmal and his team specialized in window and door fittings. Their clients were mainly other construction companies, individuals renovating their flats, apartments, and houses or those building new ones.

Akmal was able to cut back on his taxi driving. He nevertheless still very much relied on his car to get to work and to commute between different construction sites. He often was stopped by the traffic police for a regular document check, and was sometimes fined for speeding or not wearing a seatbelt. The tickets were never higher than 500 roubles (approximately £6). Akmal never had a serious collision; he never drove under the influence of alcohol. He was a careful and experienced driver. He accepted the tickets as part of his business, and paid them on time.

With regard to his immigration papers and work permit, Akmal followed a typical pattern of a migrant worker in Russia. Initially, when he arrived in Moscow, he resided legally, on the basis of the free movement (no visa) regime between Russia and the former Soviet republics, but he worked without a permit. A work permit was too expensive to obtain for a first-time migrant worker in Moscow. Gradually, however, he legalized his work, obtained a work permit via an intermediary, and renewed the permit more or less regularly. There were times when the money was short due to delays in getting paid, so Akmal would seek different means of regularizing his stay – he would leave Russia for one day, return and enjoy a renewed grace period of three months for arranging a new work permit. As Akmal became more experienced and knowledgeable about the migration papers market, he would omit the intermediaries and apply for a work permit directly at the FMS.

In February 2014, during what he thought would be a routine renewal of the work permit, for the first time his application was rejected. The local FMS officer told Akmal that his name had been placed on a blacklist (*chernyi spisok*; see Reeves 2016), and that he was forbidden entry to the RF (*v'ezd zakryt*). He was asked to leave Russia in the shortest possible time. Akmal was not given a reason why this had happened. With various construction projects underway, money still owed to Akmal and his team, a wife and a child living with him in Moscow, leaving Russia seemed impossible.

Akmal wanted to find out why he had been issued the re-entry bar. This involved a painstaking process. There are only a few FMS offices in Moscow that offer such a service, and they are open only twice each week and are understaffed. He had to wake up at 4 a.m. in order to register himself in the queue (the so-called *zhyvoi ochered*). Akmal arrived at 5 a.m., five hours before the office opened, and was already tenth in the queue. Six hours later, an FMS officer confirmed that the three-year entry bar had been issued for administrative offences committed within the last three years. He found out the exact date of the issuance of the re-entry bar, when the bar information had been forwarded to the border guards of the RF and which local FMS office had issued it. The information also included the date when the re-entry bar would automatically be lifted. When asked about the exact nature of the administrative offences committed, the FMS officer did not have this information on the database, except for a general reference to the relevant statutory provision. He advised Akmal to contact the Federal Bailiff Service[6] for detailed information. However, a quick look at the open database of the State Inspection of Road Safety[7] demonstrated that Akmal had earned himself three tickets (two for speeding and one for not wearing a seatbelt) between 2011 and 2013. He promptly paid the fines for two out of the three tickets. The entry bar would have therefore been administered partially in a retroactive manner as the law sanctioning the entry bar on the basis of two or more administrative offences was only introduced in July 2013.

Akmal asked the FMS officer about the possibility of removing the entry bar. He was told that if any of his close family members were Russian citizens, he could apply for the removal of the bar by writing a letter to the head FMS office in Moscow and submitting notary-certified copies of the marriage certificate and/or passport or birth certificate of the child. Akmal was fortunate that he fit the criteria: he was married to a Kyrgyz woman with Russian citizenship, and his son, born in Moscow, was also a Russian citizen. Akmal was lucky; he could appeal the entry bar, relying indirectly on art. 8 (the right to private and family life) of the European Convention of Human Rights (ECHR), to which Russia is a party. Many other migrants, however, do not have this advantage and, upon receiving the entry bar, they join a growing group of legally produced (de Genova 2004) 'illegal' or deportable people.

This story of Akmal illustrates how many migrants experience the entry bar in everyday life. Taking the story of Akmal as a broad canvas, in the remainder of the chapter I present my analysis of the entry bar as an immigration law sanction, focusing on its four most important socio-legal characteristics.

The Entry Bar as a Form of Social Control Deportation Model

Daniel Kanstroom, in his seminal essay *Deportation, Social Control and Punishment*, introduced an important distinction between two basic models of deportation laws and practices: border control and social control (Kanstroom 2000: 1897). The border control model envisions deportation as 'the consequence of a violation by a non-citizen of a condition imposed at the time of entry' (Kanstroom 2000: 1898) – in other words, it sanctions deportation as a consequence of a violation of the contract between the migrant and the host country as inherent to immigration law.

The social control deportation model rests on a different assumption – it is conceived of as a method of continual control of the behaviour of non-citizens

6 *Federal'naya sluzhba sudebnykh pristavov*, this federal executive body is primarily responsible for security in courts of law and the enforcement of court rulings.

7 *Gosudarstvennaya inspektsiya bezopasnosti dorozhnogo dvizheniya.*

for their alleged post-entry misconduct. It is normally issued by courts as a result of a non-citizen breaking some sort of laws on the territory of the host state (usually criminal in nature or attracting a relatively long imprisonment). In the United States, for instance, deportation follows from being found guilty of committing crimes classified as aggravated felonies (sanctioned by the Antiterrorism and Effective Death Penalty Act (AEDPA) and the Illegal Immigration Reform and Immigrant Responsibility Act (IIRIRA), both of 1996). In the United Kingdom, the 2007 UK Borders Act made deportation non-discretionary when the jail sentence was over one year.[8] These immigration reforms have expanded the class of deportable offences and limited judges' authority to alleviate deportation's harsh consequences. The drastic measure of deportation or removal is now *virtually inevitable* for the vast number of non-citizens convicted of crimes.

Kanstroom (2000) argues convincingly that, in the latter sense, the deportation law is more analogous to criminal law and often seems more punitive than regulatory. By distinguishing these two types of deportation models, Kanstroom in fact draws a line between a regulatory/punitive and civil/criminal deportations. This distinction has been systematically denied by courts in the United States, which – until *Padilla* v. *Kentucky* (2010) – rather tautologically insisted that deportation, however harsh it may be in practice, is not a criminal sanction but a regulatory and administrative procedure (Schuck 1984; Golash-Boza 2010). With the expansion of the criminal grounds leading to deportation (since 1996), the US Supreme Court in *Padilla* has recognized deportation as an integral part of the penalty that may be imposed on non-citizen defendants who plead guilty to specific crimes.

The deportation for lawful permanent residents 'no longer serves the remedial purpose of regulating the immigration process, but seeks to punish the residents for the underlying criminal behaviour' (Ortiz Maddali 2011: 6). As a result, the court established that because deportation based upon criminal convictions is *akin* to punishment – 'The severity of deportation [is] the equivalent of banishment or exile' (*Padilla* v. *Kentucky* 2010: 1486) – it requires special safeguards and protections.

The acknowledgement by the US Supreme Court that deportation *may* constitute a punishment legally recognizes Kanstroom's typology. In the regulatory or border control model, the role of deportation was supposed to be remedial (Ortiz Maddali 2011: 34), to put an end to ongoing immigration violations[9] in which one's presence on the territory of the state would constitute a continuing violation of immigration law. In contrast, sanctioning deportation for (even minor) criminal offences committed on the territory of the host state does not serve this purpose – the alleged crime has already

[8] Before these reforms, deportation was attached to a more limited catalogue of offences.

[9] 'Deportation is necessary in order to bring to an end an ongoing violation of United States law' (*Reno* v. *American-Arab Anti-Discrimination Commission* 1999: 491).

been committed and the person would have served the sentence prescribed by law. Here, deportation is, according to the court in *Padilla*, 'an integral part – and sometimes the most important part of the penalty that may be imposed' (*Padilla* v. *Kentucky* 2010: 1480). It serves a different, punitive function: it aims to control the behaviour of those migrants already admitted to the country.

The Kanstroom typology and the discussion around *Padilla* casts more light on the logic behind *zapret na v'ezd* in Russia. The evolution of the entry bar legislation and practice in Russia following the changes to the federal Law on the Order of Exit and Entry in December 2012 and July 2013 reveals how the entry bar has been transformed from a remedy for an ongoing immigration law violation to a punishment for the administrative offences of migrants legally admitted and legally residing in the country. This demonstrates a shift from the regulatory, border control model, where the entry bar sanction was indeed to control the immigration process, towards the social control model, resting firmly on the condition of deportability (de Genova 2002: 439) of a growing number of migrants, mostly already within the country. The everyday consequences of this legal shift come clearly in the story of Akmal: Russia has followed the global trend towards migration governance through expanding the conditions of deportability (de Genova and Peutz 2010).

Lex Retro Non Agit? The Retroactivity of the Entry Bar

Russia has also followed in the footsteps of other immigrant-receiving jurisdictions in the retroactive application of its immigration law. The 2013 amendment states that the entry bar should be administered to foreign citizens who 'two or more times within the three years' period were brought to administrative responsibility' (Law on the Order of Exit and Entry 2013, art. 26, para. 4). This wording leaves open the exact placement of this three-year window. In practice, immigration officials have interpreted this language to mean any three-year period of a migrant's residence rather than a three-year period since the passage of the law.

The retroactive application of the law arguably conflicts with art. 54 of the Russian Constitution, which prohibits ex post facto punishment in criminal and administrative law. However, the permissibility of retroactive laws requiring the de facto deportation of (long-term) lawful residents has so far not made it before the courts.

Russian practice resembles that of the United States. After the passage of the IIRIRA and AEDPA in 1996, deportation became a virtually automatic consequence of a criminal conviction, even if the alleged crimes were committed prior to the passage of the Act (Kanstroom 2000: 1891). The AEDPA and IIRIRA placed mandatory detention orders on all non-citizens convicted of crimes, to be applied at the time of their release from the custody of the criminal justice system with a view to removal or deportation. The retroactivity of deportation in the United States rested on an assumption that the migrants 'were not being punished, they were being regulated' (Kanstroom 2000: 1895). For example, non-citizens who committed crimes in the United States would first complete any jail or prison time that was mandated as punishment for their crimes. If those criminal convictions rendered them deportable, they were deported upon completing their sentences.

People convicted of certain crimes classified as aggravated felonies face 'mandatory deportation without a discretionary hearing where family and community ties can be considered' (United Nations Human Rights Council 2008: 8), even though these crimes have already been settled in law. Nancy Morawets illustrates the dire consequences of retroactive deportation with an example from her immigration law practice:

> Jackie H. immigrated to the United States at the age of 18 and has resided there ever since as lawful permanent resident. A few years later, she was arrested for possession of marijuana when police discovered two ounces of that substance in a car that she was driving. Although she did not know about the marijuana, she was in fact the owner and driver of the car. Seeking to avoid disruption of her work and family life, she pled guilty to a simple possession charge and was sentenced to probation.
>
> [. . .]
>
> Several years later, when she applied for a replacement of her residency card the immigration officer picked up the conviction on a computer check and placed Ms. H in deportation proceedings . . . Unless the Attorney General opts to terminate and reinitiate proceedings under IIRIRA, Ms. H will be deported regardless of how long ago she committed the offence.
>
> (Morawetz 1998: 117–118)

The Jackie H. case demonstrates how the immigration legislation that sanctions deportation or entry bar (in the Russian case) retroactively undermines the certainty of the law. Migrants could not know at the time of committing a particular crime or administrative offence that it would have immigration law-related consequences. Upon serving the sentence or having paid the fine, they would have regarded the matter as closed. The introduction of IIRIRA and AEDPA in the United States and the 2013 reformed entry bar legislation in Russia, when applied to past convictions, served to alter the legal consequences of those convictions or administrative offences. It did so either by creating a risk of deportation/deportability where none existed, or by making deportation a necessary consequence of a conviction that before only gave rise to a risk of deportation (Morawetz 1998: 122).

With regard to *zapret na v'ezd* issued retroactively for administrative offences like parking or speeding tickets, during my fieldwork in Russia in 2014, I came across numerous cases of people who, like Akmal from the case study, were affected by this harsher, retroactive re-entry bar legislation. These migrants worked and lived in Russia in accordance with the migration law – on the basis of either a work permit or a patent (labour licence). But then, during a routine visit to the FMS office to renew their documents, they could be met with a staunch refusal.[10] Due to the entry bar on the FMS database, their immigration papers could not be renewed and they were asked to leave the RF in the shortest possible time. Many felt confused – some of them had been working and living legally in Russia for many years. Now, on the basis of past speeding or parking tickets (which by and large they would have paid and regarded the matter as closed), they found themselves deportable from a country in which they had established families, lived, worked and paid taxes, sometimes for many years.

The courts in Russia have not yet taken a stance with regard to the constitutionality or broader legality of *zapret na v'ezd* issued for past administrative offences. Some immigration lawyers with whom I spoke in Russia dismiss the potential unconstitutionality of *zapret na v'ezd.* One said that 'theoretically it has not been designed as a supplementary punishment for past offences' (interview with professional advocate, 13 April 2014). The entry bar, another said, should rather be perceived as 'a limitation of one's right to re-enter the territory of RF' (interview with *pro bono* lawyer for migrants, 1 April 2014). This argument is based on a normative principle that the state, as a sovereign, should have the full right to decide who should be admitted and who should be prohibited entry *also* on the basis of that person's conduct on the Russian territory. The entry bar does not void migrants' current immigration papers, it 'only prevents them from renewing them, applying for an extension of a residence or a work permit' (interview with *pro bono* lawyer for migrants, 1 April 2014).

The Russian immigration lawyers' arguments about the re-entry bar for past administrative offences not being a punishment but a limitation of one's right to re-enter Russia echo the circular arguments on the side of state authorities elsewhere in the Western liberal-democratic jurisdictions, holding that deportation is not a punishment but an administrative procedure. However, from the migrants' perspective, the entry bar as issued in Russia for past minor administrative violations nevertheless comes across as a double punishment for the same wrongdoing. As one frustrated migrant said:

> Look, these tickets. I paid for them. I paid them. Why now the *zapret* is added as well? (Migrant Uzbekistan, male, 17 April 2014)

The discussion about the retroactivity of the entry bar in Russia demonstrates once again that this sanction is not necessarily tied to the border or to the admission process, but follows what might be termed an eternal probation or perhaps an eternal guest logic (Kanstroom 2000). This suggests that non-citizens, including lawful residents, may be subject to a shifting, even retroactive regime of deportation and the government's absolute and unqualified

10 'The FMS of RF has reasons not to allow your entry into the Russian Federation'. This is a statement that appears on the FMS website, where migrants can enter their passport details and find out whether or not they have an entry bar.

right to exclude on the basis of alleged post-entry misconduct. In Russia – in contrast to the United States – the state does not physically expel migrants (thus saving on precious resources), but removes any possibility of regularizing their stay. It uses a subtle mechanism of closing off the internal borders by making the renewal of immigration and employment documents dependent on one's traffic offences record. The aim of the re-entry bar regulation is not necessarily to enforce general compliance with immigration law – it is to control, police and ultimately exclude those who happened to transgress those rules before they were even part of the law. The practice of barring re-entry on the basis of past administrative offences literally pushes migrants outside the inner ring of legality, resulting in a 'border at the door' phenomenon (Kubal 2016b). It makes their stay illegal.

Appeal Structures

The slogan repeated by the FMS officials at almost every public meeting – 'the entry bar database does not take bribes' (*Baza vzyatok ne beret*) – illustrates the modern, technocratic style of administration of this new sanction. However, it also brings to mind the potential miscarriages of justice that could happen due to conscious or unconscious human and technical errors. A leading human rights activist in Russia expressed this in the following terms:

> OK, so the database does not take bribes. Fine. But what if the database gets something wrong? What if an FMS officer clicked the wrong button? As the database is this impersonal machine which does not take bribes, it is also difficult to argue with, to appeal, to correct its potential mistakes. A human life is involved; migrants have families, jobs, and children in Russia; what if they find themselves in the database by mistake, by a technical error?
>
> (Interview with head of an NGO, 25 May 2014)

This raises an important question about the checks and balances inscribed in the enforcement of the new legislation and the modes of appealing or challenging the entry bar. These, in Russia, still remain rather broad. Article 46(2) of the Russian Constitution provides that decisions and actions (or inaction) of state authorities, bodies of local self-government, public associations and officials may be appealed against in a court of law. Courts tend to regard as unconstitutional any statutory restrictions of this right (Burnham et al. 2012: 669). The FMS guidelines therefore state that the 'decision on the re-entry bar into the territory of the Russian Federation may be reviewed in accordance with the legislation of the Russian Federation' (Federal Migration Service 2014). There are two main ways of challenging the entry bar in Russia – administrative review and judicial review, using district-level (first instance) and regional-level (second instance) courts as arbiters between the FMS and foreign citizens.

As the case study of Akmal illustrated, a person who wishes to challenge the entry bar via administrative review must write a letter to the head office of the

FMS explaining the reasons why the bar should be lifted, accompanied by documentary evidence (in originals) that would support the plea. The formal basis for the administrative review, as described on the FMS website (and also included in correspondence between the FMS and one of Moscow's legal NGOs), is rather broad.[11] This includes, for example, the presence of close relatives who are citizens of Russia (as spouses, parents, or minor children), valid temporary or permanent leave to remain, a valid work permit or patent, and a need for emergency medical treatment or full-time study at Russian universities. These grounds explicitly result either from the national law or international obligations to which Russia is a party, such as the ECHR. The FMS has 30 days to respond to the letter with its decision. My fieldwork demonstrates, however, that the practice of entry bar removals is inconsistent. Despite clear FMS policy, some grounds for entry bar removal are more likely to be granted than others. For example, entry bar challenges on the basis of permanent residence documents or a valid work permit are often refused. In contrast, petitions on the basis of art. 8 of the ECHR have been more successful.

If denied under administrative review, one can appeal the entry bar directly in a regular district court, challenging not only the decision itself, but also the legality of the decision taken by FMS officials (e.g. procedural violations in arriving at the decision) (Solomon 2005; Trochev 2012). Generally, citizens do not have to exhaust the remedies within the administrative hierarchy before going to court (Burnham et al. 2012: 661). The scope of Russian review of administrative action includes a review of both the law and fact issues, as the courts are not obliged to accept findings of fact or conclusions of law made by officials or other state bodies (Burnham et al. 2012: 672).

As courts in Russia follow the territorial jurisdiction principle, the appeal must be submitted either to the court in a district where the applicant is registered or the district court where the FMS office that took the decision about the entry bar is located. Since in Moscow there are difficulties for migrants proving their residence registration, appeals are usually filed in the district courts where the main FMS offices are based. These courts have developed expertise in migration law-related cases. Filing the case to court usually suspends the implementation of the challenged action or decision while the case is pending (Burnham et al. 2012: 672).

There is also a right to appeal from the decision of the first-level district courts. The appeal must be lodged within seven days of the day the court judgment is rendered. The filing of an appeal automatically suspends execution of the court's judgment or ruling. The appellate (regional) court can uphold the judgment, annul the judgment and return the case for further

[11] Two letters, from 19 August 2014 by FMS Russia and from 26 December 2014 by FMS Moscow Oblast, are in the author's archive.

investigation, annul the judgment and terminate the case or modify the judgment (Smith 1996: 146).

The rather broad formal appeal structures in Russia contrast with the more limited appeal rights that have become the main feature of immigration law in Western liberal jurisdictions. In the Immigration Act 2014, for example (which repealed the Immigration Act 1999), the United Kingdom reduced the number of grounds for appeal from 17 to just 3 (Sayeed 2014). There is only a right of appeal against a decision of the Home Office to refuse a protection or human rights claim, or against a decision of the Home Office to revoke a protection status. Every other immigration decision made by the Home Office does not attract a right of appeal, with the remedy in those circumstances being administrative review and/or judicial review (Sayeed 2014).[12] Furthermore, the Immigration Act 2014 enables the secretary of state to require any appeal against deportation to be brought only after the act of physically removing a person from the territory, both in UK and EU law cases (Yeo 2014).[13] Any person with no leave to remain (and who is required to have it) may simply be removed from the United Kingdom with no further notice or legal step being required. The new provision should be seen as a simple power to remove rather than a type or species of immigration decision (Hoshi 2014).

With regard to the appeal structures for the entry bar, Russia's relatively broad rights of appeal distinguish it (for now) from other immigration-receiving jurisdictions. Although there is variation in how the formal appeal rights work in practice, the interviews with immigration lawyers in Russia demonstrate that they are definitely relied upon. As one stated:

> You do go to court. You do appeal. Whether you succeed or not – mostly you do not – is another matter, but as a principle you do appeal to court.
>
> (Interview with human rights lawyer, 16 April 2014)

Proportionality of Punishment

Notwithstanding the broad appeal structures, the introduction of the three-year entry bar in response to alleged migrant illegality in the areas of traffic or other administrative offences raises rather serious questions concerning the

[12] In the United Kingdom, judicial reviews are distinct from appeals, in that an appeal is usually brought to challenge the outcome of a particular case. The judicial review process, on the other hand, analyses the way in which public bodies reached their decision in order to decide whether or not that decision was lawful. See *Courts and Tribunals Judiciary* at www.judiciary.gov.uk/you-and-the-judiciary/judicial-review. In that sense, the review of the entry bar decision by the Russian administrative justice system is broader.

[13] However as with 'manifestly unfounded', 'clearly unfounded', various 'safe third country' and other types of appeal-limiting certificates, a judicial review of the decision to impose a certificate is possible. This will usually have the effect of suspending removal. See Yeo (2014).

proportionality of these sanctions in relation to the violations for which they are usually administered. I conceptualize proportionality in a socio-legal, empirical manner – by focusing on the disruptive effects this bar has on immigrants' livelihoods. If the entry bar is often administered while a person resides in the country (e.g. with a valid residence permit and/or a work permit), works there and has children and family ties – as illustrated by the case study of Akmal earlier in the chapter – the entry bar makes it impossible for that person to further renew his or her immigration documents and forces him or her to leave Russia for a period of three years. It therefore results in a disproportionate sanction in a common-sense meaning of the word. These specificities of the *zapret na v'ezd* concerning the proportionality of this practice demonstrate how global migration governance practices reflect the strictness and punitiveness that are long-standing elements of the Russian legal tradition.

The various legal reforms in Russian criminal and civil law since the 1960s were aimed at dismantling, at least partially, the draconian elements of the Stalinist system (Smith 1996: 141). A set of incremental changes in the 1960s and 1970s under the auspices of Soviet legality were designed to guarantee the procedural and substantive rights of citizens and to ensure the professionalism of the courts (Smith 1996: 141). And yet, while the same judicial system was capable of professional and fair handling of routine cases (Feifer 1964; Smith 1996: 142; Hendley 2011), it was also used as a repressive and arbitrary tool to punish individuals in order to protect the state. With the changes of the *perestroika* period and the greater legal reforms that followed – e.g. introducing the new Criminal Code (1997) that formally decriminalized a number of victimless offences, ameliorated the severity of sanctions, and articulated preference for non-custodial sentences – came, however, the chaos of the 1990s, preserved in collective social memory as the breakdown of public order and a rapid increase of violent crime.

The early 1990s were characterized by soaring rates of murder (*Izvestiya*, 2 October 1992, quoted in Smith 1996: 154) and rape (*New York Times*, 3 January 1994, quoted in Smith 1996: 154), as well as an explosion of white-collar and property crimes. It is perhaps not surprising that, in this period, the Russian legal system retained strong punitive elements. These 'stubborn legacies' of the Soviet past – the 'punitive mindset' and an inclination to seek solutions to societal problems in repressive measures (Pomorski 1998: 392) – were preserved well into the twenty-first century.

Russian immigration law, in contrast to the British (Aliverti 2012) or US systems (Chacón 2009; Romero 2010) has not, however, been formally criminalized. The three-year entry bar or *surreptitious* deportation does seem to follow the logic of the social control deportation model (Kanstroom 2000), but it does not constitute a migration-related mechanism of enforcing criminal law (Legomsky 2007). It remains attached to administrative offences. Examining Russia's legal tradition helps to explain this phenomenon: there was no need to criminalize Russian immigration law, as its repressive functions could be equally accommodated within the existing framework of historically *punitive* administrative law. Although formally within the ambit of the administrative law, if analysed from the perspective of the severe impact on migrants' lives, *zapret na v'ezd* actually constitutes a quasi-criminal sanction, a form of punishment. The punitive aspects of Russian administrative law more broadly have also been recognized by the European Court of Human Rights in the case of *Mikhaylova* v. *Russia* (no. 46998/08, judgment of 19 November 2015). The Court decided that the administrative proceedings brought against Ms Mikhaylova – according to the Code of Administrative Offences (CAO) – could be classified as 'criminal' within the meaning of art. 6 of the ECHR. The fine imposed on Ms Mikhaylova for failing to comply with a police order, and for taking part in an unlawful public gathering 'had been punitive and deterrent in nature' rather than characteristic of a mere pecuniary compensation connected with administrative law violations (para. 64, *Mikhaylova* v. *Russia*).

The analysis of the entry bar in Russia therefore invites a deeper reflection about the nature and the consequences of the civil and criminal labels in immigration law more broadly. With the expansion of punitive administrative sanctions, the division of legal sanctions into these two categories is perhaps misleading, as punishment seems no longer to be the distinctive attribute of criminal law (Ortiz Maddali 2011: 8). Keeping in mind that the civil/administrative law sanctions might actually be more severe and harsher than actual criminal sanctions imposed helps to interrogate the actual aims of the ever-expanding criminalization of migration law in the United States and the United Kingdom. The incorporation of criminal law into the immigration domain in Western liberal jurisdictions can rather be viewed as an instance of symbolic law (Aliverti 2012). These policies aim to placate public concerns with undocumented immigration, sending a loud and clear political message that action is being taken (Aliverti 2012; Kubal 2014). I argued elsewhere that even when the criminalization of migration is stripped of the attributes of formal judicial power, courts and lawyers, it nevertheless exercises a real power over people's lives. Indeed, extra-legal manifestations of criminalization may be even more 'effective' tools of social control (Kubal 2014: 3). Once the message of criminalization of certain aspects of migration law reaches the public discourse, it gains a life of its own, with factors such as penal politics, media coverage and the extensive discretion exercised by criminal justice and immigration officials, effectively blurring the boundaries between undocumented migrant, asylum seeker and criminal.

In Russia, the blurring or destabilization of the criminal–civil distinction is partially explained by its historically punitive law, partially by the current hybridization of legal institutions and practices and 'the slipperiness of the operations of state power as they seek to name the various modalities of its exercise' (Sarat et al. 2011b: 14). The FMS, the agency responsible for immigration law enforcement in Russia, has been moved in and out of the MVD on numerous occasions in its most recent institutional history (see Chapter 2). This complex relationship between historical legacy and institutional change lies at the root of the current instability of the criminal–civil distinction in all of its messy manifestations in immigration law and practice (Steiker 1997).

* * *

This chapter examined the evolution and the socio-legal characteristics of the entry bar legislation in Russia, with reference to the legal developments in the areas of deportation and removal in the United States and the United Kingdom. I adopted a comparative perspective to cast more light on the migration governance processes in Russia and to move away from the intellectually dead-end explanations that exoticize Russia and invoke arguments about how law does not really work there. The comparative perspective demonstrates that the entry bar legislation follows a similar logic to the developments surrounding deportation and removal orders of the United States and the United Kingdom: a shift from remedial to increasingly punitive sanctions, from putting an end to an ongoing immigration law violation to punishing migrants for their post-entry misconduct. Both sanctions are also increasingly retroactively applied. This analysis reveals how the most recent changes in Russian migration law stay very much in tune with more global migration governance developments.

The disproportionality of the entry bar in relation to the actual offences for which it is administered demonstrates, however, that the global developments are very much combined in Russia with the local legal specificities and the legacy of its punitive and repressive legal system. This, in turn, helps to question the criminal/civil labels in migration law more broadly – suggesting, in particular, the danger of extending criminal liability to what are essentially regulatory violations. With the increased criminalization of migration law in the United States and the United Kingdom, this comparative analysis suggests that serious deterrent sanctions can effectively be imposed under an administrative system provided that due process safeguards are in place.

5

Tracing the Case File

Culture of Materiality in Immigration and Refugee Law

Introduction

The previous chapter looked at the everyday experiences of immigration law in Russia through the case study of an entry bar, an increasingly popular sanction. The story of Akmal also illustrated how an experience of immigration law could give rise to a legal grievance and – potentially – a legal case. This chapter moves one level up and examines the various forms of legal cases that migrants, refugees and asylum seekers might be part of in Russia. How do these cases feature in the lives of the different actors in the migration process: immigration and human rights lawyers, Russian judges and the Federal Migration Service (FMS) officers? Reflecting on their everyday experiences, these various actors often speak with completely different voices, profess different ideologies and hold diametrically opposite worldviews. The thing they have in common, however, is the centrality of the paper and the written formal documents in how they conceptualize and experience 'a legal case'. To put it differently: a great majority of immigration and refugee legal cases are experienced through the medium and materiality of the case file. In my ethnographic pursuit I therefore turned to the different documents, letters, appeals, stamped envelopes, formal explanations, affidavits, reports, protocols, pieces of legislation, authorities' decisions, court judgments, legal texts and other forms of discourse that make up the lived experiences of these cases. This chapter, by following the case file and on the basis of observations in courts, aims to address three sets of questions. First, what sort of grievances give rise to case files in immigration and refugee law in Russia? What do the different case files look like? Second, how are the files put together and by whom? What is the role of the immigration lawyers in compiling the case files? What is the role of FMS officials in deciding which cases can proceed and which cases should be terminated? Third, how are case files that make it to court considered and treated by the judges?

As I progressed in my fieldwork, I realized more and more the importance of the written word, the documents, the multiple *spravkas* or reference letters, the police protocols, identity papers or registration certificates. To analytically frame these various materialities (or simply 'things'), I turned for inspiration to the approach pioneered by Bruno Latour and advanced by others (Michel Callon, John Law, Steve Woolgar, Anneliese Riles) that emphasizes how assemblages of human and non-human objects shape the experiences of the law and law-in-the-making (Latour 2009). I did not rely on actor–network theory (ANT) as a classic social theory to explain the behaviour of my informants. Actor–network theory's primary focus on the process and ethnographic description of the different elements of social reality makes it a weak and literally unsubstantial social theory (Blok and Jensen 2011); in the words of Lezaun, 'it is a social theory that is not meant to make theorizing any easier' (Lezaun 2017: 25). Many commentators of Latour suggest that ANT is actually the opposite of a theory, 'it is the gesture that refuses all theorizing about "the social" or "the political" in favour of specific, concrete analyses that attempts to be as dynamic and as sensitive to contingency as the process being analysed' (Levi and Valverde 2008: 812).

I find it helpful, however, to refer to Latour's sociological tradition as I ontologically embrace in the study of law's everyday experiences the texts, people, architecture, concepts and everyday office objects without the initial claims about the relative importance played by human or non-human entities in shaping the different experiences of the law (Riles 2000). In this collective body of humans and artefacts, the latter are not just merely passive instruments of social agents but are 'active in the creation and maintenance of those agents' (Hull 2003: 290); they hold, order and fix the social (Woolgar 2002: 261). To follow the things themselves and reveal a practice of intimate hybridization between humans and artefacts is not to render legal documents into ethnographic objects by exoticizing them (Riles 2000), but to open the question of the material constitution of culturally different forms of social and legal order (Pels et al. 2002: 6).

This chapter is structured around the 'performative and integrative capacity of things' (Woolgar 2002: 261) that mediate the different legal processes unfolding in the social experiences of immigration and refugee laws in Russia. I start by introducing and describing the two types of case files that result from immigration and refugee cases in Russia. I then trace how the different documents that give rise to the case file are put together at an immigration lawyer's office and are ultimately used by the different immigration and human rights lawyers to heuristically position and rank their clients (migrants, refugees or asylum seekers). I also invite the reader to accompany Bahrom, an Uzbek asylum seeker in desperate need of legalization in Moscow, to an office of the FMS. The FMS officers are important gatekeepers of the case file: they decide which documents (and which case files) are strong enough to deserve fresh consideration, and which have exhausted their performative capacity, and can be ignored without further action. Lastly, this chapter follows the case file to the courts, where it is presented before the judge to examine its role in the process of adjudication and decision-making. Tracing the case file at the different stages of its evolution and consideration sheds more light on the ultimate focus of this chapter; namely, what can the tracing of the file process tell us about the culture of materiality in immigration and refugee laws in Russia?

What Are the Migration Case Files in Russia?

The case files, which I observed in Russia, could be divided into two general types: immigration and refugee law case files. The work on the immigration law case file is usually instigated by the police or immigration authorities when these law enforcement bodies suspect a foreign national of an administrative (immigration) offence. There are two primary types of immigration offence that warrant a file being put together. The first is offences against art. 18.8 (part 3) of the Code of Administrative Offences (CAO) – not possessing a valid residence registration (the legacy of the Soviet *propiska* system). The second is against art. 18.10 (part 2) of the CAO – when a foreign national is found working without a valid work permit.[1] The files are put together usually following an immigration raid at a workplace, or when migrants are 'randomly' selected on the street for documents checks by the police.[2] These case files usually consist of protocols from immigration raids, personal immigration documents collected by the immigration authorities or the police, and handwritten or printed affidavits (signed by the defendants). An important element of the file is a printout from the FMS central database of foreign nationals[3] confirming the defendant's 'documentary trail' in Russia. It features the foreign citizen's photograph, date and mode of entry into the Russian Federation (RF), migration card details, residence registration, work permit, any exit details, information about the employer and the place of work in Russia, information about residence permits and a list of administrative or criminal offences committed so far. This printout also includes information about potential entry bars (Kubal 2017). Aside from these two documents, the case file contains a very important clarification of rights memo, in which the defendant confirms with a signature that the state representatives have informed them of their constitutional and procedural rights in Russia: the right to be silent, the right to an interpreter and the right to a legal representative. The file also contains reports by the FMS and formal letters sanctioning police custody for 48 hours. Finally, it may also include other case materials such as pictures or short video clips from the immigration raids, which serve as evidence of the immigration offence being committed (e.g. pictures of men

[1] For a more detailed legal overview of these administrative immigration offences, see Chapter 2.

[2] I put the 'random' selection in quotation marks, as police's racial profiling for these checks is widely documented – see Open Society Institute (2006).

[3] *Avtomatizirovannaya Sistema Tsentral'noy Bazy Dannykh uchota Inostrannykh Grazhdan* – Automated System of the Central Database of Foreign Citizens.

sitting around a table of the raided apartment; men operating heavy machinery on a raided building site, etc.).

The second type of case files arises from refugee law cases. They originate when a foreign national (an asylum seeker) submits a written application to the local immigration authorities asking for asylum. These case files are largely built with reference to the Russian Law on Refugees (1993) and the regulations of the FMS (since 2016 the Main Directorate for Migration of the Ministry of Interior of Russia), which decides on asylum applications. The documents that make up the file consist of letters provided by the applicant together with written proof of the individual's persecution and problems in his or her country of origin. The file contains an interview questionnaire completed by the asylum applicant and the decisions by the FMS/Main Directorate for Migration of the Ministry of Interior of Russia. As this decision is mostly negative – a refusal of refugee status – the file also includes appeals to that decision, together with new evidence usually submitted by the asylum applicant and his or her lawyer. These documents collected in support of the applicant's case are contrasted with official objections by the FMS defending the legality of their original decision (refusal of refugee protection), which are also deposited in the file. As these cases usually have their finale in court, the complete file also contains the court's decisions and appeals to these decisions by both parties (depending on the result). The file also contains reports and analyses by human rights organizations such as Amnesty International and Human Rights Watch, which are presented as evidence in court. Finally, the file might also include individual assessments of the applicant's case by the United Nations High Commissioner for Refugees (UNHCR) local field office workers based in Russia, who are called into court as experts by the asylum applicant's legal representative.

The immigration and refugee law case files differ with regard to their physical and material appearance: immigration law case files are usually thin; refugee law case files are paper-heavy and fat. The different physical appearances result from the genealogy of these files: immigration case files (prepared by the immigration authorities) are put together usually within 24–48 hours. During this time, law enforcement authorities work under immense pressure to process these cases quickly and effectively, supply copies of immigration database printouts, complete reports from the raid and gather all the necessary signatures. The rushed way in which the immigration case file is put together encourages all-too-frequent procedural irregularities, human mistakes in assessing the evidence and opening up of gaps in the facts of the case. Refugee law case files, on the other hand, are collected over several months; it is the refugee lawyers and the asylum applicants who drive the creation of the file and meticulously add formal pieces of evidence to it, until the case file reaches the trial stage. At the trial stage, it is the judge who has authority to add or remove materials from the case file. While the judge's decisions do not lead to the case file becoming any thinner (evidence material is never retracted), the asylum applicant's lawyer has to seek the judge's formal permission to append new supporting evidence – yet another formal letter, yet another *spravka* or expert report.

Russian Lawyers and the Culture of Paper Production

Bez bumazhki ty bukashka...[4] Anna was one of the immigration lawyers I shadowed while doing my fieldwork in Moscow. She often met clients who were seeking legal protection in Russia (refugee status or temporary asylum) or were trying to appeal an expulsion order for their administrative violations of the immigration law. Whenever a client entered her office she would first – upon a greeting – ask them for their papers. She would take the passport and put the details into a computer, then she would take their residence registration, then migration card (a form of landing card that migrants fill in while crossing Russia's border), then work permit, then employment contract (if it existed). She would carefully update her computer record for her client, and then pass these documents to me to be photocopied and filed (thereby commencing a case file and paper trail for the client). It is only upon this initial ritual of documenting the client that she would ask a question: 'How can I help? What seems to be the problem?' Quite often after the initial interview about the legal problem, a request for more documents followed: 'Have you brought anything else? Do you have any other documents?' It is these documents – passports, residence registrations, work permits, letters and decisions by the immigration authorities, court judgments, appeals, different forms of *spravkas* and applications – their formal quality but mainly quantity that ultimately seemed to dictate how the relationship between the immigration lawyer and their client was structured and unfolded in the consultation room. The content of the case file was a great predictor of the nature of the relationship between the client and their lawyer.

The clients seemed to be placed on a spectrum, depending on the thickness of their case file. Migrants with many documents, especially if they were in some logical or chronological order, were relatively easy to deal with for the lawyers. The lawyers used the documents to locate their clients within the legal procedure and decided what sort of a 'new document' was required, be it a reference letter or a court appeal. The lawyers knew how to attend to these cases due to their extensive paper trail, and these clients were relatively well integrated within the broader 'paper production' culture in Russia (Kubal 2018). It does not mean, however, that the clients with these handsome-

[4] Part of a Russian popular saying. In its full form, it is *Bez bumazhki ty bukashka/a s bymazhkoy chelovek* – Without a piece of paper, you are a bug/And with a piece of paper – a man. The saying comes from the 'Song of the Bureaucrat' written by Vasily Ivanovich Lebedev-Kumach (1889–1949). The meaning of the expression is: without a paper document, it is difficult for a person to prove sometimes even the fact of his existence (after Serov 2003).

looking bundles of documents were actually any closer to solving their legal problems. In my time shadowing the lawyers, there was one man, Abdusami – a refugee from Tajikistan – who had a wonderful file according to the lawyers' standards. He had a thick black plastic folder that looked like a book; each individual page consisted of a transparent sleeve containing a copy of some document. Abdusami kept originals and the Russian notary-certified translations from the Tajik language, linked to the original file by a red thread. Many lawyers who saw Abdusami congratulated him on his folder. At the same time, Abdusami had exhausted all the domestic remedies to appeal the refusal of his refugee status. His passport, deposited with the Russian immigration authorities, had expired. Abdusami was in limbo – he could not return to Tajikistan, but at the same time he was in desperate need of more evidence, new papers and reference letters from Tajikistan that could help him re-open his case and apply for temporary asylum in Russia on new grounds.

At the other end of the spectrum there were people with very few documents, or just their passports evidencing their basic identity. These clients were also relatively easy to deal with for the lawyers: they had to be sent back. These migrants would often hear from a lawyer: 'You are in the territory of Russian Federation illegally. There is not much I can do to help you.' I observed a situation in which a lawyer refused to write an appeal relating to the client's case as the client did not bring with her the receipt of the court's decision – an envelope in which the judgment was posted to her. The client was sitting in front of lawyer with the actual judgment in her hand, but the lawyer refused to take on this case until the client returned with 'proper documents'. That envelope (and the date printed on it) was crucial for calculating the appeal times, and whether the deadline for appeal had already been exceeded and should first be reinstated. There are usual procedural delays between the time of announcing the judgment in court and delivering it to the interested parties, hence the date of the court's judgment (instead of its actual delivery) was useless to the lawyer and was actually working against her client. To an outside observer that was a curious moment – how can a lack of envelope stall the progress on the client's case? However, the lawyer was adamant; with a long line of clients still waiting to be seen, she sent the women back to find and bring the official envelope.

These empirical vignettes illustrate the extreme ends of the spectrum of how the lawyers relied on the formal case files to heuristically position their clients. In the middle, though, there were people with incomplete documents, with documents, that did not follow any chronological order, or with court decisions for which the appeal times had lapsed. In this middle category, there were also those whose documents had spelling problems, or whose court decisions were missing and could not easily be located. These cases were the messy (or complex) ones and took the most time to get to the bottom of. Sorting out these cases meant restoring the chronology of the paper trail – reinstating the appeal times, correcting formal mistakes and preparing appeals.

This usually meant writing formal letters to the respective authorities and procuring more documents. *Bumaga vse sterpit*, a Russian version of Cicero's 'the paper does not blush' – literally meaning that the paper will endure all – was a saying I came across multiple times when various lawyers encouraged each other to try yet another appeal, to try yet another formal letter to the authorities. Quite often, however, due to the complexity of these cases with incomplete paper trail or simply due to too many questions in the formally (documentary) established facts of the case there was nothing that could be done to help.

The focus on the documents and on the file was central to many of the consultations I observed. There were different styles with which the lawyers dealt with the paper work – some would examine the client orally, photocopy new evidence and proceed to the next client, leaving the writing and completion of the documents for later (outside of office hours). Others would fill in the gaps in the paper trail during the consultation. The latter scenario meant that some of these consultations were rather quiet and uneventful; there were few words spoken and not much of a social interaction. Writing the appeals and the letters often appeared a routine and mundane job; they simply had to follow a particular format. Due to the volume of refugee and immigration law cases handled in Moscow, there is a scripted pattern of paperwork that needs to be included in the file; the lawyers refer to this as the 'scheme' (algorithm) of the case file. This scheme was the main structuring force behind the lawyers' work, the file's way of exerting agency and commanding the lawyers what to do. With many people to be seen around similar legal issues, some lawyers would just turn to the paper work rather than explain the intricacies of the case to the clients in front of them. Often, in communicating with their clients, they would use the exact legal phrases from the official legal documents and papers.

For example, an asylum applicant from Ivory Coast arrived at the NGO with a handsome bundle of documents. The lawyer had a look at the documents in silence; he examined the most recent court decision in particular. All he said to the client was:

> You can go out now, have a walk for an hour, and I will prepare a letter for you, which you would then take to court.

The client asked:

> But could you explain to me what will you be doing? What will you be writing?

The lawyer did not initially feel obliged to explain to the client the content of the letter due to the clarity of the situation appearing from the documents. He had approached the case rather mechanically:

> OK, see, we have a negative court decision; we need to prepare an appeal.

It was only the client's direct question and interest in the matter that prompted the lawyer's explanation:

> I would be appealing the court's decision to a court of a higher instance based on the mistakes in the decision.

The lawyer then explained that he would not dispute the law, nor the facts of the case, but the procedural and formal mistakes. The court's decision refusing asylum (or rather affirming the legality of the decision by the FMS to refuse asylum to the applicant) looked extremely general to the lawyer. It consisted of four pages, and only one paragraph (four lines) was actually devoted to the specific details of the client. It was therefore a typical 'mass-produced' refugee status rejection, which the lawyer would have come across many times in his professional career. The lawyer planned to launch a new appeal and base it on the fact that the court had not given due consideration to the individual circumstances of his client and the specific risks of persecution and violence he could encounter upon return to Ivory Coast.

The lawyers, in their everyday file work make sure that no immigration authorities' decision is left without a formal response, a grievance letter or an additional explanation. They make sure that no court judgment is left without an appeal, and that all the potential irregularities of the legal procedure are complained against. Due to the largely *pro bono* character of their work, the lawyers do not engage in gathering the multiple *spravkas*, reference letters or decisions by immigration authorities. This obligation to extend the paper trail is passed onto migrants and asylum seekers. The lawyers, in turn, take it upon themselves to address and respond to any loopholes in the authorities' decisions. This specific professional regime 'structures the embodied capabilities, assumptions, and routines' (Scheffer 2007: 69) of taking care of the file. The immigration lawyers know that first and foremost they need to respond to the paper requirements of the case file, as this is what it means to take part in the case, to 'play the game' and 'do their jobs properly'. The ongoing casework constantly entangles papers, the lawyers and their clients, creating an intimate hybridization between humans and artefacts. As observed by Thomas Scheffer (2007) in the British context:

> The file notes confront [the lawyer] with the unwritten rule of instructions. They co-define what counts as completed work. They require attendance. They employ the case-worker as much as he employs them. The author is not the sole master or initiator of the text. He delegates mastery and initiative to the file. The file is not authored by the lawyer and his cognitive/corporal efforts, but in sequences of lawyer–file encounters. (Scheffer 2007: 62)

Towards a Cultural Analysis of Case Files

Is there anything special about the materiality and the function of case files in Russia? At first glance, these files do not differ much from case files in other jurisdictions and national contexts. They are put together with varied attention to detail, and they all share the standard markers of formal legality: stamps, signatures, original documents and their notary-certified translations connected by red threads, seals and dates through which documents and communications are 'reflexively and diachronically linked with other communications' (van Oorschot and Schinkel 2015: 517).

Irene van Oorschot and Willem Schinkel analysed ethnographically the everyday and mundane case files used in 95 per cent of Dutch petty criminal offences decided upon by the 'police judges' (2015: 509). They focused on performativity of the case file, the way it mediates law's 'epistemic access to the persons and events in question' (van Oorschot and Schinkel 2015: 503) in the Dutch inquisitorial context. The file becomes a border object between the 'world of law' and the 'world out-there' through its agential powers that sometimes surpass those of the humans who put the file together (van Oorschot and Schinkel 2015: 523, 516). What makes the material file acquire such a notion of agency? Van Oorschot and Schinkel indicate that it is the file's operation constituted by self-reference (through stamps, autographs and communication tracing) that give rise to its agential capacities and credibility for 'other-reference': the mediation between the outside world and the courtroom (van Oorschot and Schinkel 2015: 516). The case files are exercising this agency by 'bringing events into law' and translating, 'doubling' or even fabricating the empirical reality for the needs of the trial (van Oorschot and Schinkel 2015: 518). The case file in the courtroom context simplifies the complex reality to make a judgment possible (van Oorschot and Schinkel 2015: 507) by 'mediating epistemic access to the persons and events in question' (van Oorschot and Schinkel 2015: 503).

I have found much inspiration and complementarities in how van Oorschot and Schinkel (but also van Oorschot 2014) see the case file and my Russian immigration law context. Perhaps it is not surprising: these two jurisdictions share the civil law tradition (and the inquisitorial system) and the Dutch researchers and I have both approached these case files from the everyday, ethnographic perspective.

At the same time, the role of the file in mediating the outside reality for the purpose of the trial seems to go as far back in history as the funnel justice metaphor (Boyes-Watson 2013: 88). The formal quality of the file – its content, stamps, signatures, photocopied and original documents, photographs, dated envelopes – as the indicators of how 'well' the file can do its job of domesticating the messy and complex empirical reality to fit the strict logic of the legal process seems to be a common trope in much Western (and non-Western) scholarship. The files are performing their epistemic mediation of the outside world nearly universally across many different legal contexts – in British and continental European courts (Tuitt 2005; Scheffer 2007; van Oorschot 2014), travelling up and down the different levels of Pakistani or Indian bureaucracies (Hull 2003; Cody 2009) or in the transitional justice setting of rural Paraguay (Hetherington 2008).

The epistemological role of files in mediating reality has also been the focus of the rich and long-standing anthropological scholarship on how documents construct subjects and forms of sociality (Hull 2012: 256). This anthropological scholarship on documents and files puts van Oorschot and Shinkel's findings in a slightly different light. While precursors of such work in socio-legal studies, they are rather latecomers to the realization of the capacity of the case file to 'make things come into being' (Frohmann 2008: 1573) if we look beyond the disciplinary boundaries. Anthropologists have long documented how formal medical records and legal documents were used to distinguish 'mad' or 'normal' persons so that they could be diverted into the 'regimes of rehabilitation or punishment' (Rhodes 2004; Reed 2006). 'Trauma portfolios' were used as governance technologies by international aid agencies to make 'victims' of those Haitians who suffered political violence (Caple James 2004). The medical paper files turned immigrants in France into deserving citizens, placing illness at the centre of their identity (Ticktin 2006). The dry records of neonatal cases brought to life the biographies of children and sustained the sentiments and commitment of families (Heimer 2006, as quoted in Hull 2012: 260). The colonial railway files mediated for many American Indians the intimate stories of family genealogies and were used to define family origins and status (Bear 2007). All these accounts demonstrated how the files as the epistemic reference link effectively bridged and constituted 'a will to connection' (Simmel 1994: 6, as quoted in Pels et al. 2002: 6).

This chapter posits that the questions pertaining to the very nature of the mediation of the outside reality that give rise to the file's agency and epistemic qualities are very much cultural ones. How does the file mediate the outside world for the purpose of the trial? How exactly is the production of 'persons and events in law' occurring? If the files indeed ritually constitute a collective agent, what exactly are they doing? To put it differently, the nuances and subtleties of how exactly the files are constructing, capturing and translating (or even fabricating) the empirical reality for the purpose of the trial are culture- or context-specific. Therefore, despite the general (generic?) similarities between the markers of legality among the different case files and their reliance on self-reference and self-validation – the translation and mediation of reality by the case file and, subsequently, into the trial reflects varying socio-cultural conditions.

What can an enquiry into the Russian immigration and refugee case files tell us about this cultural specificity of the case file's epistemic translation work? After all, case files everywhere construct reality by rendering it judgment-compatible (van Oorschot 2014). In some jurisdictions, however, the paper files construct reality more actively than in others, beyond a mere legal translation. This active production of reality, the folding of complex, interrupted and messy events into a linear narrative, happens in Russia in response to the very high standards of legal formalism and the literal reading of the law. 'Quod non est in actis, non est in mundo' – What is not kept in the case file does not exist (see also Kahn 2010). The performativity and function of the Russian case file has to, therefore, be placed within the broader legal culture characterized by extreme legal formalism (Kurkchiyan 2009). The *po zakonu* (meaning: literal, strict and direct) reading of the law, paying attention to the exact wording of the black-letter law, which does not encourage discretion nor flexible interpretation of the law ('law as a living instrument') (see also Kubal 2016a; Hendley 2017). This broader culture of legal formalism exacerbates the case file's epistemic mediating function in the courtroom and beyond. I would go even further – the culture of legal formalism makes the case files' epistemic function hyperbolic in Russia. The truth or falsity of documentary claims can be beside the point for individuals (Kelly 2006), and documents can serve as grounds for official actions even when they are shown to be ultimately false. The case files in the Russian context attain this hyperbolic reality-mediating function through how they are composed, read and interpreted by different legal professionals and in courts.

Further specific cultural traits of the Russian case file could be traced back to the more general features of the legal system and the legal process. The Russian legal system could be characterized by high levels of inconsistency ('patchiness') when it comes to the legal outcomes of individual litigants (Kurkchiyan and Kubal 2018a). In a similar vein, Kathryn Hendley coined the term 'legal dualism' to explain how ordinarily most of the everyday life mundane cases progress through the different levels of the court hierarchy, adhering to the principles of justice, but equally there are a few cases where justice is diverted because specific political interests in play (Hendley 2011, 2017). The cases of Khodorkovsky, Pussy Riot or the Greenpeace Arctic 'pirates' are handy illustrations. To reiterate, the law is not always corrupted and distorted and the judges are not always at the whim of political authority. However, cases in which justice is diverted do happen and the system as a whole does appear to be inconsistent at best. That 'patchiness' extends to all the elements of the legal process. The case file is not immune to this trend.

The material Russian case files seem to reflect this general inconsistency of the legal system. They appear as an interesting and complex mixture of hyper-formality and informality. Most documents contained in the case file are highly formal. They have no traces of judges or lawyers actively studying or reading them in order to 'arrive at a picture of the case' (van Oorschot 2014). In other words, the documents are clean – they have no highlights or scribbles. Except for the formal markers of legality, the documents contained in the case file overwhelmingly consist of orderly typed and left–right aligned text, with extra space between the words if necessary. Legal professionals would not allow themselves to add personal notes to the file, to highlight or code fragments of text in the process of reading the documents. The hyper-formality of the large portion of the file is assured by original blue or purple ink stamps or notary-certified translations attached to the original piece of evidence. At the same time, in different places, the file contains documents that have handwritten inserts by the defendants beyond the standard self-referential markers. This happens when the typed original forms and letters are deemed to possess insufficient information, or to expose the party who wanted to proceed on the bases of this document to potential allegations of breaching the formal procedure. These half-typed/half-handwritten documents look rather sloppy in contrast with the other, hyper-formal documents contained in the case file, but the judges are willing to turn a blind eye to their visual appearance, given the substantive information contained in them that is crucial for the case to proceed (see also Hendley 2017).

A good illustration of this mixture between hyper-formality and informality – intrinsically linked into the systemic inconsistency of Russian justice – is the clarification of rights memo (*Ob'yasneniye*), a separate document normally contained in the immigration case file.[5] This document could be compared to the Russian version of the US Miranda rights, where the defendants confirm with their signature that the law enforcement officers have explained their rights, particularly the constitutional right to remain silent, and not to testify against themselves, their spouse or close family members. This document also lists other procedural rights stipulated by art. 25.1 of the CAO – the right to review the case materials, 'to give explanations, present evidence, file petitions and challenges' as well as to rely on professional legal and linguistic assistance (for non-Russian speakers). This formal adherence to strict procedural rights in the first part of the clarification of rights memo is quite often coupled with handwritten inserts by the defendant in the second part of the document. These handwritten texts stipulate, for example, that the defendant has declined the right to an interpreter and confirmed their working knowledge of the Russian language. The defendants also by hand confirm that the explanations they have given with regard to establishing the chronological facts of their case are voluntary and truthful. This clarification of rights memo thereby also doubles as an ad hoc affidavit through which the defendants basically admit their responsibility for breaking Russian immigration law and confirm (with their signature) the truthfulness of an abridged version of the principal facts of the case.

The third, most characteristic, trait of Russian immigration and refugee case files could be located in the broader culture of paper production in Russia. The heuristic tool of a spectrum of how Russian immigration and refugee lawyers interact with their clients on the bases of their case files strikes familiar chords with the debates among the Western legal scholars against seeing 'clients as files', or conflating the complex cases and personalities to the 'bits of memoranda or fee notes' (Tuitt 2005: 122). Patricia Tuitt interrogates this statement from the critical legal scholarship angle; she argues that 'treating peoples as

[5] Its full form in Russian is *Ob'yasneniye litsa v otnoshenii kotorogo osushchestvlyayetsya proizvodstvo po delu* – the explanation of the person against whom the proceedings are being conducted.

files' may be rendered less problematic if we stop treating the case file in a simplistic and anachronist way. She suggests therefore to approach the case file philosophically, not only as 'a mere instrument to which no degree of emotional attachment should be extended' (Tuitt 2005: 123), but as 'one of the multiple points of reference in any moral or ethical exploration of the practice of law' (Tuitt 2005: 122).

I find it helpful to draw on Tuitt's arguments in the Russian context of immigration and refugee law cases. These are special cases, but the statistics in Russia and around the world demonstrate that the great majority of these cases are also lost cases.[6] The lawyers I spoke with called them *besperspektivnyye* – unpromising, or outright hopeless. Why do the lawyers therefore care so much about what is in the case file? Why do they insist on clients providing copies of documents with formal-looking stamps, envelopes with dates and notary-certified translations? Why do they care to keep the file in pristine condition? Here again, the culture of legal formalism that constitutes an inseparable (if not dominant) trait of the broader Russian legal tradition (Kurkchiyan 2009; Kubal 2016a) is helpful to explain it. But something else and more specific might be at work, too. If we return to Tuitt, she sees the case file as invested with agentic capacities, where 'human passions cannot be entirely extinguished' (Tuitt 2005: 125), as the file folds in it the human character that 'will always thwart law's attempt to make of the individual an object' (Tuitt 2005: 125). Perhaps therefore, as Tuitt proposes, the *duty of care towards the file* in the lawyers' offices could be – by extension – an expression of the *duty of care towards their clients*. In the Russian context, I would put it slightly differently: the file and the paper evidence are invested with such agentic capacities that the clients and their stories cannot be constructed differently than through the file. This is qualitatively different from saying that the client is reduced to the file. Here, the client, their picture, their persona, their story and character emerge from the piles of paper that have been meticulously put together. The file brings the defendant to life. These migrants and asylum seekers are constructed through the very act of their representation (collating the file) (Cody 2009). In this sense, the different elements of the case file do not only represent and mediate a reality 'out there', but are constitutive of it. The clients' cases are as strong and rich in detail as their corresponding personal case files.

Qualifying the Power of the Paper: Which Case Files Go Forward?

Immigration lawyers were not the only legal professionals who put together and scrutinized the clients' files. There were also the immigration authorities (at the time of my fieldwork this was the FMS officers) who were producing

[6] For statistical information on the historical and contemporary refugee recognition rate in Russia, see Chapter 2.

their decisions and extending the paper trail, and who had a great deal of influence on which cases actually proceeded to court. They also examined and evaluated the evidence produced in the client's file. Their actions of simultaneously 'thickening' and filtering the case file thereby marked another important stage of the file acquiring the epistemic capacity of translating the complex empirical reality for the needs of the future trial. The FMS officers were also the gatekeepers of the system – granting or refusing access to the refugee or temporary asylum procedure, issuing work permits or work licences, notifying migrants about entry bars and registering immigration violations. What were their experiences of handling the file?

Bahrom is a citizen of Uzbekistan; his family took part in the Andijan uprising of 2005. His brother is currently in prison in Uzbekistan, serving a sentence for politically motivated crimes. Bahrom is religious; he is a Sunni Muslim. He cannot go back to Uzbekistan for fear of persecution – either political or religious. In Russia, Bahrom has applied for refugee status, but his application was refused. By the time I met him he had already exhausted all the domestic legal remedies and instances of appeal. The immigration lawyers advised him of the alternative procedure of seeking protection in Russia – temporary asylum status. Temporary asylum is a subsidiary form of protection, not linked to the Geneva Convention. It is given in Russia for one year, and has to be periodically renewed (Kubal 2016a).[7] I volunteered to go with Bahrom to the FMS to file an application for temporary asylum. I thought it would be a simple matter. Catherine, the lawyer, equipped me with the 'papers'. She printed out the FMS regulations (*reglament*) on the procedure for applying for temporary asylum status. I had studied the regulations beforehand, as it seemed an extremely detailed, complex and long document.

We arrived at the FMS shortly before opening time at 10 a.m. The doors were still closed and we were fifth or sixth in the queue. The two FMS officers on duty were also in the corridor, smoking. When the door opened, people started queuing directly in front of different offices. There was no one to administer or direct the general enquiries. Things were a bit disorganized and I felt a little confused. Petitioners waiting in the corridor seemed to know personally the FMS staff; some of them were shaking hands with one, important-looking officer in glasses, Mr Lisov. Bahrom remarked that this was the officer we should speak to.

There was a small queue at Mr Lisov's office – four or five people. We waited. Mr Lisov was busy with meetings but he was going in and out of his office. On one of those occasions that he was out in the corridor, he turned to Bahrom:

> And here you are again, citizen Bahrom! What are you hoping for this time? What do I owe the unlikely pleasure of seeing you again? Do you have any

[7] For the legal overview of temporary asylum status in Russia, see Chapter 2.

> papers? Do you have a residence registration in Moscow oblast that you turn with your business to FMS for Moscow oblast? Are you here legally? I have serious reasons to suspect you are illegally at the territory of Russian Federation. You are illegally here. Have you ever been here legally? Have you ever had a work permit?

Mr Lisov knew very well that Bahrom had by now exhausted all the instances of appeal for refugee status. Bahrom's Uzbek passport had been deposited at the FMS for many months (it had also expired), so there was no real possibility for him to apply for legitimate residence registration. Bahrom responded that he was trying to apply for residence registration but he was refused and . . . Mr Lisov was not listening; he repeated again:

> Are you here legally? I have serious reasons to think you are illegally at the territory of Russian Federation. You are illegally here. Therefore, you have no business here today, citizen Bahrom.

Mr Lisov turned to me: 'This man has been taking far too long to regularize his status in Russia, and there is nothing we can do to legalize him.' The FMS often conceives of Central Asians applying for asylum as a nuisance, as the vast majority of people from Central Asia in Russia are indeed migrant workers. The immigration authorities' default position is therefore that they all should regularize their status using the migrant worker route: apply for a residence registration, a work permit or a labour licence (patent). The FMS officers see Central Asian migrants choosing the asylum route not as genuine applicants in need of refugee status, but as free riders on the system of humanitarian protection. The immigration authorities often think that Central Asian migrants turn to the asylum route as the last resort to avoid being issued with a removal order for breaking Russian immigration law. In the past, they would have fallen through the cracks of the complex immigration system: missed deadlines for a residence or work permit applications, missed deadlines for labour licence fee payments. The questions Mr Lisov asked of Bahrom were also predicated upon this premise. Mr Lisov asked for residence registration, he asked for a work permit – the conventional attributes of a migrant worker from Central Asia in Russia – only to conclude that Bahrom was really an 'illegal immigrant' and was ultimately using the humanitarian protection route as a strategy for regularization. Russia is definitely not the only country in the world with systemically entrenched 'culture of disbelief' towards asylum applicants (Anderson et al. 2014; Campbell 2017), especially as the lines between refugees and migrant workers can often become very blurred (Van Hear 2004; Van Hear et al. 2009; Long 2013). The situation of Central Asian asylum seekers seems to be further complicated by the past colonial-like relationship with Russia, and the broader image of Central Asians as 'our migrants' (*nashi migranty*) or migrants from the 'near-abroad' – moving within one geo-political space – thereby lacking Convention-prescribed reasons for protection and humanitarian claims.

Finally, Mr Lisov agreed to speak with us – 'OK, come on in, we will talk' – and invited us to a different office. When I pointed out that the FMS regulations said nothing about having a residence registration in Moscow or Moscow oblast as a prerequisite for applying for temporary asylum in Russia, Mr Lisov skilfully navigated the conversation towards other, 'stronger' in his opinion, arguments that were also contained in the written documents. From that point our entire conversation focused on papers – Mr Lisov dissected Bahrom's handsomely thick case file. He seemed well acquainted with the contents of Bahrom's file; he knew where to look for past FMS and court decisions, he knew what passages to quote back at us. He assessed Bahrom's case file and found no well-grounded reasons that he should allow him to apply for temporary asylum:

> Good, I can see you are prepared with the documents ... Do you have any others? Let us look at the court decisions.

He took all the photocopied court decisions concerning Bahrom's (refused) refugee application. He went through them very quickly. Reading the original FMS refusal, he quoted:

> Look, his mother and his sisters live in Uzbekistan. They are fine. Why should he be afraid of coming back?

Bahrom responded:

> They are not religious ... they were not politically involved. My sister was ten years old in 2005, when the Andijan uprising happened.

Mr Lisov continued:

> See, the first court judgment upheld the refusal [of refugee status] and confirmed the legality of the FMS decision. It says that Bahrom's brothers live in Russia. Are they here legally? If they were – why Bahrom cannot regularize his status as well?

Bahrom responded:

> They went back to Uzbekistan.

Mr Lisov turned to me, almost laughing:

> You see, they went back to Uzbekistan. They feel safe there, why this man cannot simply return?

Bahrom tried to explain:

> My brothers are not a laughing matter. They have been asked by the national security services to collaborate; they have to collaborate with the authorities, otherwise they will be also put in prison.

Mr Lisov was not at all convinced; he was equally not convinced that Bahrom had any valid claim to humanitarian protection in Russia. Mr Lisov was very skilful at performing his function as a gatekeeper for access to the asylum procedure. He was very confident at playing the 'paper game'. At one point, Mr Lisov even mentioned the European Court of Human Rights as a possible avenue for Bahrom's grievances, only to make a broader point about weak paper evidence brought by Bahrom to support his asylum claim:

> Why don't you then apply directly to the European Court of Human Rights? Why don't you apply to the Strasbourg Court, citizen Bahrom? Do you know why? It is because you have no documents, no written proof. You say that your brother is in prison, but *there is no written proof for it* [my emphasis]. How can we trust your words? If we did that, anybody could just come in and say they need refugee status in Russia.

Finally, Mr Lisov turned to the final court judgment in Bahrom's case, the decision of the Moscow City Court that again confirmed the legality of the FMS's refusal of refugee status. The court's decision brought to light different sets of arguments relating to Russia's security concerns originating from Bahrom's alleged participation in an extremist Muslim religious organization that was banned in Russia:

> Look the Moscow City Court clearly stated that this man is a member of a terrorist organization, aren't you [here, Mr Lisov turned to me] afraid of supporting extremists? Is Europe not afraid of Muslims?

What the court decision actually said was that Bahrom was suspected of membership in a Muslim extremist organization – Hizb ut-Tahrir – by the national security services of Uzbekistan, a charge which Bahrom himself vehemently denied.[8] Bahrom said that when he was interrogated by the Uzbek security services prior to his departure for Russia, the officers came across photos on his phone of flags and a group of people praying that made them assume he was a member of a religious organization. He otherwise admits he is religious, he goes to mosque regularly and he studies the Quran, but he is not an extremist.

By this point, Mr Lisov wanted to conclude the meeting. He quickly repeated all the arguments relating to Bahrom's unsubstantiated claim for asylum in Russia, as evidenced in the FMS decision and various court judgments laid out on the table before us. He contrasted them with no formal written evidence produced by Bahrom that he was at real risk of torture or persecution should he be returned to Uzbekistan. In conclusion, Mr Lisov stressed again the illegality of Bahrom's residence in Moscow:

> This man has no registration, I am not even sure his case comes under my jurisdiction [of Moscow oblast]. His mother and sister live in Uzbekistan, both

[8] For the description of Hizb ut-Tahrir, its political and religious ideology, see Chapter 7. There I introduce this organization in more detail as linked to broader human rights cases from Russia to the European Court of Human Rights concerning extradition of Central Asian citizens sought by their authorities back home.

of his brothers returned to Uzbekistan. He has been refused refugee status by all the instances of the courts in Russia; I really cannot see why I should accept his temporary status application. Unless I accept it and you will get a rejection within one day – would you like that?

We did not want that. We left the FMS and returned to the lawyer's office. The lawyer was not surprised by this set of events as the problems with granting access to the refugee or temporary asylum procedure were notorious in her experience (see also: Burtina et al. 2015). She was not particularly upset either – if anything, she was a bit irritated. By now, she clearly had her work cut out according to the case file logic. The lawyer immediately started typing on her computer. She filed a formal complaint against Mr Lisov, as an FMS state representative, for refusing her client's access to the temporary asylum procedure, to which he was entitled in accordance with Russian law and the FMS regulations.

A month later, I learned that Mr Lisov's manager had accepted the complaint and Bahrom received a formal letter inviting him to the FMS to submit his application for temporary asylum *ab novo*. The file got thicker, Bahrom's paper trail was extended and more documents were produced and changed hands. Realistically, however, the case has not moved forward an inch.

How Are the Case Files Considered by Judges in Courts?

The final instance of the production and evaluation of the immigration and refugee case files are the domestic courts. In my previous work (Kubal 2018), I examined the role of the case file in Russian courts to highlight two logics of adjudicating ordinary migration cases. The dominant logic was that of 'a trial by paper', where the case file and the documentary evidence it contained took centre-stage in the legal proceedings (often at the cost of examining the witnesses and asking questions of the defendant). The judge delivered the decision primarily on the bases of the documents contained in the case file. The second logic was that of human rights, where the judge took into consideration certain extenuating circumstances derived from the international human rights obligations to which Russia was a party (e.g. the European Convention of Human Rights).[9]

In the final section of this chapter I continue this work; however, my perspective changes. From describing the different logics asymmetrically unfolding in the courtroom, I want to dig deeper into the dominant 'paper trail' or case file logic and examine the role of the formal documents, reports and protocols in decision-making in Russian low-level courts (for an excellent analysis of the role of the case file in criminal law, see Kahn 2010). This section illustrates the hyperbolic epistemic function of the case file in mediating the out-of-court, empirical reality of the different judges adjudicating immigration law cases.

[9] For a more in-depth examination of the human rights logic, see Chapter 6.

In the Halls of Justice

A group of seven Central Asian men was brought into the B. District court following an FMS raid on a construction site in Moscow. The group was escorted to the court by two FMS officers on duty and charged with offences against art. 18.10 (part 3) of the CAO (working without a work permit). The men were kept waiting in the corridor. I happened to be in court at that time as I had just finished observing a different case. The FMS officers were sitting next to the Central Asian men, reviewing the documents in the case file: the pictures from the raid, the protocols and the printouts from the FMS database. After some time they collected all the case files and, together with the passports of the Central Asian migrants, they submitted these bundles of documents to the judge's assistant. The assistant took the files to the courtroom. I did not have a chance to examine the case files in detail, but from observing the FMS officers, the case files looked fairly standard in content and size. After some time, the judge's assistant emerged from the room and asked if any of the men – Central Asian migrants – were married to Russian citizens or had close family members who were Russian citizens. One of the FMS officers looked at the men but they all responded negatively. The judge's assistant went back to the courtroom. The FMS officer turned to the Central Asian migrants and said 'next time you have to do work permits, just do the work permits'. The judge's assistant emerged again from the courtroom and asked if any of these men had small children, who could be Russian citizens. Three of the men orally gave details of the gender of their children together with their dates of birth. The judge's assistant, equipped with this information, went back into the courtroom. Then, the judge started calling the men into the courtroom one by one.

This interaction between the FMS officers, the defendants and the judge's assistant – prior to the actual trial – made me think that the low-level district court judges primarily act as the auditors of the case file. They know what the law is and they know what documents should be included in the case file if the case is to be processed quickly and efficiently (see also Hendley 2017; Andrianova 2018). Prior to the trial, the judge must review (or audit) the written evidence supplied by the FMS, and the assistant's role is to make sure that all the procedurally required information is supplied and filed accordingly (and all the grounds that might have resulted in having the decision overturned on appeal are covered). About an hour later, all the defendants were handed written court judgments confirming that they have all committed administrative offences against art. 18.10 (part 3) of the CAO. The judgment specified the fine to be paid (5000 roubles) and contained an expulsion order from the RF to be carried out 'by independent means' (*samostoyatel'no*) within the next five days. With these court judgments in hand, the men were released from the custody of the FMS officers and allowed to leave the court building.

The default position of the Russian low-level courts in these immigration law cases seems to be to rely on written documents. As Kurkchiyan observed elsewhere, this phenomenon is not a contemporary development nor even a legacy from Soviet times (Kurkchiyan 2018). The use of written formal documents as the sole basis for a court judgment goes back into Russian history, when the role of the earliest judges was that of a clerk. Their main function was to write down all the testimonies and then send the whole set of documents to a superior, who would deliver a judgment (Kurkchiyan 2018). The courts from the times of Imperial Russia were also in the habit of treating their civil-service files as true representations of the facts, without much questioning of how well they reflected the complex empirical reality. Kurkchiyan links this element of the Russian legal tradition with the historical absence of professional lawyers in the courtroom. Without active lawyers in court – who could challenge the files, deliver alternative factual material, cross-examine witnesses in open court and then argue in defence of the truthfulness of evidence that contradicts the files – the logical and easy solution for a judge is to take whatever is written in the file as solid 'evidence' (Kurkchiyan 2018; see also Kahn 2010; Kurkchiyan and Kubal 2018a).

Administerial Scrutiny Short of a Challenge

At the appeals level, the higher-level judges also do not question the authenticity of the documents contained in the file. The documents produced by the FMS officers and legally affirmed by the lower court are by default correct, as the state representatives do not lie (for a discussion of this assumption as an element of legal fiction, see van Oorschot and Schinkel 2015). What follows from this is that the defence lawyers or the defendants themselves often see the judges who preside over the appeals cases as rubberstamping the decision of the lower court and reproducing the lower court's judgments. The appeal courts are seen not as an important mechanism of checks and balances on the broader institution of justice, but very much as an integral part of the legal system.

My observations point to the conclusion, however, that this is qualitatively different from saying that the appeals judges do not scrutinize the file. They do. The judges check and double-check the documents. They read and re-read the letters, reports, reference letters and printouts from the database, especially if the defence has pointed out an allegedly erroneous interpretation of some information or evidence contained in the case file. This procedure is, however, different from that observed by van Oorschot (2014) in the Dutch jurisdictional context. The Russian judges do not highlight or code different elements of the case file to 'see the case clearly' (van Oorschot 2014); they do not use sticky notes or colourful symbols to mark certain pages with particularly important or relevant information. The Russian judges keep their case files clear. In their decisions, the appeals judges adhere strictly to the rules of formal legality and reproduce the hyper-formal aspect of the file.

I once observed a case in front of the Moscow City Court, where the defendant's labour contract dates were deemed incongruent with the dates of his residence registration in Moscow. It was a variation of an art. 18.8 CAO case. At the appeals stage, the defendant's lawyer questioned the alleged incongruence, and appended to the appeal a written contract of employment, a copy of which had been deposited at the FMS. Ahead of the trial, the judge made an independent enquiry with the FMS to double-check the contract of employment dates and included a copy of the contract as evidence in the case file. As a result, the formal trial took no longer than three minutes. Everything was very quick. Upon taking a written power of attorney from the defendant's lawyer and explaining the processual rights and obligations to the defendant's party, the judge turned to the documents in front of her. She spent a moment corroborating the dates from the two types of documents (the appeal and the case file). She did not take any statements from the defendant or his representative. Upon having checked and cross-referenced the dates, making sure they were the same on both documents, she ended the case, acquitting the defendant. Prior to the lawyer's leaving the courtroom she advised him that in the court's main office they could receive a *spravka* confirming the acquittal (as the full judgment would only be ready in two weeks). This was a simple, typical case adjudicated in accordance with the case file logic (Kubal 2018); the decision was driven by the formal documents contained in the case file. The judge's inquisitorial role was limited to making a formal enquiry with the immigration law enforcement agency (the FMS) for a copy of a particular document, so that the challenge of the appeal could be corroborated against what was already contained in the official state documents.

The judges in these cases largely stay within the remit of the case file logic. They scrutinize the individual documents, they check the documents provided by the defendant vis-à-vis the documents supplied by the FMS and contained in the case file. They corroborate various pieces of formal written evidence, but they do not overall challenge or question the authenticity of the evidence. Staying firmly within the confines of the case file becomes particularly problematic in immigration law cases where the incriminating evidence relies entirely on the affidavits signed by the defendants.

For example, Elerbek, a migrant worker from Tajikistan, was found guilty of offences against art. 18.10 (part 3) of the CAO by the lower court on the basis of a photograph provided by the FMS – in which he was sitting in a car behind a steering wheel – and an elaborate affidavit, in which he confirmed that he had been working as a driver (without a work permit). He attempted to clarify this evidence before the appeals court saying that he was sitting in the car but he was *waiting* for a friend, who was also present in the courtroom, ready to testify if needed. The judge did not seem to give much credibility to this explanation, nor attempted to hear the witness brought before her. Instead, the judge turned everyone's attention to the signed affidavit already contained in the case file:

> Judge: But I have an affidavit signed by you, saying you were hired to work by company X, you were supposed to drive and deliver a package from this place to

this place, it was an oral contract and you were to be paid 4,000 roubles per day…

Elerbek [interrupting]: But I have never earned that much, anywhere in Moscow. This is not a day's going rate of pay – it is far too high!

The man was not trying to be disrespectful to the judge – he, indeed, interrupted the judge, but actually made an important observation about the artificiality of the affidavit-only-based evidence. He was genuinely astonished by the figure quoted in the testimony. Elerbek was attempting to challenge the affidavit for what it was: a piece of paper with all the correct signatures and official stamps to make it look like formal evidence, but which was in no way connected to the reality of the situation. It did not account for what had happened on that particular day, nor was it true in general when it described the context of going wages for migrant workers in Moscow. The judge responded:

But you have signed it. This is your signature. I have to expel you, as this is the minimum penalty.

In these affidavit-only cases, which are adjudicated in accordance with the case file logic, we see an acute conflation of the written subject and the agent. It is clear that for the Russian appeals judges (just like for the immigration lawyers earlier in the legal process) the construction of those agents that would be represented is in fact a product of the very act of representation (Cody 2009). The migrants, the defendants, the agents are rarely seen as the people pleading before the judge, who physically come to the court trying to clarify evidence and appeal the decision of the lower court. Instead, to the judges the agents in those cases are those of whom the documents contained in the case file speak, who are portrayed in the photographs, or who signed the affidavits (sometimes under duress or without working knowledge of the Russian language). The case file constitutes and constructs these legal subjects. The way the judges read and interpret the case file in courts is crucial for the file to attain this hyperbolic reality-mediating function: the written files and documents are always a clear reflection of facts of the case.

At the same time, I do not want to portray the Russian judges as heartless in their case file work. In the breaks before the different cases, or immediately upon the conclusion of the formal legal proceedings, I would often hear the judge saying:

I cannot really change the decision of the lower court; it was legally taken.

I feel sorry for you, you work hard here, you live where possible, but Moscow has a different [immigration] regime. I have to follow the law.

You are all so modest (*skromnyye*), I really feel pity for you but I cannot give any other decision.

The judges, by focusing solely on the case file and the written evidence before them, make the delivery of justice look administerial (Kurkchiyan and Kubal 2018a). The oft-perceived rubberstamping on the written evidence before the appeals judge leads to the conclusion that the delivery of justice does not seem to be related to hearings in a courtroom, but rather accumulated gradually through the various stages of document gathering. It starts when the FMS forms a suspicion and begins to investigate, and continues through the several phases of the pre-trial and court proceedings (Kurkchiyan and Kubal 2018a). The appeals courtroom in this administerial model of justice is merely the final point in the chain of events. The collateral effect – particularly vocal in the corridors of the various court buildings immediately after the trial – is that the appeals court is often blamed for the procedural injustices of the pre-trial stage and all the different (arguably autonomous) elements of the legal hierarchy are conflated into one big, oppressive and unjust institution. In the long career of the immigration or refugee case file in Russia – from the offices of the grass-roots immigration lawyers, through to the FMS law enforcement agencies, low-level courts and courts of appeal – the judges are not seen as an authoritative professional body ready to provide a system of checks and balances on the paper production in Russia. They are rather perceived as an integral part of this culture.

* * *

Comparing the Russian case file model of delivery of justice with Western models of fact-finding and truth-determining can easily and consistently result in a very critical conclusion (Kurkchiyan and Kubal 2018a: 275). Instead, it might be more productive to acknowledge that the traditionally developed file-based model of delivering justice embedded within the culture of paper production, materiality and high formalism exists at different stages of the legal process and is routinely relied upon by different parties to the case.

This chapter identified the three main features of how the Russian case file mediates the empirical or out-of-court reality for the purpose of the legal process and actually physically and materially constitutes the legal subjects. The hyperbolic reality-mediating function of the case file means that it is rarely contested; the written documents reign supreme and their fact-finding role is taken for granted and valued above all oral statements from the witnesses present in the courtroom. The second feature focuses on the mixture of hyper-formality and informality in how the case files are put together. Documents such as formal reports and notary-certified translations are intertwined in the case file with various memos or affidavits, and handwritten inserts by the defendants or the law enforcement agents are used to 'patch up' initial procedural or fact-finding omissions. The third important trait of the case file is that it cannot be separated from the broader culture of paper production in Russia, at all stages of the legal process – in the grass-roots immigration lawyers' offices, the FMS buildings and, finally, the different courts. The lawyers may appear heartless as they conceptualize their duty towards the client through their duty towards the case file and prioritize building up a paper trail for their client (Tuitt 2005). The FMS law enforcement agents qualify and filter what documentary evidence counts as strong, thereby exercising their gatekeeper function in granting or preventing access to a particular legal remedy or procedure. The judges may audit and administerially scrutinize the file, but they do not question or challenge the quality of the formal evidence produced before them and generally trust the legality of the previous decisions. These different elements bring us closer to understanding the culture of materiality in immigration and refugee law in Russia.

6

The Use of Human Rights in Russian Courts

Analysis of Judgments in Immigration and Refugee Law Cases

Introduction

In the remainder of the book, I stay within the broad area of access to justice and the everyday experiences of the immigration and refugee laws, but particularly focus on the realization of human rights for migrants and refugees in Russia. The purpose of this chapter is to use Russian domestic court judgments in the areas of immigration and refugee law as a lens to better understand Russia's multifaceted relationship with the European Convention of Human Rights, and human rights more broadly.

This chapter analyses the texts of different legal judgments and their underpinning ideologies to cast more light on how, when and to what extent Russian judges rely on reference to the different human rights conventions, and with what consequences for the defendants and parties involved. I have carefully examined a selection of judgments by the Russian courts of general jurisprudence – at district and regional levels – and how they make references to European and international human rights law when deliberating and deciding immigration and refugee law cases.[1] I have also included certain opinions of the Russian Supreme Court and regional supreme courts, and analysed the most recent decision of the Russian Constitutional Court relating to the right to liberty for stateless persons confined in deportation centres (23 May 2017, No. 14-P). I believe that looking at the plurality of Russian courts offers a fresh perspective vis-à-vis much of the existing scholarship that particularly focuses on the role of the Russian Constitutional Court as the leading enforcer of the European Court of Human Rights (ECtHR) judgments (Marochkin 2017). At face value, it makes a lot of sense to focus on the Constitutional Court due to the direct correlation between the European Convention on Human Rights (ECHR) and the Russian Constitution (see, e.g. art. 15(4) or art. 17 of the Russian Constitution as defining this relationship). Both legal instruments focus on the status of individuals, their rights and freedoms; hence, as Marochkin argues, 'a direct link between the two courts is obvious: both deal with cases on the implementation and violation of the

[1] For an overview of the methodological approach of working with the different court judgments, see Chapter 1.

Convention and the Constitution' (Marochkin 2017: 96). This does not mean, however, that the Russian Constitutional Court is the only 'domestic interpreter' (Marochkin 2017: 97) of the ECHR. Many studies have shown that focusing on the broader judiciary is the most effective way for examining the introduction and implantation of international law in the Russian legal system, especially when compared to the legislative and executive branches of power (Starzhenetskii 2014; Burkov 2017; Marochkin 2017: 97). In this chapter, I look at different judicial opinions, stemming from the different levels of the court system, demonstrating that this legal professional group is not as monolithic as many commentators perceive it to be. At the same time, I am acutely aware that this work is by no means exhaustive or representative of how all Russian judges invoke, rely on or ignore ECtHR jurisprudence – the judgments I relied on in immigration and refugee law cases were selected based on the courts actually making *some reference* to ECHR jurisprudence and human rights law.[2]

Analytically, therefore, this chapter is a continuation of Chapter 5 and my earlier work, where following ethnographic observations of cases involving migrants in Russian low-level courts in Moscow (Kubal 2018), I distinguished two logics according to which the courts render decisions in these cases. The primary trend was to adjudicate these cases according to the 'trial by paper' logic, paying utmost attention to documentary, written evidence presented by both parties to the trial and deposited in the case file. I have developed this argument in depth in the preceding chapter of this book, looking at the hyperbolic epistemic function of the case file in translating and mediating the empirical reality for the needs of the trial. While the case file logic dominates most of the decision-making in immigration and refugee cases, in certain exceptional circumstances the judges rely on and invoke different sets of arguments, which I dubbed the human rights logic (Kubal 2018). This is when consideration is given to the fact that migrants or asylum seekers cannot be deported to a place where they might find themselves at risk of torture, inhumane and degrading treatment (art. 3 of the ECHR), or when the return may mean a grave risk to their lives (art. 2 of the ECHR). Along the same lines, the judge may give due recognition to the fact that the deportable migrant has close family members in Russia, and that the imminent expulsion would violate their right to private and family life (art. 8 of the ECHR). Another type of human rights argument is invoked by setting the time limits of detention pending administrative removal (expulsion) or extradition; in order not to endanger the human right to liberty (art. 5 of the ECHR). Drawing on a close textual analysis of the different domestic court judgments, my approach focuses on how, when and to what extent these judgments mention, frame and style the different human rights arguments. *If* the judges did refer to human rights, *then how exactly did they do that?*

[2] In other words, my sampling of the judgments was purposive.

The Importance of Looking Beyond the High-Profile Cases

This chapter starts from the premise that the relationship between Russia and the ECHR is much more multifaceted than many commentators portray it to be. First, Russia is often depicted as the greatest abuser of human rights law, given the number of cases that originate from Russia.[3] However, may it also be interpreted as evidence that the Convention has been well received in Russia, given how often ordinary citizens rely on it in their disputes with the state? Also, Russia is the biggest country in the Council of Europe, with some 144 million people; so relative to the size of its population Russia ranks ninth in the number of pending cases before the ECtHR (per capita, as of 1 October 2018).

Second, the main axis alongside which the arguably strained relationship between Russia and the ECHR is primarily analysed are two high-profile cases: the so-called Yukos case (*OAO Neftyanaya Kompaniya Yukos* v. *Russia*, no. 14902/04, judgment of 31 July 2014) and the case concerning prisoners' voting rights (*Anchugov and Gladkov* v. *Russia*, no. 11157/04 and 15162/05, judgment of 4 July 2013) (Sakwa 2009; Fura and Maruste 2017; Mälksoo and Benedek 2017; Kahn 2018a, 2018b; for notable exceptions, see Kahn 2001, 2004, 2006). I argue that this focus presupposes a rather skewed conclusion about the Russian relationship with the ECHR. *Yukos* was a politically sensitive case that resulted in approximately €1.9 billion compensation – the largest ever awarded by the ECtHR. The human rights violations concerned art. 6 of the ECHR (right to fair trial), and art. 1 of Protocol No. 1 ('Every natural or legal person is entitled to the peaceful enjoyment of his possessions') with regard to the unlawful, arbitrary and disproportionate imposition and enforcement of the 2000–2003 tax assessments on Yukos. While it is beyond the scope of this chapter to go into a detailed analysis of this judgment, the unprecedentedly large compensation has to be put in context of the compensations awarded in arguably more serious human rights violations in which the ECtHR ruled against Russia. In the infamous 'Chechen cases' concerning torture (art. 3 of the ECHR), enforced disappearances and extrajudicial executions (art. 2), in conjunction with Russia's failure to properly investigate these crimes (art. 6), the compensation awarded by the Strasbourg Court to the applicants ranged from €5,000 to €40,000 – a mere fraction of what the ECtHR awarded to Yukos (see, e.g. *Musayev and Others* v. *Russia*, nos. 57941/00,

[3] Russia ranks second among Council of Europe member countries in numbers of complaints made to the ECtHR and ranks first in the number of violations of the ECHR, according to annual report on the court's work from 2017 (see European Court of Human Rights 2018). In 2017, the ECHR rendered a total of 1,068 decisions: 305 of these decisions, or 29 per cent, concerned complaints from Russia. As of 1 January 2018, 7,747 cases from Russia were underway at the ECtHR. Only Romania has supplied the court with more cases: 9,920. In 2017, the ECtHR deemed 49 per cent of all the applications against Russia admissible – that is, deemed worthy of consideration.

58699/00 and 60403/00, judgment of 26 July 2007). It begs a rhetorical question: would a Chechen life be worth less to the ECtHR than the property of Mr Khodorkovsky?

The question of prisoners' voting rights and the non-enforcement of the ECtHR decision in *Anchugov and Gladkov* by Russia also needs placing in comparative perspective as it resonates clearly with cases against other European countries. Russia is not the only country where problems are observed in particular cases. Since *Hirst* v. *United Kingdom (No 2)* (2005) – the first case in which the Court ruled that a blanket ban on British prisoners exercising the right to vote was contrary to the ECHR (as incompatible with art. 3 of Protocol No. 1) – seven other applications to the ECtHR followed from the United Kingdom due to the non-enforcement of the original judgment and lack of corresponding legislation.[4] Nine years since the *Hirst* judgment the British government attempted to introduce legislation that would give the prisoners right to vote (see *Firth and Others* v. *United Kingdom*, nos. 47784/09, 47806/09, 47812/09, 47818/09, 47829/09, 49001/09, 49007/09, 49018/09, 49033/09 and 49036/09, judgment of 12 August 2014). However, the bill was explicitly rejected by the British Parliament and the government has repeatedly stated since then that prisoners will not be given the right to vote in spite of the ECtHR repeatedly ruling to that effect (BBC 2012). The conflict over prisoners' voting rights together with the *Othman (Abu Qatada)* v. *United Kingdom* (no. 8139/09, judgment of 17 January 2012) case, in which under art. 6 the United Kingdom could not lawfully deport Abu Qatada to Jordan because of the risk of the use of evidence obtained by torture, led then Home Secretary Theresa May to say that the United Kingdom had to leave the ECHR altogether (*Guardian* 2016). The Home Secretary staunchly criticized the Strasbourg Court as posing an impediment to the United Kingdom's constitutional autonomy and national security: 'the ECHR can bind the hands of parliament, adds nothing to our prosperity, makes us less secure by preventing the deportation of dangerous foreign nationals' (as quoted in the *Guardian* 2016).

Perhaps, therefore, Russian resistance to certain ECtHR judgments is not unique but rather reflects a broader trend among other Council of Europe countries (see Benedek 2017: 395)? I would go even further to say that these contestations and conflicts to some extent prove that the Convention as a 'living instrument' is taken seriously by the state parties, who engage with it and the ECtHR jurisprudence, contest and co-shape it rather than simply rubberstamp on the Court's decisions or – worse – ignore them. At the same time, whenever the British and Russian relationships with the ECtHR are compared, the rather patronizing arguments are brought up: 'one [Britain] thinks it knows better; the other [Russia] does not want to be told that it

[4] Out of the seven separate applications launched with ECtHR (one had over 1,000 applicants) the ECtHR found three inadmissible. For details see: Press Unit ECtHR (2017).

knows worse' (Mälksoo 2014: 222). Not surprisingly, therefore, some Russian commentators see the ECtHR judgments as biased against Russia. Russian delegates at the different meetings of the Parliamentary Assembly of the Council of Europe (PACE – the parliamentary arm of the Council of Europe) have often repeated that:

> From the outset, the European Court of Human Rights judgments left people perplexed by its inconsistency, contradictory nature, subjective stance and flagrant political bias. That said we invariably proceed on the basis that *the decisions of the Strasbourg court must be executed.*
>
> (Parliamentary Questions for Oral Answer, Addendum 1, 4 October 2006, quoted in Preclik 2014: 61; my emphasis)

Third, the arguably strained relationship between Russia and the ECtHR is often seen through the prism of the recent legal position of the Russian Constitutional Court, which in its decision from 14 July 2015 (which later became law, see Federal Law No. 7-FKZ of 14 December 2015) gave itself a supervisory role over enforcing ECtHR judgments if they were to violate the Constitution of the Russian Federation (RF). In other words, if the Russian Constitutional Court were to conclude that a given ECtHR judgment was incompatible with the RF Constitution, it would not be implemented (Burkov 2017: 66). This prerogative has only been used three times so far – in relation to the above-mentioned, either highly politicized (*Yukos*) or constitutionally contested cases (*Anchugov and Gladkov*, *Konstantin Markin* v. *Russia*, no. 30078/06, judgment of 22 March 2012) (Marochkin 2017: 114).[5]

The Constitutional Court, in its ruling from 19 January 2017 on the refusal to fulfil the judgment in the *Yukos* case, again repeated that such refusal was 'an exception' rather than a rule (Marochkin 2017: 119). And yet many legal and socio-legal analysts were quick to portray the 14 July 2015 Constitutional Court judgment as Russia 'distancing itself from certain liberal (Western) values to follow its own concept of Russian sovereign democracy and traditionalist (Orthodox) ideology and culture' (Fura and Maruste 2017: 223). I believe these conclusions are not only alarmist but also premature, as for a large number of cases Russia appears to be no less cooperative than some other states of the Council of Europe (Benedek 2017: 398). Perhaps, therefore, the focus on the high-profile cases as a litmus test of Russia's relationship with the ECHR is

[5] The high-profile politicized cases, or cases demonstrating conflicts between Russian constitutional law and its self-imposed international law obligations, need to be distinguished from a separate group of ECtHR cases against Russia that have pointed out structural and systemic deficiencies in the Russian legal system since its accession to the Council of Europe. The latter primarily concern cases relating to the obstruction of the enforcement of ECtHR judgments (*Burdov* v. *Russia*, no. 59498/00, judgment of 7 May 2002; *Burdov* v. *Russia* (No. 2), no. 33509/04, judgment of 15 January 2009; *Konstantin Markin* v. *Russia*, no. 30078/06, judgment of 22 March 2012), or the conditions of confinement in Russia (*Kalashnikov* v. *Russia*, no. 47095/99, judgment of 15 July 2002). I am grateful to Jeffrey Kahn for this insightful observation and comment.

epistemologically wrong. Perhaps we are focusing on the wrong or impossible cases – cases that start from assumptions about Russia's exceptionality.

The Use of European Human Rights Law Domestically

How about we leave these high-profile cases and see what lies beyond them? There is an emerging socio-legal and empirical scholarship looking at the use of European human rights law in Russian domestic courts. Anton Burkov, in a very influential and empirically informed chapter examining the reception of ECtHR jurisprudence in Russian domestic courts (2017), argued that Russian judges have little regard for the ECtHR, despite the fact that the ECHR is firmly integrated within the Russian domestic legal system. The Russian Constitution in art. 15(4) gives priority to Russia's international legal obligations, and said article has been given broad interpretation by the Russian Constitutional Court to the effect that 'all ECtHR case law is deemed a source of Russian Law':

> Judgments of the ECtHR are supposed to be recognized as sources of Russian law and law enforcement practices, and must be taken into account by national courts hearing domestic cases.
>
> (Russian Constitutional Court judgment of 5 February 2007, No. 2-P, as quoted in Burkov 2017: 64)

That was the consensus at least until the above-mentioned 14 July 2015 Constitutional Court ruling, which made Russia's position and the question of legal supremacy much more ambiguous.

Separately, the explanations by the Plenum of the RF Supreme Court (Regulation No. 5 of 10 October 2003, and Regulation No. 21 of 27 June 2013) addressed the issue of the relationship and implementation of the ECHR in national courts, clarifying the position *about which ECtHR judgments exactly* should be recognized as sources of Russian law. The 2003 regulation recognized it as mandatory for domestic courts to follow all ECtHR judgments delivered against Russia, while the 2013 regulation left it to judicial discretion to further consider the judgments against other parties to the Convention 'if the circumstances of the case under examination are similar to those which have been the subject of analysis and findings made by the European Court' (Regulation No. 21 of 27 June 2013, §2, para. 2 as quoted in Burkov 2017: 68).

However, despite this deep black-letter law integration of the Convention into Russian domestic law, Burkov's own assessment of the use of European human rights law by domestic courts is rather sceptical, if not outright negative:

> In practice lower-court judges as well as Russian Constitutional Court judges ignore the convention, and the Russian Federation Supreme Court judges have not followed their own Plenum's regulations when ruling on particular cases.
>
> (Burkov 2017: 69)

This is a rather sombre conclusion. This observation is based on Burkov's empirical examination of three 'test cases' pursued by Russian human rights lawyers through the different levels of the domestic courts: the case of Alina Sablina against secret organ harvesting (*Sablina and others* v. *Russia*, no. 4460/16, lodged on 28 December 2015), the case of Korolevs on the right to conjugal meetings during long-term imprisonment (partially addressed in *Khoroshenko* v. *Russia*, no. 41418/04, judgment of 30 June 2015) and the case of Valentina Mikhaylova, a pensioner who was refused free legal assistance when charged with a criminal offence in administrative proceedings (*Mikhaylova* v. *Russia*, no. 46998/08, judgment of 2 May 2016). Burkov's research revealed that Russian domestic judges at different levels of the legal system (from justices of the peace, via district and regional courts, all the way to the Constitutional Court) adjudicated these test cases 'based on national law in favour of the state authorities when the case should have been decided for the applicant based on the Convention and ECtHR case law' (Burkov 2017: 71). The domestic judges, for various reasons – such as lack of motivation, political will and fear of having the decision overturned on appeal (Burkov 2017: 70) – 'simply did not follow the Constitution, legislation, or even relevant Supreme Court Plenum Regulations' with regard to the ECtHR jurisprudence and its applicability (Burkov 2017: 91). Conducting my fieldwork among the human rights and immigration lawyers in Moscow, I have collected similar observations – the great majority of immigration and refugee law cases had to reach the ECtHR for a successful conclusion or, as the lawyers put it, 'for justice to be achieved'. One lawyer, remarking on her experience of the low-level domestic judges' reluctance to apply the ECtHR jurisprudence, alluded to the judge's potentially significant misunderstanding of the idea of a precedent. She explained:

> The judge ignores my arguments when I refer to the previous cases decided by ECtHR against Russia in extradition or expulsion proceedings with similar or nearly identical facts by simply saying: 'What do you mean here – you are referring to a completely different person' [*Chto Vy imeyete v vidu – eto voobshche drugoye litso*].
>
> (HR Lawyer, 25 May 2014)

While, on the whole, I am therefore highly sympathetic to Burkov's argument, I would say that a different picture could be painted by a different collection of cases. While I limit my observations to immigration and refugee cases, I would say that in certain circumstances the domestic courts did invoke the human rights arguments – mostly by directly citing the relevant articles from the European Convention. I will evidence this claim later in the chapter. Furthermore, Burkov's work shows a vibrant group of human rights cause-lawyers operating in different regions of Russia who select and take on specific cases as 'test cases' to challenge Russia's domestic (non-)compliance with ECtHR law. These cases reveal conflicts between domestic legislation and international treaties that Russia has ratified. These committed human rights lawyers intentionally pursue these cases to bring about transformative changes for the legal system as a whole – to pressure the Constitutional Court to introduce a clearer interpretation of the domestic law in relationship to Russia's international human rights obligations and ECtHR jurisprudence. The acknowledgement of these different groups of cause-lawyers and their work also constitutes an important puzzle in addressing Russia's relationship with and use of the European human rights law domestically (see Chapter 3). The focus on these lawyers breaks away from the portrayal of Russia as a legal and ideological monolith and demonstrates the plurality of views and opinions within the legal profession more broadly.

A similar argument for the plurality of the domestic legal scene, and a rather more complex relationship with the ECtHR, is made by Vladislav Starzhenetskii, whose long-term study of the Russian Arbitrazh court system revealed that Russian courts:

> borrow much from the Convention and ECtHR practice; in a substantial number of cases, they frequently use the same language, legal tools and approaches as the ECtHR. (Starzhenetskii 2014; see also Bocharov and Titaev 2018: 209)

To support this observation, Starzhenetskii offers a long list of Russian Higher Arbitrazh Court cases adjudicated between 2004 and 2010, all of which referred to either the specific rights and freedoms contained in the ECHR or the Strasbourg Court jurisprudence (Starzhenetskii 2014: 209). My contextual study of the use, application of and references to the European human rights law in the domestic immigration and refugee law cases complements this picture and takes this analysis forward.

How Do Domestic Courts Refer to Human Rights Arguments in Immigration and Refugee Law Cases?

The use of European human rights law in the domains of immigration and refugee law and the operation of the human rights logic in domestic court judgments is not uniform. To help better understand how exactly the human rights arguments are invoked and the variation of Russian domestic courts' approaches to ECtHR decisions, I constructed the following typology.

First, there are a number of judgments that could be characterized by an *explicit use* and implementation of the ECHR – literal quotation and citation of the European Convention and its specific provisions in the domestic judicial decisions.

Second, there is the *implicit use* of the human rights arguments, where there might not necessarily be a reference to the Convention, but where nonetheless the 'spirit' of the human rights law is visible – through either the principles of justice and humanity as derived from the Russian Constitution, or the balance of public versus private interest invoked in the judgments. This is particularly characteristic for judgments that set exact time limits for detention pending administrative removal (or extradition) without specific references to art. 5 of the ECHR.

A third and distinctive type of invocation of human rights arguments – which I term as *affirmative* – can be observed in certain decisions of the high courts in Russia. It is when the low-level courts reject or ignore the human rights arguments but the importance of human rights is later assured (or affirmed) by a decision of Russian Supreme Court or Constitutional Court. As an illustrative case study I use here the recent decision in the *Mskhiladze* case (23 May 2017, No. 14-P) concerning time limits for detention of stateless persons whose administrative removal (expulsion) was de facto impossible. In this decision, the Constitutional Court significantly amended the interpretation of the domestic law (Code of Administrative Offences, or CAO) by drawing on ECtHR jurisprudence against Russia: *Kim* v. *Russia* (no. 44260/13, judgment of 17 July 2014).

However, this does not mean that the human rights arguments rule could be found in most of the Russian domestic decisions in immigration and refugee law cases. On the contrary. The last and most prevalent type of decisions is characterized by reference to and deliberation about human rights arguments followed by the *rejection* of the ECtHR law and jurisprudence. I discuss this using the domestic trajectory of *L.M. and Others* v. *Russia* (nos. 40081/14, 40088/14 and 40127/14, judgment of 15 October 2015), concerning the removal of Syrian nationals for ordinary immigration offences in the midst of the civil war in Syria (2011 and ongoing); and the dissent of Judge Dedov in *Z.A. and Others* v. *Russia* (nos. 61411/15, 61420/15, 61427/15, 3028/16, judgment of 28 March 2017), raising more general remarks about the relationship between human rights, migration and asylum in a neoliberal, global world.

Explicit Reliance on Human Rights Law

The explicit invocation of human rights logic was primarily visible in judgments concerning administrative offences (for which the minimum penalty in Moscow, St Petersburg, Moscow Oblast and Leningrad oblast since 2013 has been administrative removal or expulsion) lodged against de facto asylum seekers in Russia. The defendants could not easily be expelled to their home countries for committing offences against immigration law, as that would mean returning them to places of grave conflict where their lives could be at risk. So why did the asylum seekers even find themselves in court on charges of administrative offences? Due to the well-documented backlogs and administrative delays in processing of their asylum applications (Burtina et al. 2015), many asylum seekers would try to work to support themselves and their families. Until relatively recently, the question of access to the labour market for asylum applicants in Russia was not explicitly regulated. In practice, the authorities had actually been known, on many occasions, to 'turn a blind eye' to asylum seekers engaged in paid labour who could prove they were subject to a status determination procedure (either waiting for a decision or appealing a refusal of refugee status) (Kubal 2016a: 275). However, following legislative change No. 127-FZ of 5 May 2014, their access to the labour market has been explicitly forbidden in the Federal Law on the Legal Status of Foreign Citizens. As a result, the Federal Migration Service (FMS) could take them to district courts as casual immigration law offenders and charge them with working without a permit or work licence (art. 18.10 (part 2) of the CAO).[6] Alternatively, knowing the notorious difficulties with obtaining residence registration for migrants in Moscow and St Petersburg (Reeves 2013), the FMS would press charges of a lack of a valid residence registration (art. 18.8 (part 3) of the CAO).

Article 3 of the ECHR

Take as an example the following case, concerning a Syrian national in L. oblast, who was sentenced to administrative removal by the lower (district) court on account of a lack of valid residence registration (art. 18.8 of the CAO). The appeals court of L. oblast in its judgment from 13 February 2014 changed the decision of the lower court and excluded the expulsion from the sentence. The judge released the Syrian national from the detention centre and reduced the administrative fine from 5,000 to 2,000 roubles (the minimum fine prescribed by the CAO). The concluding decision reads as follows:

> [The court decided] to amend the decision of the judge [name of the judge] of the City Court of the L. region on [date], taken in respect of [name of the defendant] born on 20 March 1980, the citizen of the Syrian Arab Republic. [The court decided] to exclude from the decision the additional penalty in the form of administrative expulsion from the Russian Federation; the penalty in the form of an administrative fine shall be determined in the amount of 2,000 rubles. [The court decided] to release [name of the defendant] from the Special Temporary Detention Centre for Foreign Citizens of the Federal Migration Service of Russia for [name of the city].
>
> (Decision L. Oblast Court, 13 February 2014, p. 7)

The main body of the judgment consists of seven pages. Upon the introduction of the case and the reference to the applicable Russian domestic immigration law (Federal Law No. 115-FZ from 25 July 2002 On the Legal Status of Foreign Citizens, and specific provisions of the CAO), the judge reviewed the facts of the case as supported by the documentary material provided by the FMS and contained in the case file. On page 4, the judge considers the proportionality and applicability of the expulsion (removal) as part of the administrative penalty within the framework of the following test:

> The imposition of additional penalty in the form of administrative removal should be based on evidence that confirms the real necessity of applying to a person . . . such a measure . . . as well as its proportionality as the only possible

[6] For the legal overview, see Chapter 2.

> way to achieve a balance of public and private interests in administrative proceedings.
>
> (Decision L. Oblast Court, 13 February 2014, p. 4)

This balancing test is then performed on pages 4–6 with reference to different international human rights instruments. The judge invokes explicitly three major international conventions (pages 4 and 5):

- the International Covenant on Civil and Political Rights (art. 7 – No one shall be subjected to torture or to cruel, inhuman or degrading treatment or punishment),
- the UN Convention Against Torture and Other Cruel, Inhuman or Degrading Treatment or Punishment (art. 3 – No State Party shall expel, return or extradite a person to another State where there are substantial grounds for believing that he would be in danger of being subjected to torture); and
- the European Convention of Human Rights (art. 3 – Prohibition of torture, inhuman and degrading treatment).

These rather general-sounding international human rights provisions are then made relevant and applicable to the specific case by introducing the following paragraph:

> During the legal proceedings, concerning the administrative offence [the defendant] explained that he did not leave the territory of the Russian Federation within the prescribed time and did not return to Syria because of the war on its territory.
>
> (Decision L. Oblast Court, 13 February 2014, p. 5)

This particular statement by the defendant was then contextualized with reference to the reports and circulars produced by the United Nations High Commissioner for Refugees (UNHCR). The judgment cites at length the different materials urging states to treat people leaving Syria as refugees 'requiring international protection until the security situation in Syria, as well as its human rights record improves significantly so as to create conditions for voluntary return' (pp. 5–6). The judgment devotes pages 6 and 7 to the analysis of the steps the defendant has actually taken in order to apply for a refugee/temporary asylum status in Russia (with references to specific passages of the Russian legislation, e.g. Law on Refugees No. 4528-I, from 19 February 1993). The judge notes that according to the case file the decision on the defendant's application for temporary asylum in Russia was still pending at the time of the consideration of the case (p. 7). This, however, did not prevent the judge from rendering the above judgment, excluding the expulsion from the penalty for administrative offences as against the international human rights obligations to which Russia was a party.

Exactly the same human rights instruments were invoked by A. City Court in its recent decision concerning an Uzbek national, Mr R. Mr R. was charged and sentenced in Uzbekistan *in absentia* for anti-state crimes relating to alleged religious extremism, and put on an international wanted list. The Russian general prosecutor refused to extradite him to Uzbekistan due to the expiry of the statute of limitations for these crimes in accordance with the Russian Criminal Code (articles 244-2, part 1, and 159, part 1). Mr R. was, however, later found responsible for committing administrative offences in Russia against art. 18.8 of the CAO (lack of residence registration) and sentenced to administrative removal to Uzbekistan. The removal of Mr R. to Uzbekistan would have had exactly the same consequences for him as the extradition requested earlier by Uzbek authorities (see *Nizamov and Others v. Russia*, nos. 22636/13, 24034/13, 24334/13 and 24528/13, judgment of 7 May 2014), exposing Mr R. to the risk of torture, inhuman and degrading treatment given the systemic failures of the criminal justice system in Uzbekistan.

A. City Court in the administrative proceedings decided that there were no grounds for expelling the defendant from the RF. The decision was made with reference to the international human rights instruments to which Russia is a party (the International Covenant on Civil and Political Rights, the UN Convention Against Torture and the European Convention of Human Rights) and several specific positions of the Constitutional Court of the RF concerning:

> Constitutional requirements of justice and proportionality (Constitutional Court RF, decision from 15 July 1999, No. 11-P) [. . .] [specifically, the need to consider] the personal situation of the offender and the degree of the offence, thereby guaranteeing the adequacy of penalty relative to the harm caused by the administrative offence (Constitutional Court RF, decision from 14 February 2013, No. 4-P) [and] the prohibition of discrimination and the ideas of justice and humanism expressed in the Constitution (Constitutional Court RF, decision from 17 January 2013, No. 1-P).
>
> (Decision of A. City Court, 24 November 2017, p. 5)

Finally, in arriving at the final decision, the A. City Court relied on its own assessment of the risk of 'the use of prohibited methods of conducting preliminary investigation, including the derogatory treatment [of the defendant] and the possibility of using torture' in Uzbekistan (Decision of A. City Court, 24 November 2017, p. 5).

Article 8 of the ECHR

In another scenario the human rights arguments explicitly invoked by the judge concerned the removal of foreign nationals who had established family ties with Russian citizens, as their expulsion would potentially endanger their right to private and family life (art. 8 of the ECHR). Take, for example, a case I observed in Moscow City Court: two Ukrainian women were charged with offences against art. 18.10 of the CAO – working without a permit. They both arrived from areas of Eastern Ukraine affected by armed conflict (Luhansk oblast). They went to the appeals court without legal representation, spoke for themselves and were very respectful towards the judge, who heard their cases individually though both of them were present in the courtroom.

In their appeal, they asked for the expulsion order to be withdrawn from the administrative penalty. The first woman explained that she and her sister had come to the shop that had been inspected by FMS officers to ask for work. They claimed that as she and her sister looked very similar, the shop manager put ID badges on them, so as to be able to distinguish them while he was interviewing them. This is when the FMS raid took place. According to the defendants, the FMS officers wrongly understood the two sisters to be working in the shop, due to their ID badges. The two women also supported their appeal with the fact that both were married to Russian citizens, and included their marriage certificates (*svidetel'stvo o brake*) in the appeal documentation.

Despite the evident obscurity of this explanation, the judge accepted their appeal and overturned the decision of the lower court by excluding the expulsion order from the penalty. In announcing the sentence, the judge focused on the underlining human rights claims of the two Ukrainian women and relied directly on Article 8 of the European Convention of Human Rights. The women had close family ties with Russian citizens, which they had formally proven by appending their marriage certificates to the case file. Their removal to Eastern Ukraine would have been disproportionate to the offence with which they had been charged and would have been in contravention of international human rights obligations. This case seems another clear example of the application of human rights logic.

Although I have not managed to obtain this specific judgment to see how exactly the judge framed her argument, I believe the justification could not have been much different from a similar decision concerning an Uzbek national. The defendant was charged with offences against art. 18.10 of the CAO, but – in the course of the legal proceedings – was found to be married to a Russian citizen, and to have fathered a daughter (also a Russian citizen). Here, the appeals court of R. oblast, in a decision from 24 June 2015, overturned the decision of the district court with regard to the defendant and excluded the administrative removal from the sentence, upholding the remainder of the judgment (the fine).

In contrast to the decisions of the L. Oblast Court and A. City Court analysed above, the judgment of R. Oblast Court is very short – it consists of only two pages. Upon presenting the case, the relevant domestic legislation and the facts of the case (as supported by the documentary evidence contained in the case file), the judge emphasized an important new fact raised by the appeal and confirmed during the trial:

> [The defendant] has a family and shares a household with a Russian citizen, [name of the spouse]. They also have a common child, [name of the child], born on 28.08.2001.
>
> (Decision R. Oblast Court, 24 June 2015, p. 2)

Upon acknowledging this new fact as relevant for the case at hand, the judgment then in full and verbatim cites the relevant provision of art. 8(2) of the ECHR (right to private and family life):

> There shall be no interference by a public authority with the exercise of this right except such as is in accordance with the law and is necessary in a democratic society in the interests of national security, public safety or the economic well-being of the country, for the prevention of disorder or crime, for the protection of health or morals, or for the protection of the rights and freedoms of others.
> (Article 8(2) of the ECHR, as quoted in decision of the R. Oblast Court, 24 June 2015, p. 2)

Given the facts and the law, the court concluded that:

> The expulsion from the Russian Federation violates the [defendant's] right to respect for family life as guaranteed by Article 8 of the above-mentioned Convention and is a premature measure of administrative responsibility.
> (Decision R. Oblast Court, 24 June 2015, p. 2)

There was also an interesting variation within the group of art. 8 ECHR cases, where Article 8 was explicitly relied on by the domestic court to prevent removal of family members of recognized asylum seekers in Russia.[7] Mrs K., an Uzbek national, one day found out that the Main Directorate for Migration (MVD) of the Ministry of Interior of Russia[8] had introduced a ten-year entry bar into Russia against her. She had been residing in Russia for the last four years with her husband, Mr K., and two minor children. The entry bar was a result of the fact that Mrs K. in the past had committed a number of administrative offences against art. 18.8 of the CAO (lack of residence registration). Mrs K. appealed the decision of the entry bar to A. City Court following the procedure prescribed in the Code of Administrative Procedure. She argued that she and her husband were de facto refugees in Russia, though the authorities on numerous occasions had refused to grant them temporary asylum status. Mr K., Mrs K.'s husband, was placed by Uzbekistan on an international wanted list in relation to alleged charges of religious extremism, and the general prosecutor of the RF refused his extradition due to the expiry of the statute of limitations. Furthermore, A. City Court in its earlier judgment had excluded the expulsion to Uzbekistan of Mr K. for administrative offences relating to art. 18.8 of the CAO, as the removal would put Mr K. at risk of torture if he were to be tried in Uzbekistan in relation to the crimes imputed to him by the state authorities. Mrs K. argued that due to the impossibility of her husband's removal to Uzbekistan without the violation of art. 3 of the ECHR, the Russian authorities' decision to introduce an entry bar against her violated

[7] Personally, I am not aware of more than one judgment by Russian domestic courts that uses art. 8 in conjunction with art. 3 in order to prevent a removal of a foreign national – a spouse of an asylum seeker. This case also comes from a particular region of Russia (not Moscow or St. Petersburg). I find it important to include this case here due to its potential far-reaching consequences.

[8] The Main Directorate for Migration of the Ministry of Interior of Russia has replaced the FMS. The latter was disbanded by Presidential Decree No. 156 of 5 April 2016; see Chapter 2 for details.

her right to private and family life (art. 8). If she were now to leave Russia, she would for ten years be separated from her family, given that her husband cannot join her in Uzbekistan without the risk of state persecution, and that all her children are settled, live and go to school in Russia.

The A. City Court produced a detailed judgment (eight pages) in which it considered the relevant law, the facts of the case, as well as the arguments presented by the different parties to the trial: Mrs K.'s legal representative and the Migration Department of the Ministry of Internal Affairs of the RF. In making the decision, the judge balanced the Russian state prerogative to decide who can and cannot enter its borders with reference to the ECHR and the general ECtHR jurisprudence around art. 8 (without, however, mentioning any particular cases). The judgment quotes verbatim art. 8 of the ECHR and the following provisions of the Russian Constitutional Court (from 2 March 2006, No. 55-O), whereby:

> the establishment of liability for violation of residence conditions by foreign citizens in the RF . . . should meet the *requirements of justice and proportionality* (part 3, Article 55 of the Constitution of the Russian Federation).
>
> (Decision of A. City Court, 8 February 2018, p. 6; my emphasis)

With regard to the ECtHR jurisprudence and established practice, the A. City Court observed that:

> The European Court of Human Rights has repeatedly noted that the responsibility for ensuring public order obliges different states to control the entry into its territory and the residence of foreigners, and to expel the offenders [of the immigration regime], however as such decisions may lead to a violation of the right to personal and family life . . . Art. 8 of the Convention . . . [these decisions] must be *justified by an extreme social necessity and have a clear and legitimate aim*.
>
> (Decision of A. City Court, 8 February 2018, p. 6; my emphasis)

The court further noted with regard to the legality of the ten-year entry bar for Mrs K. that:

> [It] cannot be considered as proportionate to the socially significant and legitimate aim [of enforcing immigration law] and *constitutes an essential interference in private life* . . . disproportionate and inadequate in terms of its justification.
>
> (Decision of A. City Court, 8 February 2018, p. 6; my emphasis)

Given these arguments, the A. City Court quashed the decision of the Main Directorate for Migration of the Ministry of Interior (GUVM MVD) of Russia regarding the ten-year entry bar for Mrs K. and allowed her to stay in Russia with her family.

In all these judgments the different levels of domestic courts *explicitly* relied on the various provisions of the ECHR (and other international human rights conventions to which Russia is a party) by quoting in the judgments – usually *verbatim* – the specific legal instruments (articles and case law), as relevant for the cases before them.

Implicit Reliance on Human Rights Law

There were also a number of judgments in which the reference to the international human law instruments, such as the ECHR, was only marginal (without even specifying concrete points or articles) or non-existent, but the substance of the judgment seemed to give due diligence to the spirit of the human rights.

Take as an example yet another art. 18.8 of the CAO case, where Mr E., an ethnic Uzbek of Kyrgyz citizenship, was charged with an administrative offence due to lack of residence registration and given the penalty of administrative removal (expulsion) from Russia with placement in the detention centre. Ethnic Uzbeks from Kyrgyzstan have long been recognized in the ECtHR jurisprudence as a vulnerable group within the meaning of art. 3 ECHR (see, e.g. *Makhmudzhan Ergashev* v. *Russia*, no. 49747/11, judgment of 16 October 2012; *Turgunov* v. *Russia*, no. 15590/14, judgment of 22 October 2015; *Tadzhibayev* v. *Russia*, no. 17724/14, judgment of 1 December 2015). The rise of ethno-nationalism in the politics of Kyrgyzstan, particularly in the south, the growing inter-ethnic tensions between Kyrgyz and Uzbeks, continued discriminatory practices faced by Uzbeks at institutional level and the under-representation of Uzbeks in, among others, law-enforcement bodies and the judiciary have long been documented in various human rights reports from the region (Human Rights Watch 2018). The case, on appeal, reached the Supreme Court of T. Republic, which reviewed the decision of the Z. City Court. The detailed judgment is six pages long. Upon presenting the facts of the case and the relevant law, the Supreme Court judge formulated two principles defining the character of the penalty for administrative offences, which later he tested with reference to the lower court's judgment and the specific circumstances of the case. The first principle concerned the aims of the administrative penalty (as conforming to the spirit of human rights):

> When appointing a penalty in the form of administrative expulsion . . . the judge must proceed from the real necessity of applying . . . *a proportionate measure of responsibility* . . . to ensure the fair balance of public and private interests in the proceedings.
>
> (Decision of Supreme Court of T. Republic, 21 February 2018, p. 4; my emphasis)

The second principle further qualified the general rules of the administrative penalty as based on the 'principles of justice, proportionality and individualization of responsibility', therefore:

> Administrative penalty cannot have as its goal the destruction of the *human dignity* of the person who committed the offence, or causing him/her *physical suffering*, and neither cause harm to the reputation of their legal representative.
>
> (Article 3.1 of the CAO, part 2, as quoted in the Supreme Court of T. Republic, 21 February 2018, p. 3)

Based on these principles, the judgment then separately reflected on the different elements of the penalty given to Mr E.: detention, administrative removal (expulsion) and their potential consequences. Given the severity of detention and that it essentially amounted to 'nothing more than a form of restriction of the constitutional right to liberty and security of a person' (Supreme Court of T. Republic, 21 February 2018, p. 4), the Supreme Court judge expected the lower court judge to have based its decision on:

> a comprehensive and objective consideration of the relevant circumstances – the nature of administrative offence, the previous offences of the defendant, the length of his residence on the territory of the Russian Federation, the availability of a permanent place of residence, family status, health condition, etc. – *in order to avoid an arbitrary intrusion into the sphere of personal autonomy of an individual.*
>
> (Supreme Court of T. Republic, 21 February 2018, p. 4; my emphasis)

In its analysis, the Supreme Court of the T. Republic clearly stated that it failed to see these considerations being taken into account by the lower court.

With regard to the administrative removal, the Supreme Court judge argued that the Z. City Court decision had not been taken 'with the observance of the criteria of validity, proportionality and reasonableness' (Supreme Court of T. Republic, 21 February 2018, p. 5), and did not correspond with the aims and goals of the administrative penalty (as formulated previously). The Supreme Court also considered the consequences of administrative penalty, especially the relationship between returning Mr E., an ethnic Uzbek, to Kyrgyzstan and the risk of torture and persecution, the threat to his life and health that may await him in his country of citizenship. Furthermore, the court raised the issue of close family members of Mr E. who had Russian citizenship, and with whom Mr E. shared a household in Russia, particularly the situation of his four minor children.

Without therefore an explicit reference to any specific provisions of the ECHR, the ECtHR case law or other instruments of international human rights law, the Supreme Court of the T. Republic stayed very much true to the spirit of the human rights law.[9] It concluded that the decision of the lower court should be quashed and the case of Mr E. returned for a fresh consideration.

Another type of judgment that relied on implicit acknowledgement of human rights law and principles concerned placement in detention pending administrative removal following offences against articles 18.8 and 18.10 of the CAO (in two particular regions of Russia). Here, the judge would specify the timeframe for confining the defendant in detention pending administrative removal – usually between one and two months – sending the law enforcement authorities a strong signal that if they did not manage to remove the

[9] These international human rights instruments were, however, relied upon by the defence in its submissions before the Supreme Court of the T. Republic.

foreign national within the specified timeframe, his or her detention should cease, and the person should be released.

In the judgments that I have read, the district judge usually balanced the gravity of administrative removal with the personal situation of the defendant – the presence of family members (Russian citizens) and availability of resources to buy a train or plane ticket home and leave Russia 'by independent means'. If no such circumstances were present, and given that the officer representing the local Department for Migration, Ministry of Interior always raised the issue of the risk of the defendant absconding, the judge would rule that:

> the defendant should be placed in detention pending administrative removal however for *no longer than* two (2) months.
>
> (Decision of I. District Court, 19 April 2017, p. 2; my emphasis)

This type of judgment, clearly specifying the timeframe of detention pending expulsion, is in stark contrast to the majority of administrative removal judgments in Russia. In the majority of cases when the removal became for some reasons impossible (as in the situation of stateless persons, or persons whose countries of citizenship refused or could not accept them due to war, e.g. Syria), the defendants risked spending up to two years in administrative detention – until the expiry of the statute of limitations for this particular CAO offence. This de facto indefinite administrative detention, with lack of opportunity for judicial review of its legality, was recognized as a systemic problem in many cases before the ECtHR.[10] It was also at the core of the *Mskhiladze* developments before the Russian Constitutional Court, which I discuss in the following section.

Affirmative Reference to Human Rights

Mr Noe Georgiyevich Mskhiladze was born in the Georgian Republic of the USSR in 1972. In 1988, he came to Leningrad to study at a professional technical high school. Upon completion of his studies, he returned to Georgia; however, the following year he returned to Russia, to St Petersburg, married a Russian citizen (his wife passed away in 2010), and has not left St Petersburg since. Mr Mskhiladze had the right to be recognized as a citizen of the RF, but he did not receive the citizenship certificate, since on several occasions he was convicted of criminal offences. His USSR passport expired while he was in custody, and as a result Mr Mskhiladze found himself in the position of a stateless person. He was ready to leave for Georgia, but could not do so since Georgia did not recognize him as its citizen and refused to issue a certificate of return.

[10] See: *Ismailov* v. *Russia* no. 20110/13, judgment of 17 April 2014; *Akram Karimov* v. *Russia*, no. 62892/12, judgment of 28 May 2014; *Egamberdiyev* v. *Russia* no. 34742/13, judgment of 26 June 2014; *Rakhimov* v. *Russia* no. 50552/13, judgment of 10 July 2014; *Eshonkulov* v. *Russia* no. 68900/13, judgment of 15 January 2015; *Khalikov* v. *Russia* no. 6673/13, judgment of 26 February 2015; *L.M. and Others* v. *Russia*, nos. 40081/14 40088/14, 40127/14, judgment of 15 October 2015.

Towards the end of 2015 Mr Mskhiladze was stopped by the FMS authorities, charged with administrative offences against art. 18.8 of the CAO (lack of residence registration) and sentenced to administrative removal from Russia, with placement in a detention centre for foreigners. The judge of the K. District Court of St Petersburg noted that the applicant was a stateless person but held that he had to comply with a statutory obligation to leave Russia, having no valid legal basis for being there.

Mr Mskhiladze's legal representative appealed this judgment, arguing that the penalty of administrative removal could not be enforced in the absence of Georgian or any other nationality and that it was therefore unjustified to place Mr Mskhiladze in detention and keep him there. In January 2016, the St Petersburg City Court rejected the appeal and ruled that Mr Mskhiladze could still be removed to the country from which he had arrived in Russia 'if there was a readmission agreement with that country'. The court also ruled that Mr Mskhiladze could be held in detention for a maximum of two years, which was the statutory period for the enforceability of a penalty according to CAO. Two months later, in March 2016, Georgian authorities again informed the Russian migration authority that they would not assist in providing documents for Mr Mskhiladze's return to Georgia as he was not a Georgian national.

In view of this communication, the Federal Bailiffs Service turned to K. District Court with a petition to terminate the enforcement proceedings of the administrative removal of Mr Mskhiladze, and his release from detention. In July 2016, the K. District Court dismissed this petition and held that there was no statutory basis in the CAO or other legislation for granting such an application. As this decision was upheld on appeal, Mr Mskhiladze's legal representative, having exhausted all domestic legal remedies, applied to the ECtHR under art. 3 (concerning the conditions of detention) and art. 5(4) (right to speedy judicial review of legality and lawfulness of one's detention) (see *Mskhiladze* v. *Russia* no. 47741/16, judgment of 13 February 2018).

The development of Mr Mskhiladze's case before the domestic courts revealed two structural problems with the CAO in immigration cases that later became a matter of debate before the Russian Constitutional Court. First, there was the length of Mr Mskhiladze's detention pending administrative removal. Article 31.9 of the CAO had not required the trial judge to set a time limit when ordering placement in a detention centre for foreigners; as a result, and according to judicial customary practice, the time spent in detention pending administrative removal became *equal* to the expiry of the statute of limitation for a particular CAO offence. That translated to Mr Mskhiladze – and any other foreign national, asylum seeker or a stateless person – being kept in detention for a period of two years, without the possibility of judicial review of the legality and length of detention. The second structural problem was revealed by the unsuccessful petition of the Federal Bailiffs Service to K. District Court to terminate the enforcement proceedings against Mr Mskhiladze, as the removal was impossible to enforce since Mr Mskhiladze was a stateless person. It concerned the provisions of art. 31.7 of the CAO, which established an exhaustive list of grounds for terminating the enforcement of a ruling in an administrative offence case. These grounds did not include, however, the absence of an actual possibility to execute/enforce the penalty. Since there were no legal means to release the Federal Bailiffs Service from the obligation to enforce this particular judgment, Mr Mskhiladze could be kept in detention pending administrative removal potentially indefinitely.

23 May 2017: Decision of the Russian Constitutional Court

On 23 May 2017, the Constitutional Court of the RF decided the constitutionality of articles 31.9 and 31.7 of the CAO. A number of positions and observations by the competent authorities – the Supreme Court, State Duma and General Prosecutor's Office, and expertise by the Law Department of Voronezh State University – were examined at the request of the court, to aid the deliberation.[11]

The observations by the Supreme Court from 31 March 2017 fully supported the position that the CAO did not in any way regulate the time limits for which foreign nationals should be placed in detention pending administrative removal, and that articles 31.7 and 31.9 did not solve this issue in any meaningful way (Tseytlina 2018: 35). Furthermore, the submission by the Supreme Court noted that it was necessary to establish legal provisions for the possibility of imposing an administrative penalty in the form of a fine (arrest) without administrative removal from Russia. In specifying the category of persons with regard to whom these provisions should be made particularly available, the Supreme Court clearly reaffirmed the human rights obligations to which Russia was a party (without actually explicitly and verbatim mentioning the specific instruments). The Court noted that there were a number of circumstances that should be taken into account when deciding the administrative removal of foreign citizens from Russia, such as:

- strong family ties with Russian citizens;
- if there are grounds to believe that the removal of foreign citizens from Russia may put them at risk of torture, inhuman or degrading treatment or punishment in the state to which they are being expelled;
- if there are difficulties in establishing the country the person should be removed to, which makes the procedure of deportation impossible;
- if a person subject to removal had received temporary asylum in Russia;
- the complexities that entail the detention of asylum seekers, which should be used only as a last resort.

(Hearing of RF Constitutional Court, 17 May 2017, available at: www.ksrf.ru/ru/Sessions/Pages/ViewItem.aspx?ParamId=159).

[11] For a full list and detailed analysis of all the submissions, please see Tseytlina (2018).

In other words, the Supreme Court in its conclusion before the Constitutional Court affirmed the importance of the ECHR (articles 3 and 8), and the relevance of the 1951 Convention on Refugees (with regard to the special situation of stateless persons, refugees and asylum seekers). These observations are especially relevant for the argument made earlier in this chapter concerning the style of referencing the human rights instruments by Russian domestic courts at different levels.

Upon studying the different observations and hearing the parties to the proceedings on 17 May 2017, in its decision the Constitutional Court found articles 31.7 and 31.9 of the CAO unconstitutional to the extent that they:

> Did not allow to resolve in court the question of the lawfulness of continued detention of stateless persons sentenced to administrative removal and placed in detention centres ... in circumstances ... where was *no actual possibility of enforcing the removal.*
>
> (Decision of Constitutional Court of RF, 23 May 2017, No. 14-P, p. 26; my emphasis)

The Court defined the detention of stateless persons as deprivation of liberty not only within the meaning of art. 22 of the Russian Constitution, but also art. 5 of the ECHR, and ECtHR jurisprudence.[12] With reference to these legal instruments, the Court noted that deprivation of liberty 'can acquire a variety of forms that are not always identical to imprisonment in its classical sense' (Decision of Constitutional Court of RF, 23 May 2017, No. 14-P, p. 12). The Court further affirmed that:

> any deprivation of liberty must meet the [European] Convention's criteria for protecting the individual from arbitrariness of the authorities, and the base of its legality cannot be interpreted broadly, since [any deprivation of liberty constitutes an] exception to the fundamental guarantees of personal freedom.
>
> (Decision of Constitutional Court of RF, 23 May 2017, No. 14-P, p. 12)

The lack of clarity of articles 31.7 and 31.9 of the CAO concerning the detention of foreign nationals whom it was impossible to remove from Russia meant that the domestic legislation did not meet the criteria set by the Convention. In this context, the Constitutional Court made also explicit references to ECtHR jurisprudence against Russia, and the general measures specified in another case of a stateless national sentenced to administrative removal – Mr Kim, a former USSR citizen born in Uzbekistan. In *Kim* v. *Russia* (no. 44260/13, judgment of 17 July 2014), the Strasbourg Court obliged the RF to 'secure in its domestic legal order a mechanism which allows individuals to institute proceedings for the examination of the lawfulness of

[12] *Guzzardi* v. *Italy*, no. 7367/76, judgment of 6 November 1980; *Kemmache* v. *France*, nos. 12325/86, 14992/89, judgment of 24 November 1994; *Kurt* v. *Turkey*, no. 24276/94, judgment of 25 May 1998; *Aleksey Borisov* v. *Russia*, no. 12008/06 judgment of 16 July 2015; *Z.A. and Others* v. *Russia*, nos. 61411/15, 61420/15, 61427/15, 3028/16, judgment of 28 March 2017.

the detention pending removal' (*Kim* v. *Russia*, para. 71). Given the length of the detention, deemed by the ECtHR as unreasonable, the *Kim* v. *Russia* judgment also obliged Russia to take 'the necessary general measures to limit detention periods so that they remain connected to the ground of detention applicable in an immigration context' (*Kim* v. *Russia*, para. 72).

The Constitutional Court, by referring to this judgment, affirmed the necessity of these general measures in the domestic context and provided an additional important stimulus from within the domestic legal system for the Russian government to introduce specific legislation. The court obliged the national legislator to:

> immediately introduce amendments to the Code of Administrative Offences of the Russian Federation aimed at ensuring *effective judicial control over the periods of detention of stateless persons* subject to compulsory administrative removal [and placed] in detention centres, established under the Federal Law on the Legal Status of Foreign Citizens.
>
> (Decision of Constitutional Court of RF, 23 May 2017, No. 14-P, p. 27; my emphasis)

The Constitutional Court went even further and suggested that the legislator creates

> *A special migratory status for stateless persons* in respect of whom the administrative removal from the Russian Federation cannot be executed due to . . . the absence of a state willing to accept such a person.
>
> (Decision of Constitutional Court of RF, 23 May 2017, No. 14-P, p. 27; my emphasis)

Until the legislation is in place, the Court put forward an interim measure, whereby stateless persons placed in detention pending administrative removal should be granted the right to appeal to the court to review the legality of their further detention either if:

> There is no evidence of actual possibility of their removal, or *after three months from the date of the imposition of administrative penalty.*
>
> (Decision of Constitutional Court of RF, 23 May 2017, No. 14-P, p. 27; my emphasis)

According to the immigration legal practitioners, this interim legal measure 'opened the door for release from detention not only stateless persons, but all migrants who spend in detention centres more than three months and de facto can be considered stateless persons' as there was no country willing to admit them (Tseytlina 2018: 37).

Ambiguous Consequences of the Constitutional Court Decision

What was the reception of the Constitutional Court decision by domestic, low-level courts in Russia? Has the decision been enforced? How does this ruling work 'in action', given the experiences of immigration law practitioners before domestic courts? Prior to the proceedings before the Constitutional Court, the UNHCR in Moscow formally asked the GUVM MVD about the number of foreign nationals in long-term detention, who could not be administratively removed from Russia as there were no countries willing to accept them, i.e. they were in de facto stateless positions. The reply, dated 14 March 2017, stated that there were 263 such individuals (on file with the author). A report by a Russia-wide network of immigration lawyers and legal practitioners, called 'Migration and Law', deemed this to be an underestimate, and put forward its own statistics of 351 individuals in long-term detention (Burtina 2018b: 11). At the same time, due to limited resources, the practitioners concluded that even the latter estimate might be inadequate, and the total number of stateless or de facto stateless persons in Russian detention centres might be close to 500.

A quick look through the statistical profile of the detained, de facto stateless persons demonstrates that the majority of them are from Ukraine and former USSR republics: Kazakhstan, Uzbekistan, Georgia (Table 6.1). The great majority of them (92 per cent) were born before 1991, i.e. at the time of their birth they were Soviet citizens with USSR passports. Like Mr Noe Mskhiladze and Mr Roman Kim, a proportion of them were already in Russia at the time of the dissolution of the USSR, but for one reason or another they did not manage to secure Russian citizenship. Others arrived in Russia due to the

Table 6.1 De facto stateless persons in long-term detention in Russia

Country of origin	Number of persons
Ukraine	66
Kazakhstan	64
Uzbekistan	53
Georgia	52
Azerbaijan	36
Tajikistan	32
Kyrgyzstan	15
Armenia	12
Turkmenistan	6
Belarus	5
Lithuania	4
Estonia	2
Moldova	2
Others (United States, Vietnam)	2
Total	351

Source: Burtina and Tseytlina (2018; in Russian, on file with the author).

recent conflict in Eastern Ukraine, their passports have expired and the central Ukrainian authorities refuse to issue them certificates of citizenship given the 'impossibility to confirm this fact with the local authorities in Luhansk and Donetsk oblasts' (Burtina 2018b: 14). Another significant group of the detainees were people who arrived in Russia as migrant workers before 2002, i.e. before the radical reorganization of immigration regime following the Law on Citizenship (Federal Law No. 62 of 31 May 2002), and the Law on the Legal Status of Foreign Citizens (Federal Law No. 115 of 25 July 2002). These migrants established families and livelihoods in Russia, but fell through the cracks of the complex immigration law, and, at the time of checking by immigration authorities, had no documents and no countries willing to confirm their citizenship. The available data reveal that the majority of migrants spend 1–2 years in detention, with the average time being 8–9 months (Burtina 2018b: 15).

Immediately upon the decision of the Constitutional Court, immigration practitioners initiated legal proceedings to have the stateless and de facto stateless persons released from long-term detention. At the time of writing, nearly a year since the decision of the Constitutional Court, approximately 40 people have been released – a mere 11 per cent of all long-term detainees, given the above-mentioned statistics. What are the reasons for this?

There are a number of factors that could explain this rather 'less than enthusiastic' reception of the Constitutional Court judgment. One of the explanations lies in the legal culture of *inertia* and general conservatism of courts and judges in Russia, especially their scepticism and caution towards new laws – an argument already well established in the literature (Starzhenetskii 2014; Hendley 2017; McCarthy 2018). The study of the different low-level court judgments in the year following *Mskhiladze* and the experiences of lawyers cast more light on this argument. The low-level district courts would return lawyers' applications without consideration, arguing that there were 'no clear procedural bases in the Code of Administrative Offences according to which the courts could judicially review the legality and grounds of further detention' of stateless persons in the detention centres (V., immigration lawyer, personal communication, 19 April 2018). As an alternative, they suggested the lawyers follow the procedure more familiar to courts, envisaged by art. 31.7 of the CAO (the same article deemed unconstitutional by the Constitutional Court!) or directly launch the case with the higher-level court (city or regional court) using the procedure prescribed in art. 30.12 of the CAO.

The other reason for negative court decisions could be linked to the familiar culture of strict legal formalism and 'black-letter' (*po zakonu*) legal interpretation that dominates Russian low-level court jurisprudence, decision-making and everyday life experiences of the law (Kurkchiyan 2009; Kubal 2016a).[13] For

[13] For more explanation on the *po zakonu* legal culture, see Chapter 5, and Kubal (2016a).

example, the lower courts sometimes said that the legislative changes and amendments instructed by the Constitutional Court had not yet been legislated (Burtina 2018a: 51); therefore the decision to release a person from detention or review the legality of detention would have been premature and not based on actual law. The immigration lawyers and practitioners drew attention to the decision of K. District Court in Moscow, which adjudicated a case of Mr R., a former Uzbek citizen, whose citizenship has been revoked by the president of Uzbekistan; the stateless man was (indefinitely) detained in the centre for foreigners pending (impossible to enforce) administrative removal. The K. District Court refused to release Mr R. from detention as the defence has not supplied the court with the reasons why the president of Uzbekistan had revoked the citizenship of the defendant. Furthermore, the authorities have not conducted diligent checks on whether the defendant might be a citizen of other countries. Which other countries? The court had not specified. The lawyer cynically remarked that probably the court meant all the remaining 194 countries existing on the world map today (V., immigration lawyer, personal communication, 19 April 2018; also referred to in Burtina 2018a: 48).

The empirical evidence suggests that the everyday experiences following the *Mskhiladze* judgment in the low-level domestic courts are patchy and inconsistent, despite the rather clear guidelines provided by the Constitutional Court. This might lead to the conclusion about the general ambiguity around the human rights arguments, as experienced at the domestic level: the situation appears complex despite the operation of human rights logic in certain specific judgments (as demonstrated earlier in this chapter).

The following section therefore presents the final type of arguments used by the courts with reference to human rights, whereby the domestic judges upon deliberation of the human rights instruments *rejected* them and the ECtHR jurisprudence altogether. It has to be stressed that this rejection did not happen unreflexively; the judges went against the human rights logic, often in full knowledge of the human rights argument and its implications. This section complements the picture about the multifaceted and multi-layered relationship between Russia and human rights more broadly in the area of immigration and refugee law.

Rejection of Human Rights Arguments

When, in April 2014, the FMS raided a sweatshop in a town K, three Syrian men were arrested.[14] They were working without work permits, on expired

[14] An earlier version of this section has been published as Kubal, A. (2016a). 'Refugees or migrant workers? A case study of undocumented Syrians in Russia – L.M. and Others v Russia (ECtHR 14 March 2016)'. *Journal of Immigration Asylum and Nationality Law* 30(4): 265–282. For further information visit: www.bloomsburyprofessional.com/uk/journal/journal-of-immigration-asylum-and-nationality-law.

tourist/business visas, with no residence registration. Two of the men had not taken any significant steps to regularize their immigration status (e.g. apply for asylum in Russia). The FMS charged the men with administrative offences against articles 18.8 and 18.10 of the CAO and promptly took them to the district court, which sentenced them to a fine and administrative removal (expulsion). The men subsequently, via their legal representative, applied for asylum in Russia, but the domestic courts did not give much weight to this development and supported their administrative removal (expulsion) to Syria. The case reached the ECtHR, which in a precedent ruling *L.M. and Others* v. *Russia* (nos. 40081/14, 40088/14 and 40127/14, judgment of 15 October 2015), decided that returning the applicants to Syria would breach their right to life (art. 2) and prohibition of inhuman and degrading treatment (art. 3).[15] By following the developments of this case before the Russian domestic courts, I demonstrate how, when and under what circumstances the human rights arguments might be rejected by the low-level judges in immigration and refugee law cases.

Syrian Men as 'Ordinary' Immigration Offenders

The protocols from the trials and the judgments by the first low-level court that heard the Syrian men's cases – M. District Court – reveal that for the judge this was a clear-cut case of simple immigration offences against the CAO. The priority was to consider the Syrians as 'ordinary' immigration law offenders over recognizing their potential human rights claims, to protect the domestic migration and refugee law from potential 'abuse' and manipulation and to secure a clear, unambiguous outcome to this case.

From a quantitative perspective, the protocols from the M. District Court – each approximately three pages long – are a telling source. The largest share of the protocols seems to be devoted to: (1) formal explanations of the rights and duties of the interpreter (from Arabic), who was present at the trial; (2) personal information on the offenders (their ages, places of birth, places of residence in Syria and in Russia); (3) the explanation of their formal and processual rights and obligations; and (4) the list of the documents appended to the case file. These formal and procedural explanations (confirmed by the signatures of the interpreter and the defendants) take approximately two pages of the official protocol (about 70 per cent of the text). That leaves a little less than one page for the actual examination of the facts of the case and the analysis of the evidence.

It is only in the final part (approximately one-quarter of a page) that the judge assumes her inquisitorial position, characteristic for a civil law trial, and

[15] The Court also decided that the men's prolonged detention and lack of opportunity to judicially review the lawfulness of their detention constituted breaches of art. 5(1)(f) and art. 5(4) of the ECHR, respectively.

asks the men a few questions: 'When did you arrive in Russia? Why you did not leave Russia when your visa expired? Why you did not legalize your status?' In response, the men said (or what was at least evident from the protocols): they arrived in Russia to earn money; they did not legalize their status and had not obtained the required work permits as they did not know how to proceed. They promised to 'sort out' their documents and asked the court not to deport them to Syria as 'there is no work there and it is a dangerous place to live due to the war'.[16]

From the qualitative perspective, therefore, the protocols provide very succinct and important evidence of how the human rights arguments were intricately interwoven with the facts of this case, but also how they were sidestepped, ignored and, ultimately, deemed irrelevant by the judge. The only time where the implied human rights claim had a chance to be voiced was towards the end of the protocol, where the defendants, upon pleading guilty, asked the judge not to deport them due to the war in Syria:

> Please do not deport me from Russia, as I am afraid for my life. I need to help my parents and there is no work in Syria.
>
> (M. District Court protocol, 15 April 2014, p. 3)

Even when the men explicitly asked the court not to return them, their claims about the civil war and 'fear for their lives' were intertwined with livelihood arguments such as 'there is no work in Syria'. However, there is a visible imbalance between the two types of considerations in the protocols. The judge clearly decided not to pursue the human rights line of inquiry, namely what might happen to the men outside of Russia should they be returned to Syria. The case of the Syrian men was treated as a 'typical' administrative offence case; the goal seemed to be to process their case quickly and efficiently, leaving as little doubt as possible about the men's legal identity as 'ordinary' immigration offenders.

Prioritizing Domestic Law over Human Rights Considerations

In the K. Regional Court (appellate level), the question of the pending asylum applications was perhaps complicating the overall picture, but the judge was adamant that it should not be given centre-stage in the proceedings – the men filed their asylum applications via their legal representative only upon their arrests, after the M. District Court's judgments had already been delivered. They were certainly a long way from receiving asylum.

I had the chance to accompany the three Syrian men and their legal representative to the K. Regional Court. The defence lawyer was determined to introduce the human rights arguments into the appellate proceedings. The lawyer decided not to dispute the facts of the case: the men indeed were

[16] M. District Court Protocol (15 April 2014), on file with the author.

working illegally and lived above the sweatshop in contravention of the migration residence requirements, and their visas had expired. She, however, wanted to shift the focus of the case from the administrative offences of contravening Russian immigration law towards the human rights arguments centred on the civil war in Syria. This strategic shift was to help the lawyer petition the court to exclude the administrative removal (expulsion) from the sentence and to reverse the logic of the proceedings before the lower court – the men were not 'ordinary' immigration offenders, they were asylum seekers escaping the civil war. Therefore, the next argument raised by the defence in the appeal centred on proportionality – in light of the overwhelming evidence pointing directly and unequivocally to a massive, indiscriminate humanitarian crisis in Syria, the defence maintained that it would be disproportionate to go ahead with the expulsion as a penalty (or 'punishment') for simple administrative offences. In support of this argument, the defence invoked the UNHCR position on returning people to Syria, focused on the principle of non-refoulement:

> It is essential that protection provided to those fleeing Syria entails treatment which respects the fundamental humanity and dignity of the individuals concerned and guarantees minimum humanitarian standards, including: ... b. protection from refoulement.
>
> (UNHCR International Protection Considerations with regard to people fleeing the Syrian Arab Republic, Update I, December 2012)[17]

The appeal referred to other independent human rights reports on the hostilities in Syria (Human Rights Watch, Amnesty International and UN Human Rights Council). Each applicant (MA, AA and LM) had an individual assessment letter produced by the UNHCR Moscow office that supported the arguments that administrative removal of the men to Syria would breach the principle of non-refoulement.

In the course of the proceedings, the K. Regional Court judge asked the men 'Why did you come to Russia? How did you arrive in Moscow and the town K.? Did you know anyone in Russia?' The most pertinent questions were about work permits and regularization of status:

> Did the defendants know that when coming to a different country one requires a work permit to work? Why did the defendants not secure a work permit?
>
> (Judge, AA case, minutes handwritten by author from K. Regional Court 27 May 2014)

This was followed by a series of questions revealing the judge's sincere preoccupation to enforce the formal requirements and protect Russian immigration law from continuous and repeated non-compliance:

[17] Available at http://unhcr.org.ua/attachments/article/739/Condsider_SYR_Dec12_ENG.pdf (accessed 14 April 2016).

> If you do not speak the language, you do not have work permit, how would you support yourselves here if I do not expel you?
>
> (Judge, AA case, minutes handwritten by author from K. Regional Court 27 May 2014)

The judge prioritized the domestic law and again focused on the nature of the immigration administrative offences committed over recognizing the Syrian men's human rights claims.

The final judgment ultimately rejected the defence's appeal and affirmed the men's administrative removal to Syria, stressing that 'these men came to Russia to work, earn money and support their families in Syria' (K. Regional Court judgment, AA, 27 May 2014). They arrived in Russia as migrant workers, worked without documents and should therefore bear 'the full punishment' as prescribed by law. The domestic immigration law took precedence over human rights considerations:

> military operations conducted on the territory of Syria . . . cannot serve as grounds for the change of the court's decision regarding expulsion as M.L. arrived in Russia in order to seek employment and not in relation to military actions in Syria.
>
> (K. Regional Court judgment, AA, 27 May 2014)

Announcing the decision, the judge quoted the relevant passages of the Russian immigration law regarding the work permit for foreigners, and that asylum applicants/refugees can work once their legal status has been confirmed and not when it was being determined.[18] The Syrian men did not use their time in Russia to regularize their status and comply with Russian immigration law. The appellate judge, while clearly sidestepping the human rights arguments, did not deviate from the already legally established fact (in the decision of the M. District Court) that these men were 'ordinary' immigration law offenders.

Literal Reading of the Law: Response to the ECtHR

Having exhausted all domestic legal remedies, the Syrian men's legal representative turned to the ECtHR, requesting the application of interim measures – Rule 39 of the Rules of the Court – suspending the applicants' removal from Russia for as long as their case was examined before the ECtHR. The Court grants such requests only on an exceptional basis, when the applicants would otherwise face a real risk of serious and irreversible harm (Press Unit ECtHR 2018). The ECtHR responded within 24 hours, applying Rule 39 and putting a temporary injunction on the administrative removal (expulsion). In light of this development, the local Federal Bailiffs Service, responsible for the enforcement of the judgment and seeing to the Syrian men's effective expulsion from Russia, petitioned the M. District Court to stay the removal

[18] Federal Law No. 127-FZ of 5 May 2014, On Amendments to Article 13 of the Federal Law on the Legal Status of Foreign Citizens.

proceedings. The M. District Court in a closed session on 30 June 2014 dismissed the Federal Bailiffs Service petition and obliged them to continue the enforcement of the removal proceedings.

How did the low-level domestic court justify this controversial decision of, essentially, disregarding an important mechanism of the ECtHR? The M. District Court in its judgment referred to the very literal reading of the CAO. While art. 31.5 of the CAO provided for a mechanism for the postponement of an administrative arrest, deprivation of special rights or a payment of fines (which were the typical penalties for petty administrative offences), it did not contain a mechanism of postponement of the administrative removal (expulsion).[19] Because of this direct reading of the law – no postponement provision in the CAO *ergo* postponement is impossible – the three Syrian men formally remained in the highly precarious state of 'removal proceedings' for whole duration of the consideration of their case before the Strasbourg Court. They ultimately spent 20 months in the detention centre for foreign nationals in town K. – from 14 April 2014 to 21 December 2015.

The developments of the *L.M. and Others* v. *Russia* case before the domestic courts constitute a case in point for the illustration of how different levels of domestic courts may reject or ignore the human rights arguments. It is important to stress that the courts did not reject the human rights instruments without due reflection. The analysis of the judgments points to a number of considerations that the courts seemed to prioritize over the international obligations to which Russia was a party. These were considerations around 'protecting' domestic immigration law from potential and continuous non-compliance, very literal interpretations of the domestic law and finally prioritizing domestic legislation to secure a clear and unambiguous outcome to the case.

Migrants, Asylum Seekers and the State in a Neoliberal World: A View from a Russian Judge

Is the discourse of rejection of human rights arguments underpinned by some broader ideologies around the relationship between refugees, migrants and the state in a globalizing world? I believe more research is needed to address this question in an exhaustive fashion (particularly via qualitative and ethnographic methods) focusing on the perspectives of immigration policy-makers, judges, law enforcement officers and the police in Russia. As a first glimpse into this topic, let me offer an analysis of a dissenting opinion by Dmitry Dedov, a judge representing Russia in the ECtHR in Strasbourg, from a landmark case *Z.A. and Others* v. *Russia* (nos. 61411/15, 61420/15, 61427/15, 3028/16, judgment of 28 March 2017). I have introduced the case in detail in Chapter 3. It concerned

[19] Article 31.5 of the CAO was subsequently amended by Federal Law N 57-FZ of 8 March 2015, whereby administrative removal has been included in the list of 'penalties' that are subject to postponement (*otsrochka*).

four male asylum seekers from Syria, Iraq, Palestine and Somalia, who were denied entry to Russia and became stranded in the transit zone of Sheremetyevo Airport for between 6 and 23 months. The ECtHR found that the men's de facto detention in Sheremetyevo Airport led to violation of art. 5(1) (right to liberty), and the conditions of their detention amounted to inhuman and degrading treatment, thereby violating art. 3 of the ECHR.

Judge Dmitry Dedov disagreed with this outcome.[20] On account of art. 5 and art. 3, Dedov questioned the significance of the state in the proceedings altogether and pointed to the individual applicants – asylum seekers – as 'irresponsible aliens' bringing these conditions upon themselves. He questioned whether being stranded in the transit zone of Sheremetyevo Airport ever amounted to a deprivation of liberty. The applicants, after all, could have left the transit zone 'by boarding a flight'. He concluded that the 'decision to stay in the transit zone was made voluntarily by the applicants themselves without any compelling reasons' (Dedov 2017: 26). Similarly, with regard to the conditions of their stay in the transit zone, Dedov pointed out that it was 'obviously the applicants [who] placed themselves in a difficult situation [and this was their own choice]' (Dedov 2017: 26). He saw the whole case as being (mis)construed around the complaint that the 'authorities did nothing to take care of [the applicants]'. This, in Dedov's view, reflects a

> neo-liberal concept of social life, where liberties prevail over the public interest and individual responsibility, so it appears that the State becomes responsible for any difficulties in private life even if those difficulties were provoked by the individuals themselves. (Dedov 2017: 26)

This is quite a problematic statement, given the fine balance to be struck between the state's prerogative to protect its borders and its obligations towards people who are fleeing war, persecution and discrimination, and their right to claim asylum. Dedov seems oblivious to this nuance. He goes on to ask, rhetorically 'did the applicants try to solve their problems themselves?' (Dedov 2017: 27). For him, the legal identity of the applicants in *Z.A. and Others* seems to be clearly that of 'ordinary' immigration law offenders[21] who should have been aware that they 'would not be allowed to enter the State's territory without a valid visa or residence permit' (Dedov 2017: 26). By this, Judge Dedov pre-emptively denied the applicants the right to claim asylum in

[20] Judge Dedov, who succeeded the highly respected Anatoly Kovler only in 2013 as the Russian judge in Strasbourg, seems already notorious for controversial dissenting opinions. His arguably 'outrageously homophobic dissent' in *Bayev and Others* v. *Russia* (nos. 67667/09, 44092/12, 56717/12, judgment of 20 June 2017) earned him 'the worst judgment of 2017' mention in a poll conducted by an influential ECtHR watchdog-blog, 'Strasbourg Observers' (even though his was a dissenting opinion and formally not a judgment) (Lavrysen and Poppelwell-Scevak 2018).

[21] This is very similar to that put forward by the M. District Court in the *L.M. and Others* judgment.

Russia (without even considering their claim on merit), and ignored the obligations Russia has as a party to the 1951 Refugee Convention.

The great irony of this dissent lies in Dedov's complete misunderstanding of neoliberalism as an ideology, concept and a political outlook. According to Dedov, it is the neoliberal concepts and ideas of requiring 'more from governments than is necessary' (Dedov 2017: 27) that have already 'led to the current ideological and political crisis in the West triggered by mass (and mostly economic) migration' (Dedov 2017: 27). Yet, I would call Dedov's own position neoliberal throughout – promoting a transformation of the state towards the *laissez-faire* model, at the same time stressing the idea that our individual lives, identities and subjectivities should be framed by 'entrepreneurial beliefs, attitudes and thinking' (Birch 2017).

After all, what were the alternatives that Judge Dedov suggested for the applicants in *Z.A. and Others*? As 'they were all young, healthy men aged between 25 and 35', and thereby 'they did not belong to any vulnerable group', they should have sought 'independence and responsibility' and 'try to improve their life at home, make their own contribution to the national economic situation or fight for peace in their homeland' (Dedov 2017: 27). Basically, they should have tried anything that would keep them from embarking on a plane to Russia. And, since the applicants had already arrived in Russia, but were formally denied entry into its territory, instead of complaining, they should have looked for inspiration in

> the great movie 'The Terminal' starring Tom Hanks, whose character did not complain, but retained his dignity in difficult conditions, thanks to his personal qualities, his education and knowledge. (Dedov 2017: 27)

The dissent in *Z.A. and Others* v. *Russia*, especially when put into context of Judge Dedov's other opinions, does not seem exceptional, but illustrative of his unusual style of legal thinking and argumentation. It remains a question, though, to what extent can we draw conclusions from this opinion regarding broader ideas concerning the relationship between asylum seekers and the state's responsibility that are generally prevalent in Russia? Dedov's stance is by no means representative of all Russian judges deciding on immigration or refugee law cases. The analysis contained in this chapter of the complex and multifaceted ways in which different human rights arguments are referenced and relied upon by domestic courts proves this case in point. Nevertheless, I find it important to ponder this dissenting opinion as it brings to light a set of arguments and, crucially, ideological misunderstandings as to why the overall influence (potency) of the human rights logic remains rather limited in Russia as far as immigration and refugee law cases are concerned.

* * *

This chapter has demonstrated that the relationship between Russia and the ECtHR (and human rights more broadly) remains much more complex and multifaceted than the high-profile cases before the Strasbourg Court or the recent conflict over constitutional supremacy would suggest. If we leave these high-profile cases at the domestic level and see what lies beyond them, we can actually observe instances in which the human rights arguments are invoked, referenced and relied upon, even by the low-level courts. Drawing on the empirical case study of judgments in immigration and refugee law cases, this chapter revealed that the reference to the human rights logic is by no means uniform. In order to explain the significant variation in how different levels of domestic courts framed, structured and positioned the human rights arguments, I put forward the following typology: the use of human rights instruments by Russian domestic courts may be *explicit*, *implicit* or *affirmative*, but also there are often instances when the human rights logic is *rejected* altogether.

7

Who Are the Humans Behind the Human Rights Cases?

Migration Cases from Russia to the European Court of Human Rights

Introduction

The previous chapter looked at the complex and diverse logic of human rights application in domestic judicial decisions concerning migrants, refugees and asylum seekers in Russia. It focused on legal reasoning and judicial discourse. However, this analytical approach left an important question unanswered. Who are the humans behind these and other migration cases from Russia? Who are the people these judgments are about? What are their stories, their narratives and their subjectivity?

Migrants and refugees are some of the main actors behind human rights cases that reach the European Court of Human Rights (ECtHR) from Russia. However, the judgments of the ECtHR do not allow the reader to get to know the applicants before the court. Their personal experiences are often reduced to a few words under the heading 'facts of the case' and are barely visible from under the piles of parties' submissions, legal arguments and descriptions of the domestic legal proceedings. The information about them is usually captured in a few lines:

> The applicant was born in 1988 in Uzbekistan. He arrived in Russia in 2005. He is currently detained in Moscow.

Or:

> The case originated in an application … by two Tajikistani nationals. The applicants were born in 1972 and 1976, respectively, and live in Moscow. The applicants are married and have three minor children. They are practising Muslims.

Sometimes, despite the laconic nature the information, it still can have an unsettling effect, especially when one reads:

> The applicant was born in 1985. He is presently serving a prison sentence in Tajikistan.

This last one-line statement hides as much as it reveals. The man in question could not have launched his application before the ECtHR directly from Tajikistan, as that country is not a party to the European Convention of

Human Rights (ECHR). In the meantime, he must have spent some time in Russia. How did he find himself back in Tajikistan, and in prison? He could have been arrested in Russia at the request of the Tajik authorities, or because he broke Russian immigration law. Was he extradited? Was he administratively removed (expelled)? Perhaps he was abducted?

These formal-sounding excerpts from the different judgments do not tell us much about the people behind these human rights cases. Given the gravity of the charges, in the documents contained in the case files and presented before the ECtHR, it is the state's official, formal and largely accusatory narrative against the defendants that comes across most clearly. The purpose of this chapter is to revert this imbalance: to give voice to migrants themselves and use this chapter as a conduit, as a platform to let them express their side of the story. How does it feel to be detained on the same day as your claim for asylum has been refused? How does it feel to be released from detention pending extradition just to be re-arrested on the charges of breaking domestic immigration law? How does it feel when the only document proving your identity in Russia is a letter of interim measures issued by the ECtHR? What do you think of first when migration authorities and anti-terrorist forces raid your apartment at 4 a.m., when your three children are sleeping? Finally, how do you even start arriving at a decision: is it better to be detained together with my children, leave them in the custody of Russian social services or somehow send them across to relatives in Tajikistan, and risk never seeing them again?

At an analytical level, these stories and narratives bring in the complexity and richness of detail, and illustrate certain broader features and characteristics of the *Garabayev* group[1] of cases before the Strasbourg Court. The *Garabayev* group comprises immigration and refugee law cases from Russia concerning alleged violations of art. 3 of the ECHR (if Russia was to go ahead with the extradition or otherwise an administrative removal of a foreign national), and art. 5 of the ECHR (regarding the length of detention pending extradition or administrative removal). In 2014, when I started being interested in this topic, the *Garabayev* group before the ECtHR concerned approximately 40 cases. In 2018, there were already 81 decided and pending cases before the Strasbourg Court concerning extradition, administrative removal and deportation from Russia with human rights implications (see Figure 7.1).

The applicants in the *Garabayev* group before the ECtHR could roughly be divided into two, often overlapping, groups. The first group concerns people accused by state authorities in Central Asia (Uzbekistan, Tajikistan, Kyrgyzstan, Kazakhstan or Turkmenistan) of politically motivated crimes – 'attempt to overthrow a constitutional order' or 'conspiring to commit a crime against

[1] This group of cases concerns different violations related to extradition/expulsion (articles 3, 5, 13 and 34 of the ECHR). For the list of all the cases as of 2018, see Appendix 2. In this chapter, I offer a socio-legal analysis of the *Garabayev* group of cases. For the full legal reference and case details, see the ECtHR at: http://hudoc.exec.coe.int/eng?i=004-14088.

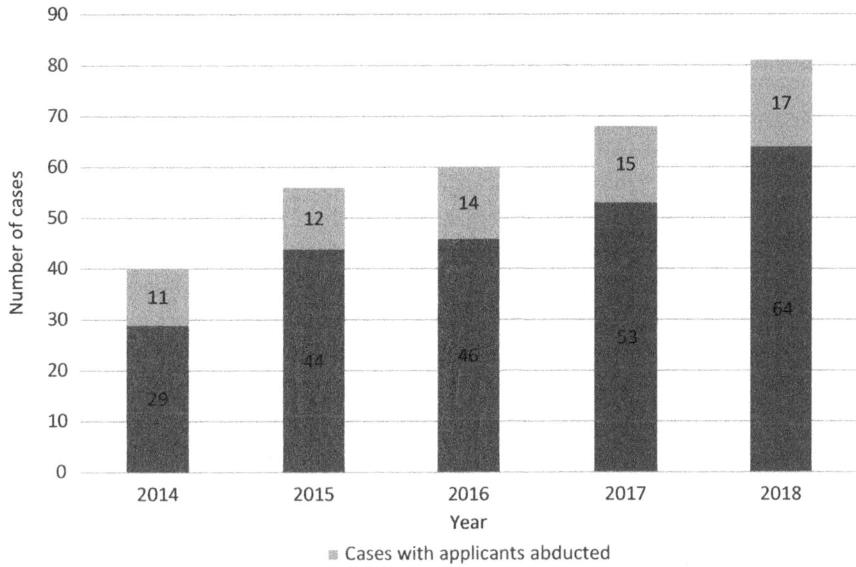

Figure 7.1 *Garabayev* group of cases before the ECtHR, 2014–2018.

the state'. The second group concerns people accused of religious extremism, participation in an allegedly extremist Muslim organization (e.g. 'Hizb ut-Tahrir'[2]) or possession and dissemination of literature of a religiously extremist nature. According to Daria Trenina, a prominent human rights lawyer and scholar of Russian refugee law:

> Most of [these people] were intimidated by local police or security service officers at home for being 'too religious' i.e. practicing their religion openly, celebrating Muslim marriages . . . or practicing religion outside the official framework (Trenina 2014: 17).

At the face value, these charges sound very serious; they often borrow from the language of terrorism law. However, they have to be placed in the context of the actual political situation in Central Asia. Given the authoritarian nature of these regimes, any form of political activism or opposition could easily be framed as an 'attempt to overthrow the constitutional order'; the activist and international NGO literature presents ample evidence to support this

[2] Hizb ut-Tahrir is a political and ideological movement with a fundamentalist Islamic inclination that translates into English as a 'Party of Liberation'. It was founded in 1953 in Jerusalem by Muslim cleric and jurist Taqiuddin al-Nabhani, in reaction to the establishment of an Israeli state and the subsequent expulsion of Palestinians. Hizb ut-Tahrir rejects democracy, secularism and all Western models of state. It calls for the establishment of an 'Islamic state' based on the early Islamic model of caliphate. However, unlike jihadi groups such as al-Qaeda and Islamic State (ISIS), Hizb ut-Tahrir rejects the adoption of violence. Hizb ut-Tahrir has followers in the Middle East, Central and Southeast Asia, and some Western countries; see Mamouri (2015).

interpretation (Amnesty International 2013, 2015, 2016b; Human Rights Watch 2017). Similarly, because Islam as a religion in Central Asia is strictly sanctioned by the state authorities, any deviation from the state-prescribed norms of preaching, reading *namaz* outside the state-sponsored mosques, at home or with a group of friends, can often be branded as 'religious extremism' (Heathershaw and Montgomery 2014; Rasanayagam 2014; Yusupova and Ponarin 2016; Kudaibergenova and Shin 2018).

The personal life stories of selected individuals from the *Garabayev* group play an important role in the process of understanding the developments of migration, asylum and refugee cases from Russia before the ECtHR. Epistemologically they break the monopoly of the Strasbourg Court to decide what a violation of human rights is by bringing to light unique individual experiences of inhuman and degrading treatment, arbitrary detention or deprivation of liberty. They demonstrate that a comprehensive understanding of human rights (and human rights violations) goes much beyond the legal sphere – it should also embrace the different elements of the social: narratives, meanings, understandings. These are much richer, complex and at times contradictory; they are contextually situated, relational and embodied. These narratives are not about locating 'the truth' (absolute and universal), but instead they seek and bring to light 'a truth' (provisional and positional). By their very nature, they cannot be squeezed into the confines of the linear formal legality without a significant loss for our epistemological process. These stories pay attention to the ordinary, everyday and mundane things that never make news headlines or court judgments, but may affect ordinary people's lives significantly. As such, they also constitute sites of resistance to formal legal authority; they can be read as examples of claims-making about human rights, justice and morality that present viable counterpoints to the Court's renderings of reality. My interviewees told their stories and asserted their version of the events as a form of resistance. These narratives created a world in which they continued to live and affirm their agency and not be reduced to simply a few lines of the Court's judgment. These narratives also provide a much-needed thick description to an intricate dialogue between the Russian domestic courts, Russian migration authorities and the ECtHR, and demonstrate the evolution of Russian immigration law and its enforcement practices under the influence of the ECtHR jurisprudence. This evolution of Russian immigration law has been well documented in the legal literature (Trenina 2014; Trenina and Zharinov 2017); however, it has so far been missing from the broader socio-legal analysis – much to the detriment of a comprehensive understanding of the issue.

What can these legal narratives tell us about the broader legal developments in the sphere of migration cases from Russia to the ECtHR? The main argument of this chapter, drawing on an in-depth study of the *Garabayev* group of cases, is that the evolution of Russian immigration law practices could be understood in terms of its *adaptability* towards the emerging and consolidating ECtHR jurisprudence. This unique adaptation follows a rather ambivalent pattern: the law enforcement authorities may reform one set of domestic practices given the established ECtHR case law, but then they do not extend these reformed procedures to deal with future and subsequent immigration cases. Instead, new and innovatory practices from a plethora of domestic options are relied upon. These 'new' domestic practices usually come with fewer legal assurances for the migrants involved. This, in turn, leads to the development of new case law before the ECtHR and, given the systemic nature of the domestic problems in the immigration sphere, often prompts the Strasbourg Court to instigate further changes in the Russian legal system (via general measures).

In retelling the stories of migrants and asylum seekers in Russia – applicants before the ECtHR – I have to note the following limitation: in the course of my fieldwork, I could not obtain detailed narratives from those individuals who were prematurely removed from Russia and transferred to their countries of origin. Their life stories have been interrupted or lost, as they had been secretly apprehended, abducted and extra-judicially removed – a practice similar to a secret rendition (see *Savriddin Dzhurayev* v. *Russia*, no 71386/10, judgment 25 April 2013). Figure 7.1 shows a steady growth in the number of cases in the *Garabayev* group before the ECtHR with a proportion of applicants abducted between 2014 and 2017. Therefore, I primarily focus on the experiences of those who were still in Russia at the time of my field research, managed to escape the risk of forcible return with the help of an NGO or were subsequently relocated to one of the European countries.

This chapter proceeds in three parts. The next section introduces two detailed legal narratives, each representative of one of the two sub-groups in the *Garabayev* group of cases before the ECtHR. The story of Myriam and Farrukh Nizamov[3] is that of a married Muslim couple charged with offences of alleged religious extremism in Tajikistan and their experiences of dealing with the extradition requests, Russian migration authorities and arrests in Moscow. The story of Khumoyun Umidov[4] gives an account of a person charged with anti-state and political crimes in Uzbekistan, his application for asylum in Moscow, subsequent detention and the threat of extradition and deportation. Both cases have found conclusion in the ECtHR. The second part of this chapter analyses these stories in the context of the broader socio-legal scholarship on legal narratives, addressing the questions: what are these particular stories actually useful for? How do they contribute to a more comprehensive understanding of human rights? The final part uses these stories as a background to trace the adaptability and evolution of Russian immigration law to ECtHR jurisprudence.

[3] These names have been changed to protect the anonymity of my informants.

[4] The name has been changed to protect the anonymity of my informant.

The People and Their Stories

Mrs and Mr Nizamov

Myriam Nizamov is an ethnic Uzbek, born and raised in Tajikistan. I met her in the headquarters of the NGO where I was conducting my fieldwork. An immigration lawyer introduced us, knowing I was interested in the stories of people whose cases reached the Strasbourg Court. I recognized Myriam from the judgment I had studied before I came to Russia. Even though her case was decided back in 2013, her residence in Moscow and temporary asylum status in Russia were still 'under consideration' by the migration authorities and she was trying to attend to this matter with the help of the NGO. At the time of writing in 2018, Myriam still had no legal status in Russia. When I introduced myself and my research, and mentioned that I knew her case from the ECtHR database she thought it was a bit bizarre (she told me about this later, though, once we became more acquainted). Why would someone be interested in reviving her memory of events, which she was trying to put behind her? We stayed in touch, however, and a couple of weeks later Myriam agreed to an interview and invited me to her flat in Moscow. We had tea and cooked traditional dishes together – Myriam taught me how to prepare manti, Central Asian steamed dumplings filled with minced lamb. Her daughters were with us in the kitchen, so she could not always talk freely. Myriam started her story after the girls went outside to play. She and Farrukh got married in 1998 in Tajikistan; soon after, their children started arriving – a son who is now 15 and two daughters aged 14 and 11. Farrukh had a small carpentry business back home; he was doing well – even too well, as at some point, according to Myriam, the local police officers started demanding their 'cut' of the profit:

> My husband was telling them – give me some time to develop my business and I will start paying you all – but they did not listen.

It is at that time that Farrukh got interested in Hizb ut-Tahrir. All his close and distant family members from the mosque would read *namaz* together and talk, exchange information and religious literature:

> It was a way to be free from the stagnation and corruption of everyday life.

Myriam remembers that after rediscovering Islam her husband became a much calmer man, he stopped drinking any alcohol, was coming home on time, became quieter and more responsible, more loving towards her and the family. When she saw this change in him, she also started studying the literature and the ideas of this organization. In 2003, the Tajikistani authorities arrested Farrukh, having found leaflets published by Hizb ut-Tahrir in his carpentry workshop. Farrukh was beaten up in detention; the police officers broke his heel bone in an attempt to extract a confession from him concerning Hizb ut-Tahrir's activities:

> When Farrukh was released, he went into hiding. He closed the business. It was not a life but a mere existence. In 2005, we decided he leaves for Russia.

Myriam and the children joined Farrukh a year later, in 2006:

> Until 2010, these four years we had a normal life. My husband was working, earning money; I was looking after the house. At that time, I was even thinking, 'Oh God, I wish I could get a break from all of that routine, from the children, from all the cooking and cleaning.' And God works in mysterious ways: indeed I was soon to get a break from all that, and sleep in a single bed, in a prison cell...

In December 2010, at 4 a.m. in the morning, the Nizamov's apartment was raided by the police and FSB security services. The children were sleeping; the older boy woke up and was very scared, seeing men in black uniforms with masks on their faces and heavy guns. The two smaller children were half-asleep and did not realize much of what was happening:

> They searched our flat, yes they found religious literature, which they thought was 'extremist'.

Mr Nizamov had just come home from a night shift and was very tired.

> They took us to the police station, initially as witnesses. I remember sitting next to Farrukh at the police station, he was handcuffed and very tired; all he could think of was to get some sleep.

The same day the police officers arrested Mr Nizamov. In the course of the investigation it transpired that back in 2005 (after the incident with the Tajik authorities) Mr Nizamov was charged in Tajikistan *in absentia* with 'involvement in a criminal organisation inciting racial, ethnic or religious hatred or hostility and publicly calling for the overthrow of the political order or breach of the territorial integrity of the Republic of Tajikistan'.[5] The Ministry of Security of the Republic of Tajikistan ordered Mr Nizamov's arrest and put his name on an internationally wanted persons list requesting his extradition. The extradition order stated that Farrukh, being an active member of Hizb ut-Tahrir, had on numerous occasions disseminated extremist leaflets and literature for that organization.

Mr Nizamov was arrested in Russia with a view of extradition to Tajikistan, given Russia's obligation under the 1993 Minsk Convention[6] and in accordance

[5] All the quotes concerning legal material (charges, legal proceedings, excerpts from decisions by different courts) come from the original case of Myriam and Farrukh Nizamov (names changed) before the ECtHR, published in the HUDOC database.

[6] The CIS Convention on Legal Aid and Legal Relations in Civil, Family and Criminal Matters. It was signed in Minsk in 1993 by Armenia, Belarus, Kazakhstan, Kyrgyzstan, Moldova, Russian Federation, Turkmenistan, Tajikistan, Ukraine and Uzbekistan. The Convention provides the rules for legal cooperation between member states' courts in civil, family and criminal matters. In particular, it sets forth the rules regarding jurisdiction of member states' courts, recognition and enforcement of foreign court judgments and conflict of law rules.

with the Russian Code of Criminal Procedure. The M. District Court in Moscow ordered Mr Nizamov to serve one month's detention, which was later extended for another six months as:

> There were no grounds to alter the preventive measure, as the extradition check in respect of Mr Nizamov had not been completed, and therefore without extending the detention it would not be possible to ensure his extradition to Tajikistan.

The M. District Court noted that Mr Nizamov was charged with serious criminal offences in Tajikistan, which were also punishable under Russian criminal law, he had no residence registration in Russia, he had never been granted the status of refugee or temporary asylum in Russia and there were sufficient reasons to believe that he might abscond if at liberty. Half a year later, in July 2011, the same M. District Court further extended Mr Nizamov's detention for another six months.

When the authorities initially arrested Farrukh, Myriam, through friends of friends, got a telephone number of a prominent human rights lawyer in Moscow:

> When I called her she instructed me not to tell my story via telephone, not to contact anyone, stay at home and she said she would be in touch with further guidelines. A few days later, she called back saying that our lawyer would be a woman named Hope.[7]

Hope met with Mrs Nizamov and explained to her that her husband could stay in prison up to 18 months, for her to be prepared.[8] The lawyer also mentioned that Myriam should look after herself, keep a low profile and always tell her family members and friends of her whereabouts – if she was going to a shop or dropping the children at school – as her safety was also in danger. If she were on the internationally wanted persons list, the Russian authorities could also arrest her and start extradition proceedings.

At the same time, Hope started representing Farrukh Nizamov before the Russian authorities; she asked the Russian Prosecutor General's Office to refuse the Tajikistani authorities' request for his extradition, stating that he ran a serious risk of being subjected to torture if extradited. The Russian Prosecutor General's Office rejected this petition and proceeded with the extradition order. The lawyer later appealed to Moscow City Court, citing already established case law before the ECtHR of other presumed members of Hizb ut-Tahrir, where the Strasbourg Court had found that extradition would breach art. 3 of the ECHR. The Moscow City Court refused the appeal, stating

[7] In text, I am relying on the English translation of the Russian name Nadezdha to specifically highlight the role this lawyer played in the lives of Myriam and Farrukh Nizamov.

[8] In accordance with art. 109 para. 4 of the Code of Criminal Procedure. 'No extension [of pre-trial detention] beyond eighteen months is permissible and the detainee must be released immediately' (art. 109 para. 4).

that there was not enough evidence to corroborate the allegations of ill-treatment in Tajikistan, and that 'Tajikistani authorities had provided the necessary assurances, in accordance with international law'. The lawyer appealed again, this time to the Supreme Court of Russia, which denied the appeal.

In early December 2011, one year into Mr Nizamov's detention in Russia, and having exhausted all domestic remedies in the extradition proceedings, Hope applied to the ECtHR for interim measures, Rule 39 of the Rules of the Court, to place an injunction on the extradition order until Mr Nizamov's case could be heard before the Strasbourg Court. Rule 39 was granted, and the following day Mr Nizamov was released from detention at the request of the General Prosecutor. He was released under a written undertaking not to leave his place of residence in Moscow and to appear at the Prosecutor's Office every week.

Throughout 2011, when Farrukh was in prison, the security services summoned Myriam for questioning on many occasions:

> I was going, but always with my three children. They were my insurance. They were small, so I knew that finally the authorities would let me go, as the kids were making noise, and I needed to give them food and attend to them.
>
> Immediately prior to my arrest, the leading officer asked me to come to questioning alone. This is when I got truly scared. I tried to argue that it would be difficult given that my husband was in prison and I had no one to leave my children with.

At some point in mid-May 2011, when Farrukh had already been in detention for five months, a car arrived in front of the Nizamovs' block of flats. Myriam had 'a bad feeling'; her intuition told her to avoid this car. Then, it seemed the car had driven off. When she went out to buy some bread, it turned out that the car was still parked in the vicinity, but behind a corner; therefore, Myriam could not see it from the windows of her apartment. Two security service officers were in the car and they requested Myriam to accompany them for questioning. Myriam did not want to go without Hope, the lawyer. However, the men forced her into the car and drove her away.

Now we come to a point in the story when my argument about hearing migrants' voices becomes particularly relevant. According to Myriam, the security service officers who pushed her into the car have ultimately abducted her. In Mr and Mrs Nizamov's case before the ECtHR we read, however, based on the reports by officers Z. and L. who arrived to summon Myriam for questioning, that Myriam herself 'asked for a lift to the questioning session'. The security officers simply 'agreed to do so'. The documents officially sanctioned by the Russian state and contained in the ECtHR judgment elaborate on the event as follows:

> Officer Z. was driving, officer L. was in the front passenger seat while the applicant was in the back seat by herself. Her freedom was not restricted in any way, and during the journey, she was talking on a mobile phone and sending text messages. She did not show any anxiety concerning the questioning and did not make any requests, such as to contact her lawyer or her family.

According to Myriam, however, the incident was very different to the official reports and protocols:

> When they got me into the car, I dialled the number of the lawyer but it went to voice mail. So I kept the phone on, and was loudly asking the men where they were taking me. I discretely recorded the address on the phone, so Hope could find me once she became available. When Hope came to the security services headquarters and called the officers on the intercom – they were not picking up; when they finally picked up, they said 'no Mrs Nizamov is not here'. I could hear this as I was sitting just nearby, so I shouted: 'Hope, I am here!'

The officers finally let the lawyer in to be with Myriam during the questioning. During the questioning, it became apparent that the Tajikistani state authorities instituted criminal proceedings against Mrs Nizamov on suspicion of her membership and active involvement in the activities of Hizb ut-Tahrir. She was charged with involvement in a banned extremist organization, and her name was put on an internationally wanted persons list. This is how Myriam remembers the questioning:

> The investigative officer showed me a book and asked me whether I knew it. I really did not know it; it was not one of ours. They asked me to read it. I responded that if it had really been our book they would have already found my fingerprints on it, hence now there was no need for me to touch it . . . Hope showed me a big 'thumbs up' under the table.

The following day the M. District Court in Moscow ordered Myriam's detention for a period of two months. In the court, Hope argued that the detention of Mrs Nizamov was unlawful and unjustified:

> She had good character references; she had not been subject to criminal prosecution in Russia; she had a permanent place of residence in Moscow where she resided with her three minor children.

The court stated that Mrs Nizamov's detention was necessary in order to ensure her extradition to Tajikistan. The lawyer appealed but the Moscow City Court rejected the appeal. The M. District Court further extended Mrs Nizamov's detention by four months. Hope again appealed that decision to Moscow City Court, arguing that:

> the [lower] court had failed to indicate the progress of the extradition proceedings . . . the grounds for the extension of detention had not been sufficiently specific [and] the court had not attached due weight to [Mrs Nizamov] being the mother of three minor children.

The Moscow City Court rejected the appeal, stating that: 'the extension of detention as a preventive measure was justified in view of the ongoing extradition proceedings, and that Mrs Nizamov's children had been placed in the care of Russian social services'.

Myriam has spent six months in detention altogether. This is how she remembers it:

> I was put in a cell with a 19-year-old Russian skinhead girl who was being charged with a murder of a Tajik migrant. I was crying in my bed, crying and regretting that 'break' I yearned for earlier on. Always be careful what you wish for . . . I was biting my cushion, missing my husband's touch, missing the smell of my children.

Initially Myriam was frightened of her skinhead cell mate; she thought it must have been some horrible joke, a form of torture on the side of the detention facility management or the FSB security services. Later on, she and the girl became 'friends':

> She was very young and beautiful; she received 20 years in prison. She told me she was drunken and drugged when she committed that horrific act. Later on, the girl was even telling others to turn down the TV when I was reading *namaz.* The funny thing was that at the end of my stay in prison I had a feeling we could have become friends if we only met under different circumstances.

Five months into Myriam's detention, in October 2011, Hope petitioned the Russian Prosecutor General's Office to refuse the Tajikistani authorities' request for Mrs Nizamov's extradition, stating that 'she ran a serious risk of being subjected to torture if extradited'. A month later the Prosecutor General's Office refused the extradition order owing to 'the expiry of the statutory limitation period in respect of the offence [Mrs Nizamov] was charged with'. Myriam was released from prison on the same day, in November 2011.

The ECtHR decided Myriam and Farrukh's case in June 2012, a little over six months since their release from detention in Russia. It was a partial victory. On the positive side, the Court decided that if the order to extradite Mr Nizamov to Tajikistan were to be enforced, it would be a violation of art. 3 of the ECHR (prohibition of inhuman and degrading treatment). This provided an impetus for the Russian immigration authorities to issue Mr Nizamov with temporary asylum in Russia, which has been subsequently prolonged. With regard to Myriam – as the Russian Prosecutor General's Office terminated the extradition proceedings of their own accord due to the expiry of the statute of limitations – the Strasbourg Court could not rule on a violation (or potential violation) of art. 3. As a result, Myriam's repeated requests for temporary asylum have been denied in Russia. Her legal status and the status of her three children is still precarious. On the disappointing side, the Strasbourg Court found no violation of art. 5 with regard to the prolonged detentions of Mr and Mrs Nizamov, as these were always based on a decision of a court in accordance with domestic criminal proceedings.

The part of the judgment that shows the greatest limitation of the ECtHR towards comprehensive treatment of Myriam's human rights claims concerned, in my opinion, her alleged abduction by the security services. The

Strasbourg Court found 'no evidence that would enable it to depart from the findings of the domestic courts' which established that Mrs Nizamov had asked the security service officers to 'give her a lift in their car' to the questioning. The Court further noted that:

> Regrettable, as it is, the authorities' failure to accurately indicate the time of [Mrs Nizamov's] deprivation of liberty in the record of arrest did not entail a breach of procedural guarantees against arbitrary detention.

In the light of further developments, this procedural and formal legality applied by the ECtHR in this case has opened the doors to the practice of secret abductions and renditions of migrants that now constitute an infamous but significant proportion of the *Garabayev* group of cases (around 20 per cent, see Figure 7.1).

Mr Umidov

Mr Khumoyun Umidov is an Uzbek national. He came to Russia in July 2010 using the visa-free regime. According to the statement of the facts of his case before the Strasbourg Court, 'he arrived in Moscow with a view of finding a seasonal job and marrying'. In an interview, Khumoyun told me he had to flee Uzbekistan as the Uzbek security services were preparing a case against him. He had learned about this from one of his university colleagues who was doing an internship at the local security service office in Bukhara. Khumoyun was in his forties when he arrived in Moscow. Back in Uzbekistan, he received university degrees from Bukhara University and was also studying at Tashkent University (now the University of World Economy and Diplomacy – 'the place to train future leaders of the country' – according to the website). Throughout the 2000s, Khumoyun had a close group of friends from university; they met regularly, often – especially on Fridays – praying together or reading *namaz*. He comes from a quite politically involved family: his grandfather was shot in 1938 for anti-Soviet opposition. While at university, Khumoyun protested against the students being 'forced to gather cotton', a practice in Uzbekistan that Human Rights Watch compared in its 2013 report to 'forced labour' (Human Rights Watch 2013).

While in Moscow, Khumoyun soon learned that his brothers were arrested and charged with 'participation in an extremist religious organisation'. One of his brothers, Abdusami, is still in prison; he originally received a six-year sentence for alleged 'religious extremism' (art. 244-2 of the Criminal Code of Uzbekistan) and 'attempts to overthrow the constitutional order in Uzbekistan' (art. 159 of the Criminal Code of Uzbekistan). Shortly after this, Khumoyun learned that he was suspected of similar charges by the Uzbekistani authorities – in September 2010, Bukhara Town Court opened a criminal case against him. At this point, Khumoyun had found out about the United Nations High Commissioner for Refugees (UNHCR) in Russia, and its partner organization in Moscow, the NGO where I conducted my fieldwork. With the help of the lawyers from the NGO, in October 2010 Mr Umidov lodged a request with the Moscow Division of the Federal Migration Service (FMS) seeking refugee status in Russia.

Mr Umidov's refugee status application was refused. Inadvertently, however, it also triggered Russia's response to the Uzbek authorities' extradition request. According to the facts of the case before the ECtHR, Mr Umidov

> was arrested at the FMS's office where he had gone to receive the copy of the decision in his [asylum] case. The Moscow police informed the Uzbekistani authorities of the applicant's arrest. On the same day, they received a copy of the arrest order . . . and documents confirming that the applicant had been put on the internationally wanted persons list.

For Khumoyun, the outcome of the refugee application was indeed most unfortunate. This is how he remembers it:

> One day in February 2011, I received a phone call to come and collect the decision on my refugee status application. The woman on the phone insisted that I came that very day, and alone. At the FMS office, it was not only the woman who awaited me and gave me the refusal of my application, but there were also three men from Moscow police and international extradition division. I was arrested and taken straight to the police station. There, they gave me a document to sign stating that I no longer required protection in Russia and wished to be returned back to Uzbekistan. But knowing what happened to my brothers back home, of course I refused to sign it. That is how I ended up at the General Prosecutor's Office. He assured me that my rights would be protected and my case would be dealt with in a civilised manner.

The following day, I. District Court in Moscow ordered Mr Umidov's detention pending extradition; no time frame was set for this detention. The domestic court noted that:

> [Mr Umidov's] name is on the internationally wanted persons list in connection with a crime he committed in the Republic of Uzbekistan. He has not been recognised as a refugee in Russia. Nor have any other circumstances preventing his extradition been identified.

One month later, the same court extended Mr Umidov's detention for a further four months, thereby reaching the six-month period of detention pending extradition – exactly as in the case of Myriam Nizamov. If no progress was made in the extradition proceedings, Mr Umidov would need to be released by the prosecutor.[9]

Mr Umidov was indeed released from detention pending extradition; however – as we can read in the facts of his case before the ECtHR – 'on the same

[9] I discuss this trend in more detail in the following section when analysing the evolution of Russian immigration law practices under the influence of ECtHR jurisprudence.

day he was arrested for his alleged failure to comply with the administrative rules governing residence of foreigners in Russia'. We learn more about what really happened that day from Khumoyun:

> The NGO lawyer could not be present at my release. She had another important case pending in court. And I did not want to leave the detention centre without her. I have heard about numerous cases of asylum applicants being forcibly removed to Uzbekistan by Uzbek security services operating on the territory of Russia. I was holding onto anything I could find not to be removed from the centre; the detention guards took my hands and legs and moved me down the stairs. I banged my head repeatedly on the stairs, until I lost consciousness. When I awoke, I was lying on the floor. I was not bleeding . . . In that state, they released from the detention centre.

Immediately outside the detention centre, on the street, a couple of police officers asked Khumoyun for his immigration papers in Russia. As an Uzbek citizen and according to the immigration law he had to have a valid residence permit, and either a work permit or a work licence (patent). Khumoyun could not show any of these documents as he had spent the last six months in detention pending extradition. The police officers accused him of staying in Russia illegally, without residence registration, and passed his case to the FMS, leading to administrative removal (expulsion) proceedings. Two days later, the I. District Court found Mr Umidov's stay in Russia to be in contravention of the Russian immigration law and ordered his removal according to art. 18.8 of the Code of Administrative Offences (CAO). Khumoyun was to remain in custody pending the enforcement of administrative removal. No time frame was set for this administrative detention – the judicial practice had it that it was equal to the expiry of the statute of limitation for the art. 18.8 offence of CAO, i.e. two years. As a result, the detention pending extradition following the criminal proceedings was conveniently substituted by the detention pending expulsion following the administrative proceedings. In either case the goal was to have Mr Umidov removed from Russia.

Having exhausted all domestic legal remedies, Mr Umidov's lawyer petitioned the ECtHR for interim measures, Rule 39 of the Rules of the Court, to stop Mr Umidov's removal from Russia until his case could be heard by the Strasbourg Court. The ECtHR had granted Rule 39 in Mr Umidov's case with a view to both the extradition and expulsion proceedings pending against him.

As in the cases of Mr and Mrs Nizamov, the ECtHR intervention had profound implications for the development of Mr Umidov's case before domestic legal bodies. The Moscow City Court quashed the decision of the lower court and, given that the ECtHR had put an interim injunction on Mr Umidov's removal from Russia, and ordered the release of Mr Umidov. Khumoyun was finally free. The General Prosecutor's Office of the Russian Federation, in turn, refused to extradite Mr Umidov to Uzbekistan. The following year the FMS granted him temporary asylum (a subsidiary form of protection in Russia) 'due to consideration of his case by the European Court of Human Rights and the application of an interim measure'.

These developments definitely demonstrate the responsiveness of the domestic Russian legal authorities towards the interim measures of the ECtHR. The ECtHR intervention together with the reaction of the domestic legal authorities have made the situation of Mr Umidov more secure in Russia. However, it has not solved it. Due to the temporary (one year) duration of the temporary asylum status, Mr Umidov had no means of regularizing his residence in Russia and making his livelihood in Moscow more permanent.

A year on from Mr Umidov's release from detention, the ECtHR delivered a judgment in his case. As in Myriam's case, it offered a halfway solution, or rather, demonstrated the serious limitations of the ECtHR as a court that could attend to the complex needs of migrants, asylum seekers and refugees in Russia. On the positive side, the ECtHR ruled that the first detention of Mr Umidov – from under the FMS office – violated his right to liberty (articles 5 (1) and 5(4) of the ECHR) as it did not contain specific time limits, nor allowed for a speedy judicial review of the detention. The ECtHR awarded Mr Umidov compensation in lieu of non-pecuniary damages.

On the rather troubling side, the ECtHR, having regard to the General Prosecutor's Office decision refusing to extradite the applicant to Uzbekistan, concluded that Mr Umidov was 'no longer subjected to the risk of removal to Uzbekistan and, accordingly, was no longer at risk of ill-treatment'. The complaint under art. 3 was dismissed and the interim measure was lifted. As an immediate response, the Russian migration authorities refused to prolong Mr Umidov's temporary asylum in Russia, referring to the Court's finding of the applicant's complaint under art. 3 of the ECHR being manifestly ill-founded. Mr Umidov's temporary asylum was effectively terminated and he was back in legal limbo.

I personally met Mr Umidov when he was in the process of appealing the termination of his temporary asylum in Russia before the domestic courts. He came frequently to the NGO to consult his lawyer, and kindly allowed me to accompany him and the lawyer to court to observe the appeal proceedings. However, all the court instances refused his appeal, agreeing with the FMS (and the ECtHR). Given the General Prosecutor's refusal to extradite Mr Umidov to Uzbekistan, he was no longer 'covered' by art. 3 of the ECHR and should find different means of legalizing his stay in Russia. But how? This was a true conundrum. Practically, Mr Umidov could not leave Russia to any of the neighbouring states without risking a repeat of the extradition ordeal, as they were all parties to the Minsk Convention and had his name on the internationally wanted persons list. Khumoyun was trapped in Russia. When we put this argument to the lawyer representing the FMS during one of the numerous chats we had in the courtroom corridor while waiting for the hearing, he seemed equally puzzled. At the same time, he stood firmly on the position that the FMS decision to terminate Mr Umidov's temporary asylum in Russia was legal (*zakonnaya*) and defendable in court. The FMS lawyer in a personal chat admitted that he 'had nothing against' Mr Umidov; he went as far as to suggest that:

> If it was up to me I would have given him status in Russia – Mr Umidov's religious extremism charges were probably fabricated in Uzbekistan, he speaks good Russian and is well integrated here.

The FMS lawyer even alleged that instead of the Russian migration authorities, Mr Umidov should rather fear the Uzbek security services, confirming the tacit knowledge of the widespread violations and abductions from Russian territory.

When Mr Umidov had exhausted all the domestic remedies in his temporary asylum proceedings, his lawyer again petitioned the ECtHR for interim measures, stating that while the refusal to extradite him may remain in effect at present, the status of the administrative removal decision was *much less definite*. The lawyer relied on the final FMS letter terminating Mr Umidov's temporary asylum, which stated that 'if the person refuses a voluntary departure from the Russian Federation, he will be administratively removed or deported together with the family members'. The ECtHR once again adopted interim measures and put an injunction on Mr Umidov's removal from Russia to Uzbekistan. Mr Umidov was facing an imminent second case before the ECtHR that could lead to establishing a precedent in cases concerning 'failed' asylum seekers from Central Asia in Russia facing politically or religiously motivated criminal charges in their home jurisdictions.

The ECtHR letter awarding interim measures became Mr Umidov's primary identity document in Russia. He had the English original copy and the Russian translation attached to it – both stored in a plastic sleeve. His legal situation in Russia was very precarious and his freedom of movement severely limited. The Moscow police stopped Mr Umidov on numerous occasions during routine documents checks. As the officers did not understand the intricacies of international human rights law (and the ECtHR letter looked nothing like the documents issued by the domestic migration authorities), Khumoyun inadvertently found himself countless times in a prison cell for 48 hours at a time until his lawyer could come and demand his release.

After approximately eight months of this ordeal, an opportunity came to have Mr Umidov relocated to one of the Schengen countries, drawing heavily on the personal networks and charismatic capital of the chairwoman of the legal NGO that was handling his case. Khumoyun seized this chance. Russian migration authorities agreed to Mr Umidov's departure, and at the same time informed the ECtHR that Mr Umidov was no longer in Russia. In response, the ECtHR struck Mr Umidov's second case from the register. A chance to attend to the matter of legal status of 'failed' asylum seekers in Russia, who were implicated in religiously extremist or political charges in Central Asia, was lost. But the life, health and livelihood of Mr Umidov could now flourish, as he received refugee status in one of the European Union countries. Setting the legal precedent before the ECtHR had to wait.

Legal Narratives: What Are They Useful For?

What do the narratives of Myriam Nizamov and Khumoyun Umidov tell us beyond supplying a number of details, evoking emotions and intricacies of their personal experiences? What are these stories actually useful for? When legal scholars read the ECtHR judgments, they feel comforted: legally we know where the case stands, what human rights have been deemed violated (or not) by the courts and on what legal bases. We can see what arguments were raised by the parties to the trial, underpinned by what type of reasoning and how the Court considered them. Finally, we may agree or disagree with the judgment, but we can be fairly certain we know what the case was about. But do we really? After all, the law occupies only a small part in the lives of the people; it is embedded in the broader context of the 'social' with all its richness, complexity and controversies (Feenan 2013). It is only through embracing the 'social' that we can find out 'what really happened' in a particular case. The road to comprehending the 'social' most often leads through the narrative and the personal story.

The 1980s and 1990s saw the explosion of the debate about the value of storytelling, lay narratives, meta-narratives, dialogues, parables and lived experiences for legal scholarship (O'Barr and Conley 1985; Delgado 1989; Massaro 1989; Scheppele 1989; Baron 1993; Ewick and Silbey 1995, 2003; Natapoff 2005; Taylor 2007; Levit 2010; Di Donato 2011; Fielding 2013). These, then 'non-traditional' forms of legal expression were deemed especially relevant to capture the voices of the 'outsiders' to the legal system – women, people of colour, immigrants, ethnic minorities, LGBT communities. Retelling of the stories was used as a tool to heal trauma among women who experienced domestic violence (Espinoza 1997; Hunter 2006) or to illuminate stereotypes about third- and fourth-generation Asian Americans ('You speak such good English') (Chon 1995, quoted in Levit 2010: 753). The stories, mediated by feminist and critical legal researchers,[10] helped people in legal academia to see what 'scholars in other disciplines had known for a long time – that people comprehend events in narrative form' (Levit 2010: 751). Building of a narrative became a powerful tool in obtaining the full facts of the case (Espinoza 1997: 907). The legal story has become an inseparable building

[10] The journal *Michigan Law Review* hosted the first symposium on the role of narratives in the legal scholarship in 1989 (Vol. 87, No. 8, entitled: 'Legal Storytelling'). *Stanford Law Review* featured an important article offering an appraisal and critique of this movement by Farber and Sherry (1993), while *Vanderbilt Law Review* in the same year published Delgado's powerful and emotional response to Farber and Sherry (Delgado 1993). In the 1990s Martha Minow and Austin Sarat developed a book series for the University of Michigan Press, *Law, Meaning and Violence*; and Foundation Press created the *Law Stories* book series (Levit 2010: 757).

block in developing the background and constructing a legal case, creating meanings and challenging social norms (Levit 2010: 757). It was also seen as a source of greater agency for the lay people in a courtroom context, demonstrating that they, too, were able to construct legal meanings and influence the way a legal story was presented by the lawyer to the judge (Di Donato 2011). The legal narrative scholarship helped to capture the perspectives of the subordinated groups, helped hear their 'voices from the bottom' (Matsuda 1989). It 'highlighted and celebrated diversity' (Scheppele 1989) not only racial or ethnic, but also epistemological as 'parables provided the manifestation of new knowledge and insight' (Taylor 2007). The storytelling movement also framed the dangers of silencing individuals in the course of the legal proceedings as 'a massive democratic and human failure' underlining the '(un)democratic features' of the justice system (Natapoff 2005).

The turn towards legal narrative faced numerous critiques from traditional legal theorists and dogmatists – narratives were deemed impressionistic, subjective, unverifiable, one-sided, emotionally charged and not analytical enough to be incorporated into legal theory and doctrine (Baron 1993; Delgado 1993; Farber and Sherry 1993). Despite this resistance, storytelling has now been firmly established in the mainstream of legal and socio-legal scholarship, playing an important role in revising and redefining the epistemological and ontological boundaries of these disciplines, pushing against the orthodoxy that 'when white folks tell stories . . . they don't seem like stories at all, but the truth' (Delgado 1996: 194).

Telling stories, like those of Myriam and Khumoyun, seems particularly important for human rights scholarship. Their accounts demonstrate the wider significance of 'giving voice' to the lay participants of the justice system and are important in at least three ways. First, listening carefully to Myriam and Khumoyun breaks the Strasbourg Court monopoly for dictating what constitutes a violation of human rights. Marie Dembour and Tobias Kelly, voicing their disappointment with the ECtHR jurisprudence, once posed a poignant question: 'are human rights for migrants?' (Dembour and Kelly 2011). Their edited volume under this very title concluded with the widespread 'reproduction of human rightlessness of migrants'; identifying 'certain messages of hope' and 'marks of hospitality' among the mainly prevalent 'sites of despair' (Baxi 2011). Comparative studies of the 'adjudicatory leadership' by the American Supreme Court and different constitutional courts across Europe contained in the volume – complemented later by Dembour's study of the ECtHR and its inter-American counterpoint – provided close analysis of the relevant case law with sociological insight and historical awareness (Dembour 2015). However, the voices and narratives of migrants – the applicants who lodged these human rights claims – were largely missing from the analysis (as they were from the texts of the judgments that the different authors focused on). The stories of Myriam and Khumoyun show how important it is to complement the reading of the judgments with the voices and experiences of migrants themselves in order to arrive at a bigger picture as to whether human rights are for migrants. Addressing this question cannot really take place without bringing to light *their* lived experiences of inhuman and degrading treatment, *their* experiences of detention as deprivation of liberty, *their* understandings of family life. Focusing on narratives and stories broadens the scope of narrow prescriptions contained in the official judgments and demonstrates how epistemologically our knowledge and conceptualization of articles 3, 5 or 8 of the ECHR cannot be detached from individual experience.

Second, Myriam's and Khumoyun's stories push back against the 'moralizing narratives of legal institutions that define world views of criminality, sanity and sexuality' (Foucault 1977). They provide viable counterpoints to state and institutional renderings of reality – shifting the dynamics and openly challenging the taken-for-granted nature of situational power relations (Ewick and Silbey 2003: 1331). Following from the established socio-legal scholarship we can therefore read these legal stories as sites and 'openings for resistance', distorting the asymmetry of power between the (legally and formally privileged) narrative of the state and that of the individual, if only for a moment (Ewick and Silbey 1995, 2003). The resistance in these stories comes through a particular order (appropriation) of events and the positioning of Myriam's and Khumoyun's voices against the language of the law of the formal ECtHR judgment.

Patricia Ewick and Susan Silbey (2003) interviewed ordinary Americans who resisted the state law and challenged the formal authority in their stories in a number of different ways. They pretended to be 'someone or something they were not', they sometimes took the rules literally, thereby causing confusion to the established bureaucratic modes of operation. On different occasions they consciously disrupted social hierarchies, they took their time and asserted themselves in spaces and places normally associated with the law by 'colonializing them' through their physical – not always welcomed – presence (Ewick and Silbey 2003: 1350–1363). The stories of Myriam and Khumoyun add to this plethora of tactics by showing how resistance can also be achieved through telling *an alternative story* that disrupts and exceeds the textual confinement of the facts of the case before the Strasbourg Court. Telling a story 'on their own terms', telling 'what really happened' constitutes a challenge to the legally affirmed sequence of events. This is shown in the example of Myriam's summons for questioning by the FSB security officers in Moscow: while the ECtHR did not recognize this as 'deprivation of liberty' due to inadequate timekeeping by the security officers and lack of other substantive evidence, Myriam kept telling and retelling her story, placing it firmly within the frames of abduction and arbitrary detention. Through this narrative, she asserted 'the truth on her side' and freed herself from the confines of the written legal form. Referred to as 'tales of the unrecognized' (de Certeau 1984: 68) or 'weapons of the weak' (Scott 1985) in the broader literature, these narratives as 'everyday acts of resistance represent the ways in which relatively powerless persons accommodate to power while simultaneously protecting their interests and identities' (Ewick and Silbey 2003: 1329). This has important repercussions for reversing the imbalance of power inherent to the legal process. As James Baldwin asserted: '[The] victim who is able to articulate the situation of the victim has ceased to be a victim: he, or she, has become a threat' (Baldwin 1998: 562 in Hobson 2012: 74).

Third, narratives by Myriam and Khumoyun are important, as they offer a rich, contextual and ethnographic illustration to an intricate dialogue between Russian immigration authorities, domestic courts and the ECtHR. They supply a number of clues that help to trace the adaptability of the Russian immigration law to the ECtHR jurisprudence. For example, the narrative by Khumoyun of his release from detention pending extradition (due to the expiry of the time limits set for detention as clarified by the ECtHR case law) was followed by his immediate arrest, on the same day – this time on charges of breaking the domestic immigration law – and placement in detention pending administrative removal. What Khumoyun's story brings to light is that Russian immigration authorities' responses to the ECtHR case law and practice contain an element of ambivalence, an element of subversion to the spirit of human rights. Cross-referencing Khumoyun's story with the stories of other migrant-applicants from Russia (and the relevant ECtHR jurisprudence) reveals that this ambivalence has a more systemic nature. I trace it in more detail in the following section.

Russian Immigration Practice: Adaptability to ECtHR Jurisprudence

Russian immigration law is responsive towards the ECtHR jurisprudence. The state party submissions to the ECtHR have over the years become more substantive, comparatively drawing on the existing and emergent ECtHR jurisprudence but also domestic legal evidence following the 'precedent' style.[11] The practices of Russian immigration authorities and law enforcement bodies have undoubtedly evolved under the influence of the ECtHR jurisprudence. This evolution, however, took a trajectory that is often referred to as a 'double-edge sword' by human rights lawyers representing migrant-applicants in domestic courts and before the Strasbourg Court. For every positive development in the domestic immigration law practice, there has been a backlash or a new strategy that would allow the state authorities to sidestep these legal

[11] For example, see the *L.M. and Others* v. *Russia* (no. 40081/14 40088/14 40127/14, judgment of 15 October 2015), a case of Two Syrians and one Palestinian (former Syrian resident) who were to be expelled from Russia on account of undocumented work. The government, in its submission to the ECtHR, used a decision of L. Oblast Court to demonstrate that in 'genuine' Syrian asylum seeker cases the domestic courts did pay attention to human rights arguments. Ironically, the government relied on the same decision that the defence lawyer tried to use (unsuccessfully) in domestic proceedings to exclude the administrative removal (expulsion) from the sentence a couple of months earlier (for background, see Chapter 6).

developments. We can see this intricate dialogue between the ECtHR, Russian domestic courts and immigration authorities as unfolding in the different phases of the *Garabayev* group of cases.

Phase 1: Extradition

The initial migration cases that reached the ECtHR from Russia and formed the original core of the *Garabayev* group were extradition cases. This first phase lasted roughly between 2002 and 2009. The year 2002 was when the case of Mr Garabayev (the case that gave the name to the whole group) was filed in the Strasbourg Court; 2009 marked the issuance of the internal circular letter by the Moscow Region Prosecutor that led to a visible transition in the types of migration cases before the ECtHR.[12]

These original cases started with charges initiated by Uzbek, Kyrgyz or Tajik authorities against specific individuals – citizens of their countries – who resided in Russia. These citizens have often also been tried before domestic courts *in absentia*. This was followed by an international arrest warrant (pursuant to the 1993 Minsk Convention), exactly as in the case of Mr and Mrs Nizamov. Migrants were then detained in Russia following the extradition request.

In the early stage of these extradition cases the detention of foreigners subject to extradition proceedings from Russia usually followed the maximum period allowed by the Code of Criminal Procedure (art. 109, para. 4), i.e. 18 months or longer (see, e.g. *Nasrulloyev* v. *Russia*, no. 656/06, judgment of 11 October 2007). The decision about detention pending extradition was often within the prerogative of the Russian state prosecutor without the appropriate oversight by the courts (e.g. *Dzhurayev* v. *Russia*, no. 38124/07, judgment of 17 December 2009, para. 17). When it was the Russian domestic court that ordered the detention pending extradition, usually no timeframe for detention was specified (e.g. *Khodzayev* v. *Russia*, no. 52466/08, judgment of 12 May 2010, para. 13; *Gaforov* v. *Russia*, no. 25404/09, judgment of 21 October 2010, para. 56), nor was it always clear whether this decision could be appealed (e.g. *Dzhurayev* v. *Russia*, no. 38124/07, judgment of 17 December 2009, para. 17). With regard to extradition procedure, Russian domestic courts relied on diplomatic assurances by the General Prosecutor's Office of a particular Central Asian republic that:

> if extradited, the applicant would not be persecuted on political, ethnic, linguistic, racial or religious grounds and that he would not be subjected to torture or inhuman or degrading treatment or punishment.
>
> (*Gaforov* v. *Russia*, para. 27)

[12] This periodization is a heuristic device based on my own analysis of the *Garabayev* group of cases before the ECtHR, and should not be considered as 'set in stone'. This periodization is rather to guide the reader about the general developments and tendencies in Russian immigration law and practice under the influence of Strasbourg Court jurisprudence.

Otherwise, when considering the risk of ill-treatment or torture upon extradition, the Russian domestic authorities stipulated that:

> Information obtained from 'official sources' had not confirmed that the ... authorities were persecuting their citizens on political or religious grounds or subjecting citizens under criminal prosecution to inhuman or degrading treatment.
>
> (*Gaforov* v. *Russia*, para. 103).[13]

As a result, the Russian domestic courts regularly dismissed the appeals against the extradition orders, and upon the exhaustion of domestic remedies the case would find its conclusion in the Strasbourg Court.

The developments in the case of Mr Nizamov could be considered as typical of the later stage of extradition cases. What I mean by 'later stage' was that there was already a critical mass of ECtHR judgments, which Mr Nizamov could directly rely on and benefit from. The Strasbourg Court repeatedly found that detention while awaiting a formal extradition request on the basis of art. 61 of the Minsk Convention required the adoption of 'domestic legal provisions establishing the grounds and the procedure for ordering detention, as well as applicable time-limits' (e.g. *Abdulkhakov* v. *Russia*, no. 14743/11, judgment of 2 October 2012, para. 171). The benefits of this jurisprudence were clear in Mr Nizamov's case – Farrukh was detained for 'only' 12 months in Russia, and all the extensions of his detention were judicially reviewed; these decisions also specified exact periods for detention. Later, given the domestic responses to ECtHR jurisprudence, the detention pending extradition in politically motivated or religious 'extremist' cases was capped at six months (e.g. *Rakhmonov* v. *Russia*, no. 50031/11, judgment of 16 October 2012). With regard to alleged risks of ill-treatment following extradition, Mr Nizamov could rely on *Gaforov* v. *Russia* and *Khodzhayev* v. *Russia* (no. 52466/08, judgment of 12 May 2010), i.e. cases of other presumed members of Hizb ut-Tahrir, where the Strasbourg Court had found that extradition would breach art. 3 of the ECHR.

Finally, under the influence of the emerging ECtHR jurisprudence, the Plenum of the Supreme Court adopted guidelines for domestic courts when dealing with extradition cases (Regulation No. 11 of 14 June 2012). This ruling clarified the domestic legislation, eliminated the erratic application of the Code of Criminal Procedure and was praised by the Strasbourg Court as 'a significant development of the domestic jurisprudence' (see *Savriddin Dzhurayev* v. *Russia*, no. 71386/10, judgment of 25 April 2013, para. 259). In the regulation the Supreme Court acknowledged other than domestic law grounds to deny extradition requests – especially highlighting those resulting from international agreements to which Russia was a party, such as the International

[13] On the limitations of the diplomatic assurances, see Hall and Weicherding (2014). See also other established case law: *Abdulkhakov* v. *Russia*, no. 14743/11, judgment of 2 October 2012, paras 149–150; *Tadzhibayev* v. *Russia*, no. 17724/14, judgment of 1 December 2015, para. 46.

Covenant of Political and Civil Rights, UN Convention Against Torture and the ECHR (Trenina 2014: 18).

However, the domestic response to these developments also had a more ambivalent character – as the story of Mr Umidov demonstrates.[14] The immigration authorities acting together with the state prosecutor in many subsequent cases decided to replace the extradition proceedings with administrative removal proceedings. Migrants would be released from detention pending extradition and on the same day arrested *de novo*, charged with ordinary offences against Russian immigration law (e.g. lack of registration, lack of a work permit) and sentenced to administrative removal. In that way the new guidelines on the interpretation of the Code of Criminal Procedure concerning the time limits of detention or specific safeguards to be followed in extradition proceedings, as developed under the influence of the ECtHR (*Yuldashev* v. *Russia*, no. 1248/09, judgment of 8 July 2010, para. 111), could be circumvented altogether and replaced by an uninhibited reading of the CAO. This practice was formalized in a circular letter – Order of the Moscow Region Prosecutor from 3 July 2009 (no. 86/81) – that legitimized this substitution arrangement:

> In every case of release of a detained person due to the impossibility of his extradition to the authority he is wanted by, it is obligatory to settle the issue [relying on the] administrative expulsion from the territory of the Russian Federation. (Cited in Trenina 2014: 21)

Phase 2: Replacing Extradition with Administrative Removal

In the second phase (2009–2016),[15] the original *Garabayev* group of cases before the ECtHR was expanded and complemented by cases in which the extradition had been effectively substituted by administrative removal (expulsion).[16] At the domestic level, the administrative removal proceedings seriously limited the individual applicants' chances of finding an effective remedy

[14] See also other cases before the ECtHR: *Rakhmonov* v. *Russia*, no. 50031/11, judgment of 16 October 2012; *Azimov* v. *Russia*, no. 67474/11, judgment of 18 April 2013.

[15] This period starts with the issuance of the Order of the Moscow Region Prosecutor formalizing the arrangement of substituting extradition with administrative removal (expulsion) in 2009. The year 2016 marks the first cases filed at the ECtHR in which the domestic authorities substituted extradition with yet another domestic immigration law practice – that of deportation, see *O.O.* v. *Russia* (no. 36321/16, pending).

[16] See, for example: *Yakubov* v. *Russia* (no. 7265/10, judgment of 8 November 2011); *Rakhmonov* v. *Russia* (no. 50031/11, judgment of 16 October 2012); *Zokhidov* v. *Russia* (no. 67286/10, judgment of 5 February 2013); *Azimov* v. *Russia* (no. 67474/11, judgment of 18 April 2013); *Nizamov and Others* v. *Russia* (nos. 22636/13, 24034/13, 24334/13, 24528/13, judgment of 7 May 2014); *Akram Karimov* v. *Russia* (no. 62892/12, judgment of 28 May 2014).

against potential risks of ill-treatment and torture upon their return to Central Asia. According to Trenina's professional practice:

> the courts did not even reflect on the arguments of alleged risk of torture in their decisions, as they clearly considered these arguments as falling outside the scope of the [ordinary immigration] proceedings. (Trenina 2014: 21; see also Kubal 2016a).

In effect, the courts were 'turning a blind eye' to the fact that the consequences of administrative removal (expulsion) and extradition were identical for the applicants, since in both cases they ended up in the hands of the state requesting their return.

Furthermore, the CAO did not specify time limits for the detention of migrants pending administrative removal. The judicial practice had it that the detention was equal to the expiry of the statute of limitations for these particular administrative, immigration law offences – i.e. two years. This led to a certain paradox: while under the (intuitively) stricter criminal proceedings individuals could spend a maximum of 18 months in detention pending extradition (later reduced to six months given the ECtHR jurisprudence); under the administrative removal proceedings individuals spent up to 24 months in detention. They were detained for that period without the possibility of requesting a judicial review of the lawfulness or timeframe of their detention (see, *Azimov* v. *Russia*, no 67474/11, judgment of 18 April 2013, paras 152–154).

The emerging ECtHR jurisprudence seemed to respond directly to these ambiguous adaptive strategies by the Russian immigration authorities. In all the subsequent judgments the ECtHR concluded that the applicants' forced return to Central Asia 'in the form of extradition, expulsion, or otherwise' would give rise to a violation of art. 3 of the ECHR (*Azimov* v. *Russia*, para. 143). Returning migrants to countries of Central Asia for their alleged political or religious 'extremist' crimes clearly violates art. 3 of the ECHR. This is now part of the established case law by the ECtHR, as observed in *I.U.* v. *Russia* (no. 48917/15, judgment of 10 January 2017) – the first case decided by the Court sitting as a committee composed of three judges.[17]

With regard to detention pending administrative removal extending up to 24 months, the Court in the *Garabayev* group has also always found a violation to art. 5 (right to liberty). The ECtHR's assessment of the prolonged detention under these administrative removal proceedings did not overlook the fact that it was adopted to 'evade the requirements of the domestic law, which set a maximum time-limit for detention pending extradition' (*Azimov*

[17] In accordance with art. 28.1(b), protocol no. 14 to the Convention for the Protection of Human Rights and Fundamental Freedoms, Amending the Control System of the Convention, from 13 May 2004.

v. *Russia*, para. 165). The ECtHR at one point also normatively questioned the proportionality of the 24-month detention as a 'preventive' measure:

> Given that the maximum penalty in form of deprivation of liberty for an administrative offence under the CAO is thirty days, and that detention with a view to expulsion should not be punitive in nature and also should be accompanied by appropriate safeguards . . . the 'preventive' measure, in terms of its gravity, was much more serious than the 'punitive' one, which is not normal.
> (*Azimov* v. *Russia*, para. 172)

However, it took the Court another year to specify general measures in order to prevent similar violations occurring in the future. In *Kim* v. *Russia* (no 44260/13, judgment of 17 July 2014), ECtHR advised Russia to introduce 'a mechanism which allows individuals to institute proceedings for the examination of the lawfulness of their detention pending removal' (*Kim* v. *Russia*, para. 71). It also recommended that Russia takes 'the necessary general measures to limit detention periods so that they remain connected to the ground of detention applicable in an immigration context' (*Kim* v. *Russia*, para 71).

The Russian Constitutional Court affirmed these recommendations in the *Mskhiladze* case on 23 May 2017 – three years later.[18] The court declared unconstitutional the relevant provisions of the CAO concerning the lack of judicial review of the lawfulness of detention pending removal. This decision drew heavily on the ECtHR jurisprudence and compared the 24-month placement in administrative detention to an arbitrary deprivation of liberty (Decision of Constitutional Court of Russian Federation, 23 May 2017, No. 14-P, p. 12). This gave an additional internal stimulus to the Russian legislature to reform specific provisions of the CAO, and to adjust the immigration practices with regard to detention of migrants pending administrative removal.

Phase 3: Replacing Extradition with Deportation?

Given that these legal developments took place relatively recently to the time of writing, it remains to be seen how they will be followed in practice by the Russian domestic immigration and law enforcement authorities. However, the scholarly work and experience of migration and human rights professionals demonstrates that since 2016 we might be entering a new phase of the *Garabayev* group of cases that rescinds administrative removal and introduces another legal mechanism from Russian domestic immigration practice to replace extradition: deportation. The fast-track deportation procedure, in which a person 'can be deliberately stripped of any guarantees and denied any remedies' is a consequence of an exclusion order, i.e. a foreigner is deemed *persona non grata* on the territory of the RF (Trenina and Zharinov 2017: 39).

[18] Ruling No. 14-P of 23 May 2017, refer to Chapter 6 for details.

An exclusion order is a formal decision issued by the Ministry of Justice or Federal Security Service in respect of a foreigner residing in Russia (legally or illegally), if such person had been found to 'pose a threat to national security, public order or public health'.[19]

Daria Trenina and Kirill Zharinov, both lawyers at the Right to Asylum project in Moscow, describe these developments in the following way, using a recent example of their client, Mr B, whom they were representing before the ECtHR:

> On 2 September 2017, Mr. B, a Tajikistani national and an asylum seeker whose extradition was sought by Tajikistan, was released from the pre-trial detention facility in Moscow as the maximum term provided by law for the detention pending extradition had elapsed. He was immediately re-arrested and then deported to Tajikistan within 48 hours due to an exclusion order of the Federal Security Service of Russia. He and his lawyers were not informed of the deportation order until Mr. B was brought to the airport; so he had no chance of lodging an appeal against the order or asking to suspend its execution. (Trenina and Zharinov 2017: 40)

Trenina and Zharinov conclude that this fast-track deportation procedure leaves vulnerable migrants and asylum seekers who might be subject to torture or ill-treatment upon return with no legal protection before Russian domestic authorities. While administrative removal proceedings regulated by CAO under the influence of the ECtHR jurisprudence might have eventually become an effective remedy against the risk of ill-treatment, 'the [fast-track] deportation proceedings provide no room for such guarantees whatsoever' (Trenina and Zharinov 2017: 40). First, the execution of the deportation order does not require a hearing before the court. Second, while the exclusion order can be appealed in a court of law,[20] filling such an appeal does not automatically have suspensive effect and 'does not anyhow prolong the three-day period during which a foreigner must leave Russia' (Trenina and Zharinov 2017: 40). A case recently communicated by the ECtHR following the fast-track deportation procedure – *O.O* v. *Russia* (no. 36321/16, pending) – proves this point: despite the appeals filed in court against the exclusion order, the applicant was still deported to Uzbekistan (see also Amnesty International 2016). Third, due to the gravity of the charges involved in issuing the exclusion order (threat to public security, public order or public health), these decisions are often classified and therefore not disclosed to the individual or even to the court if a person brings a legal action against the decision (Trenina and Zharinov 2017: 40).

[19] According to art. 25.10 of the Law on the Order of Exit and Entry from the Territory of Russian Federation (Federal Law No. 114 of 15 August 1996).

[20] In accordance with the newly introduced Code of Administrative Procedure (Federal Law No. 21 of 8 March 2015). Chapter 22 of the code regulates the appeals against the decisions of officials and public bodies.

This potential new turn towards the fast-track deportation mechanism following the exclusion order by the Russian immigration authorities makes the domestic remedies against inhuman and degrading treatment in the event of a removal few and far between. The human rights lawyers openly admit that they now operate in a very difficult legal environment with few viable options to prevent their clients' removal to Central Asia:

> A man has just been removed from Russia, he was flown away [to Central Asia]. Why? Because in the 21st century Russia the notifications about Rule 39 [of the Rules of the Court, ECtHR] are prepared in special letters with seals and delivered by pigeons. Because within the structure of the Ministry of Interior, no one understands what Rule 39 is and what does it mean that it is urgent. The notifications are not dispatched but left lying on someone's desk and wait ... Because the letters from the ECtHR are not recognized by the low ranking state officials, who stare at them like deers caught in the headlights: 'what is this bizarre document without an official stamp?'
>
> Or because everything is coordinated? And the feeling that it is coordinated does not leave me. That everything is pre-arranged: some state officials pretend to notify [their lower ranking counterparts], others pretend that they do not have time to respond in time and act accordingly. Because, as we know, when it is really necessary to act, do something for someone in the state organs, everything is done quickly in this country.
>
> (Human Rights Lawyer, via Facebook, 24 September 2018)

Given the types of questions asked by the ECtHR of the parties in the recently communicated cases concerning deportation – *S.S.* v. *Russia* (no. 2236/16, pending), *O.O* v. *Russia* (no. 36321/16, pending) – the Strasbourg Court will now turn to reviewing the newly introduced Code of Administrative Procedure (in force since 2015), and whether it provides an effective domestic remedy for complaints under art. 3 of the ECHR. In particular, the Court is interested in the procedure and time limits for challenging a deportation order, and whether lodging an appeal against a deportation order might have automatic suspensive effect, so that the applicant may obtain an 'independent and rigorous scrutiny' of his complaint of a risk of ill-treatment in the event of the return (see *S.S.* v. *Russia*, no. 2236/16, pending). It looks like, after the Code of Criminal Procedure and the CAO, the Strasbourg Court will turn to the different provisions of the Code of Administrative Procedure. The results of this deliberation and further evolution of Russian domestic immigration law practices remain to be seen.

Exceptional Circumstances: Abductions and Extrajudicial Renditions

A steady, 20 per cent of the *Garabayev* group consists of cases in which the applicants have been violently and/or against their will removed from Russia (see Figure 7.1 and Appendix 2). These cross-border transfers are commonly known as 'renditions'. While rendition is not a legal category under international law, it is 'a descriptive term to identify practices used to bypass ordinary transfer proceedings' (International Commission of Jurists 2017: 120). In these cases apprehension and cross-border transfer to Central Asian countries took place

> where extradition/expulsion of applicants through legal procedures proved impossible due to the application by the ECtHR of Rule 39 (an interim measure) or a final decision of the Court establishing violation of Article 3. (Trenina 2014: 21)

These rendition cases clearly follow the pattern of the *Garabaev* group of cases: migrants were wanted in their home countries for membership in an illegal religious organization or were charged with alleged terrorist activities or crimes that could be qualified as against national security. In all of these cases, migrants were initially arrested in Russia with a view to extradition and then released (upon expiry of the statutory time limit for such detention). Thereafter they 'disappeared' in suspect circumstances. In the majority of cases, after their disappearance they resurfaced in the penitentiary systems of the requesting countries (Uzbekistan or Tajikistan), often amid claims of torture, which the local authorities refused to investigate – as reported by local, yet anonymous media sources (Committee on Legal Affairs and Human Rights 2014: 10).

Knowledge of these rendition cases is widespread among migrants and asylum seekers from Central Asia who I interviewed, human rights lawyers as well as Russian migration authorities. These abductions are a matter of well-established case law of the ECtHR[21] subject to 'enhanced supervision procedure' of the Department for the Execution of Judgments, where the enforcement of this sub-group of cases is classified as a 'complex problem'.[22] Around 2014, during my fieldwork in Moscow, the renditions became so widespread that the general view among the human rights and immigration lawyers was that:

[21] *Kamaliyevy* v. *Russia*, no. 52812/07, judgment of 3 June 2010; *Muminov* v. *Russia*, no. 42502/06, judgment of 11 December 2008; *Isakov Abdulazhon* v. *Russia*, no. 14049/08, judgment of 8 July 2010; *Iskandarov* v. *Russia* no. 17185/05, judgment of 23 September 2010; *Yakubov* v. *Russia* no. 7265/10, judgment of 8 November 2011, *Koziyev* v. Russia no. 58221/10 (no judgment, abduction mentioned in *Savvriddin Dzhurayev*, para. 52); *Abdulkhakov* v. *Russia*, no. 14743/11, judgment of 2 October 2012; *Zokhidov* v. *Russia*, no. 67286/10, judgment of 5 February 2013; *Azimov* v. *Russia*, no. 67474/11, judgment of 18 April 2013; *Savriddin Dzhurayev* v. *Russia*, no. 71386/10, judgment of 25 April 2013 – first pilot judgment with general measures to prevent further kidnappings; *Nizomkhon Dzhurayev* v. *Russia*, no. 31890/11, judgment of 3 October 2013; *Ermakov* v. *Russia* no. 43165/10, judgment of 7 November 2013; *Kasymakhunov* v. *Russia*, no. 29604/12, judgment of 14 November 2013; *Latipov* v. *Russia*, no. 77658/11, judgment of 12 December 2013; *Mamazhonov* v. *Russia*, no. 17239/13, judgment of 23 October 2014; *Mukhitdinov* v. *Russia*, no. 20999/14, judgment of 21 May 2015; *O.O.* v. *Russia*, no. 36321/16, lodged on 27 June 2016.

[22] See Department for the Execution of Judgments of the ECtHR; available at: http://hudoc.exec.coe.int/eng?i=004-14088 (accessed 25 May 2018).

> Your clients are safest when they are in detention centres, when the centre's management is held accountable for them. Having them released should be a cause for concern – they are at risk. No one knows what might happen.
>
> (HR lawyer, 21 May 2014)

The knowledge of these secret rendition practices was independently confirmed by an FMS lawyer in the narrative of Mr Umidov's case invoked earlier in this chapter. The FMS lawyer, in a casual conversation ahead of the trial, suggested that Mr Umidov, rather than disputing the legality of FMS decisions, should remain cautious and vigilant of the Uzbek security services operating in Moscow. This advice, despite its clear double meaning, was expressed in good faith.

As these abducted individuals have been prematurely removed from Russia, their voice is unfortunately lacking from the overall narrative of human rights and migration cases. These individuals remain silent, often unable (or unwilling) to tell their stories. What we do know about their cases comes from the rather abridged version of events that could be found in ECtHR jurisprudence, or through the words of the lawyers who were representing them. For example, the case of *Savriddin Dzhurayev* v. *Russia* (application no. 71386/10, judgment of 25 April 2013) illustrates an abduction of the applicant in the following way:

> The applicant and a friend were driving in the south-west district of Moscow when their car was blocked by a mini-van in M avenue . . . The applicant and his friend got out of the car and tried to escape. They were followed by three or four unidentified men who fired two shots. The applicant's friend managed to escape, while the applicant was stopped, beaten up with a truncheon and forced into the mini-van by the same men, who did not identify themselves . . . The applicant was kept in the mini-van for a night and a day. The individuals beat him up, put a gun to his head and threatened to kill him unless he agreed to return to his home country. The applicant showed them the temporary asylum certificate delivered by the FMS, but they just laughed at him in response. The person who put questions to the applicant was of Tajik origin . . . In the evening of the following day, the applicant was taken by his kidnappers directly to the airfield of Moscow's Domodedovo airport, without going through the usual border and customs formalities and security checks. The applicant was handed over to a Tajik patrol, who forced him into a nearby aircraft without presenting a ticket or any travel documents . . . At around 4 a.m. the next day, the aircraft arrived at the airport of K. in Tajikistan, where the applicant was handed over to the Tajik authorities.
>
> (*Savriddin Dzhurayev* v. *Russia*, paras 38–41)

The great majority of the cross-border transfers were conducted by Tajikistani or Uzbek security forces operating in Russia. However, it would be surprising to think that the Russian authorities were not aware of these renditions. The human rights lawyers view these renditions as 'the last resort for those Russian forces that cannot take a loss on the legal terrain' (Trenina 2014: 21). In fact, Russian tacit knowledge of and, at times, complicity in, certain cases of abductions is now part of an established ECtHR case law:

> in six of these cases (*Iskandarov, Abdulkhakov, Savriddin Dzhurayev, Nizomkhon Dzhurayev, Ermakov, Kasymakhunov*), the Court found that the applicants could not have been abducted, disappeared or forcibly transferred from Russian territory without the knowledge and passive or active involvement of the Russian authorities.
>
> Furthermore, in four cases (*Savriddin Dzhurayev, Ermakov, Kasymakhunov and Mamazhonov*) the Court found that the authorities had breached Article 3 by failing to protect the applicants from exposure to the risk of torture and ill-treatment and also by omitting to hold an effective investigation into the disappearance/abduction incidents.
>
> ... in seven of these cases (*Abdulkhakov, Savriddin Dzhurayev, Zokhidov, Nizomkhon Dzhurayev, Ermakov, Kasymakhunov, Mamazhonov*), the Court considered that, by failing to comply with the interim measure indicated under Rule 39 which prohibited the applicants' removal from Russian territory, the authorities had hindered the applicants' right of individual petition in violation of Article 34.
>
> (Statement on the Status of Execution of the Garabayev group of cases – Enhanced Procedure, Committee of Ministers – Council of Europe; available at: http://hudoc.exec.coe.int/eng?i=004-14088 (accessed 29 May 2018)).

The case of *Savriddin Dzhurayev* – a Tajik refugee holding temporary asylum in Russia who was abducted and illegally transferred to Tajikistan – was the first in which the ECtHR decided to use the pilot-judgment procedure.[23] By relying on the pilot-judgment procedure, the ECtHR recognized this sub-group of the *Garabayev* group of cases as derived from the same underlying problem. The *Savriddin Dzhurayev* judgment speaks of these repetitive cases of abductions as 'lawless', 'a flagrant disregard for the rule of law' (para. 257) characterized by manifest arbitrariness and abuse of power and 'deliberately circumventing the due process' (para. 204). The Court proclaimed these cases to be 'anathema to the rule of law and the values protected by the Convention' (para. 204).

In specifying the general measures, the Court urged Russia to guarantee 'vulnerable applicants in respect of whom the Court has indicated interim measures ... effective protection not only in law, but also *in practice*' (para. 262; my emphasis) to ensure that they can benefit from immediate and effective protection against unlawful kidnapping and irregular removal. The Court also suggested that Russia orders 'an effective investigation into every case of breach of such measures' and 'scrutiny of such investigations at an appropriate official level ... to ensure that they are conducted with the necessary diligence and to the required standard of quality' (para. 263).

Despite this strongly worded pilot-judgment in *Savriddin Dzhurayev*, the cases of extrajudicial renditions continued, which prompted the Parliamentary

[23] The pilot-judgment procedure is a means of dealing with large groups of identical cases that derive from the same underlying problem (see ECtHR Registrar 2009).

Assembly of the Council of Europe to issue a special inquiry into these cases. The report entitled 'Urgent need to deal with new failures to co-operate with the European Court of Human Rights' was prepared by the Committee on Legal Affairs and Human Rights of the Council of Europe (rapporteur Kimmo Sasi) and published in 2014. While the report was not explicitly directed at Russia and also contained examples of cases from other countries that breached the interim measures (e.g. *Sivanathan* v. *the United Kingdom*, no. 38108/07, judgment of 3 February 2009; *Aoulmi* v. *France*, no. 50278/99, judgment of 17 January 2006; *Ben Khemais* v. *Italy*, no. 246/07, judgment of 24 February 2009; *Trabelsi* v. *Italy*, no. 50163/08, judgment of 13 April 2010; *Malevanaya and Sadyrkulov* v. *Ukraine*, no. 18603/12, pending; *Labsi* v. *Slovakia*, no. 33809/08, judgment of 15 May 2012),[24] the 'undercover' transfers of persons to Tajikistan and Uzbekistan from Russia figured prominently in the report. The report's conclusions were kept in a clearly diplomatic style. While the Committee recognized that these extraordinary renditions were a political rather than a strictly legal matter, the solutions it proposed were limited to rather vaguely sounding 'preventive actions and/or specific, sufficiently dissuasive sanctions', ultimately left to the discretion of the Strasbourg Court (Committee on Legal Affairs and Human Rights 2014: 13).

The *Garabayev* group of cases – including the sub-group concerning extrajudicial renditions – was last examined at the 1280th meeting of the Ministers' Deputies – Human Rights (DH) on 7–10 March 2017. No resolution with regard to this group of cases was adopted, meaning that the enforcement of the ECtHR judgments with regard to these cases continues to be ongoing under the enhanced supervisory procedure, defined as a 'major problem' encountered in the execution of judgments (Council of Europe – Committee of Ministers 2017).

* * *

Migrants and asylum seekers are some of the most significant and vulnerable groups of applicants who bring their cases before the ECtHR from Russia. And yet, due to the nature of the ECtHR proceedings and formality of the justice process, their voices, individual experiences and subjectivity are often omitted from the final judgments. This chapter, by retelling the stories of Myriam Nizamov and Khumoyun Umidov, once applicants before the Court, asserted their voices and their versions of the events as crucial in order to arrive at a full picture of 'what really happened'. These individual, emotional – often dismissed as idiosyncratic – legal narratives play an important role as 'sites of resistance', sometimes implicitly sometimes openly challenging the Court's epistemological supremacy at defining human rights violations. They also provide a much-needed illustration to the evolution of Russian immigration

[24] For the full list of cases, see Committee on Legal Affairs and Human Rights (2014).

law and practice under the influence of the ECtHR jurisprudence. These narratives offer a thick ethnographic description that helps us understand and contextualize the nuanced dialogue between the ECtHR, Russian domestic courts and the everyday practices of immigration authorities as part of the *Garabayev* group of cases. The *Garabayev* group constitutes one of the most significant groups of cases before the ECtHR, concerning threats of torture and ill-treatment in the event of extradition, expulsion or deportation of migrants and asylum seekers from Russia. The stories of Myriam and Khumoyun help us capture the 'double-edged sword' of the ambivalent reception of ECtHR jurisprudence in the Russian domestic immigration law practice: replacing extradition with expulsion proceedings and later with deportation, thereby reducing domestic remedies against inhuman and degrading treatment in the event of a removal. The stories that are acutely missing from these accounts are those of migrants and asylum seekers who were prematurely removed from Russia against their will. These 'lost' narratives offer a unique testimony and disturbing glimpse into the practice of extrajudicial renditions and abductions of vulnerable migrants and asylum seekers from Russia to Central Asia.

Conclusions

It comes with a great sense of responsibility to write a book about immigration and refugee laws in Russia when globally the limits of law in securing migrants' human rights and access to justice have been so clearly exposed.

Since 7 May 2018, we have observed a 'zero tolerance' policy unfolding in practice in the United States – prioritizing criminal prosecution for alleged illegal entry of asylum seekers from Latin America (Chacón 2018). Throughout the course of this policy we have learned that it was legal to separate children – some as young as a couple of months – from their parents. At the time of completing this manuscript, as many as 2300 children have been placed in special detention centres or with foster families throughout the United States (Gambino 2018). Their future as to whether, when and where these children might be reunited with their parents was largely unknown (Riva 2018). The various immigration law practices at the southern US border aiming to deter migrants from claiming asylum in the United States have remained legally unchallenged (except by individual and *pro bono* human rights lawyers). This was demonstrated by the recent ruling in a case called *Matter of A-B* by US Attorney General Jeff Sessions (27 I&N Dec. 316; 11 June 2018). This ruling replaced the earlier case law, known as *Matter of A-R-C-G* (26 I&N Dec. 338; 26 August 2014) decided by the Board of Immigration Appeals, ultimately removing a chance for asylum for 'those fleeing targeted domestic violence who lack recourse to official protection in their home countries' (Aleinikoff et al. 2015; Chacón 2018). Earlier, these migrants, victims of violence, could have hoped for asylum on account of being members of a particular social group as defined in US asylum law. While the practice of separating often traumatized migrant families remains legal in the United States (even though it violates their basic human rights), it is *not* illegal for public figures holding important political offices to openly compare migrants to 'animals' (Hirschfeld Davis 2018).

What does this vignette have in common with the situation in Russia? The United States and Russia, despite profound legal, structural and ideological differences in the immigration sphere, are two of the main migration-receiving countries globally. They also share large undocumented populations. Under both jurisdictions – especially recently – the law seems to be doing its job very well when it comes to *othering* of migrants and refugees on account of their legal status, country of origin and the degree of social, political and even human rights afforded. When combined with toxic political narratives, this *othering* takes extreme forms: by denying migrants their basic humanity. The vignette exposes the limits of the law not only with regard to the management of migration and refugee flows, but primarily with regard to the access to justice and realization of human rights in immigration and refugee contexts. These limits of law are currently visible across many national jurisdictions – not only in the United States or Russia, but also in Continental Europe re-emerging from the 2015 so-called refugee crisis. It begs the question: how did we get there? I believe part of the answer is that we lost sight of migration as an inseparable part of social life, social change and transformation. We lost sight of migration as an integral part of a society (Castles 2010, 2015).

Complexity of Everyday Experiences of Law in Migration and Refugee Contexts

This book was my response and attempt to reverse this divisive logic perpetuated in law and politics, through the discursive tool of positioning law in everyday life – reading, seeing and understanding it through the experiences of migrants, refugees, asylum seekers, immigration lawyers and law enforcement authorities (Federal Migration Service (FMS) officers and Russian judges). I wanted to demonstrate that when looked at from these everyday life perspectives, both immigration and refugee laws attain more complex forms and reveal more nuanced experiences. Migrants grapple with the law, avoid or try to bypass its complex bureaucratic structures just as ordinary Russian citizens do. Taken a step further, this conclusion demonstrates that binary analytical categories – for example, whether Russia is a 'rule of law' or 'rule by law' country – do little to cast more light on the complexities of the law as it unfolds in the everyday life experiences of ordinary people (Hendley 2017). Instead, I would like this book to be read with the understanding, in concurrence with what many anthropologists already observed, that the absence of rule of law does not necessarily entail the rule of disorder and mutual abuse (Comaroff and Comaroff 2007). This in-depth inquiry into the everyday life of immigration law reveals that the cultural expression of legality can take many distinct forms and the entire array of these should not be 'both buried and fetishized under the universal rubric of the rule of law' (Silbey 2010). Many of those situations have been discussed in detail in this book, using as an illustration the personal stories of migrants and refugees, exploring their potential for shaping our understanding of Russia 'in its own right'. I presented the case of Akmal – a migrant worker from Uzbekistan with over ten years of residence in Russia, a wife and a small family – who suddenly discovered that his past minor traffic offences had earned him a three-year entry bar to Russia (Chapter 4). The entry bar made it impossible for Akmal to further extend his legal residence in Moscow and renew his work permit. However, given the rather broad appeal structures against the decisions of state authorities in Russia, Akmal tried to have his entry bar reversed on administrative review, relying on humanitarian grounds – both his wife and child were Russian citizens. I also discussed the story of Bahrom, a refugee from Uzbekistan who the Russian FMS refused to recognize as such and suggested he legalizes his stay in Moscow relying on the precarious migrant worker route (Chapter 5). I shared the narratives of Myriam and Farrukh Nizamov or Khumoyun Umidov, who until their applications before the European Court of Human Rights could not achieve justice and obtain recognition of their claims to international or humanitarian protection before the Russian domestic courts (Chapter 7). I observed judges whose decisions to expel migrants who had clearly broken the immigration regime in Moscow were followed by the remark: 'I am sorry for you but my hands are tied. I have to follow the law' (Chapter 6). I encountered FMS lawyers who would do all they could before the domestic courts to defend the legality of the FMS decision to revoke temporary asylum of a vulnerable migrant. At the same time, they were not shy when it came to sharing the following reflection in the courtroom corridor: 'If it was up to me, I would have prolonged the temporary asylum so that the person could legalize their status in Russia' (Chapter 7). This does not mean, of course, that the operation of law in everyday life was free from abuse and examples of outright injustice. There is one particularly disturbing case, not discussed in the book, that deserves a separate mention. It is the story of Zarina Yunusova, a Tajik migrant in St Petersburg, a mother and homemaker who was charged with offences against art. 18.8 of the Code of Administrative Offences (CAO), sentenced to a fine and administrative removal (expulsion) from Russia. In the course of the legal proceedings, however, she was separated from her five-month-old baby, who died in the custody of the FMS (Sarkorova 2015). It is a case that acutely exposes the limits of immigration law when dealing with migrant families from Central Asia; it especially highlighted 'the existence of a boundary between working and nonworking family members, and the structural exclusion of the latter from Russia's legal and social space' (Nikiforova and Brednikova 2018: 142). This case speaks directly to the 'zero tolerance' or 'enforcement first' immigration policies in other Western jurisdictions.

Russia and Global Legal Trends in Immigration Law

Another theme explored in this book was how the various immigration and refugee law practices in Russia actually resembled and followed the more global trends of immigration law. However, comprehensive understanding of these various practices would not be complete without considering how these global trends are translated, transposed and ultimately received into Russian domestic immigration law. Starting from the overview of Russian immigration and refugee legal environments (Chapter 2), I tried to demonstrate that the well-rehearsed mantra that Russian law consists of 'amendments ... followed by amendments to the previous amendments and also further laws' (Buckley 2018a: 219) – actually does very little to cast more light on the logic behind these legal changes. The rapid pace of these legal developments is no different to what happens under other migrant-receiving jurisdictions. For example, the Immigration, Asylum and Nationality Act 2006, a major piece of immigration legislation in the United Kingdom, has, since its enactment, been amended 212 times; by 2018, the Immigration Act 2014 had seen 380 statements of changes.[1] The Immigration and Nationality Act (INA), the main immigration law statue in the United States, since its adoption in 1952 has been amended 117 times, often by laws that themselves were substantive self-contained immigration acts (e.g. the Illegal Immigration Reform and Immigrant Responsibility Act of 1996, or Real ID Act 2005).[2] This means that the developments in Russian immigration law (at an arguably slower pace to start with) are consistent with the general practice – immigration law is one of the fastest-changing areas of legislation globally. Repeating the stereotypes about the reckless pace and erratic developments in Russian legislation prevents us from actually grappling with and coming to terms with this complex legal environment.

In this book, I turned to the heuristic device of a spectrum to position the legal changes in the Russian immigration and refugee law between the extreme ends of liberalization and restrictionism (the latter defined with reference to legal changes observable in Western jurisdictions towards criminalizing different elements of immigration law and exposing its punitive logics). I also pushed against the orthodoxy of portraying Russia as 'a deviant other' by placing specific aspects of its immigration legal regime in comparative perspective with legal developments in other migrant-receiving countries. The analysis of the Russian practice of the entry bar (Chapter 4) takes place with reference to an increased reliance on deportation and deportability (de Genova and Peutz 2010) as a form of post-entry control of the migrant population (Kanstroom 2000) in the United States and the United Kingdom. The discussion of appeal structures and proportionality of the entry bar as an immigration law sanction reveals, in turn, the specificity of how global migration governance practices are married in Russia with the long-standing elements of the Russian legal tradition: broad formal appeal structures, the strictness of application and punitive character of administrative law. A similar observation could be made about the use of case files in Russian immigration and refugee law cases (Chapter 5). While the reliance on the case file for mediating the complex empirical reality for the purpose of the trial is recognized as the 'file's

1 As demonstrated by searches on 'Immigration, Asylum and Nationality Act 2006' and 'Immigration Act 2014' as delivered by the National Archives; available at: www.legislation.gov.uk/changes (accessed 9 July 2018).

2 US Citizenship and Immigration Services, Public Laws Amending the INA (updated through May 2013); available at: www.uscis.gov/ilink/docView/PUBLAW/HTML/PUBLAW/0-0-0-1.html (accessed 9 July 2018).

work' under many civil law jurisdictions, in Russia the case file attains a hyperbolic reality-translating role. This goes beyond the notion that the file accurately depicts the various facts or events of the case – the file actually constructs, sustains and brings them to life. This is why the lawyers in their immigration practice attend to the case file first and foremost, seeing the build-up of the documentary trail as a clear extension of their duty towards the client (Tuitt 2005). Similarly, for the Russian FMS officers (who assess which files go forward and which cases are terminated) and for the Russian judges later on in the legal process of case adjudication, the construction of agents that would be represented through the file is, in fact, a product of the very act of representation (Cody 2009). Tracing the case file helped to see how knowledge is iteratively produced in immigration and refugee law contexts in Russia.

Against 'Tribal Epistemology'

Epistemologically, therefore, this book was also my attempt to challenge the tribalism of knowledge about Russia, where the truth or falsity of a statement depends often on whether the person making it is deemed 'one of us' or 'one of them' (see also Freedland 2018). While the confirmation bias is generally unavoidable, the highly politicized and divisive topics like migration, law and Russia often warrant some conflation (or at least blurring) between 'true' and 'good for our side' (Roberts 2017). The plurality, complexity and nuance of the immigration law scene, unsettling the allegedly definitive 'us' versus 'them' divide, is captured in the chapter devoted to the immigration, refugee and human rights lawyers in Russia (Chapter 3). I wanted to highlight the legal professionals' experiences of dealing with the law, protecting their clients and standing for the rights of migrants. While it is undoubtedly true that these actors operate in a difficult and highly constricting environment, it does not mean that their everyday work resembles the proverbial *tilting at windmills*, and is destined to fail. My characterization of the immigration, human rights and refugee lawyers as a professional group in Russia extends beyond the dominant narrative and the stigma of the 'Foreign Agents' Law (2012). While many of the lawyers share the widespread cynicism about the law and are rather sceptical about law's potential to achieve justice – an expression of some broader traits within Russian legal culture (Kurkchiyan 2009) – many do not lack genuine passion for their job:

> I much prefer to stay in St Petersburg and 'live on a volcano' than work for some legal, human rights NGO in the West and write briefs and memos. Here [in Russia] I have the feeling that I can change things and really make a difference to people's lives. It is not easy, but it is possible.
>
> (HR lawyer, 14 April 2018, Cambridge)

The immigration, refugee and human rights lawyers among whom I conducted my fieldwork could all be positioned with reference to the analytical category of cause-lawyering; it does not mean, however, that they all understood, interpreted and practised cause-lawyering in the same way. The majority of them – as demonstrated by the figure of Varvara – subscribed to cause-lawyering defined as 'caring for individual clients and cases' and represented, *pro bono*, vulnerable migrants and refugees before domestic courts. For them, making a change, making a difference, meant disrupting the status quo at the level of everyday experience of the law. A small and elite group of human rights lawyers challenged the immigration law at a more systemic level, either in the international arena, before the European Court of Human Rights, or domestically, before the Russian Supreme Court or Constitutional Court. Their actions often resulted in landmark cases that stimulated important changes in national legislation, clarification of the law and legal procedures. For others, the commitment to their clients did not end when the limits of the law often exposed the limits of a particular legal case. For those lawyers, their client became the cause, and they were willing to pursue their interests by all means – both legal and beyond. This specific group of lawyers, which in the main body of the book I dubbed cause-lawyers 'with the grain', demonstrated exceptional commitment to their clients, uninhibited by the restrictionist legal environment. For them, cause-lawyering was not limited to the purely legal arena, and these lawyers often went beyond the legal representation and professional call of duty to ensure that their clients were safe, comforted and their welfare needs were attended do. This happened even at the cost of losing important legal battles or dropping cases that could lead to precedent judgments before international courts.

Similarly, the portrayal of Russian domestic judges deciding immigration and refugee law cases (Chapter 6) demonstrated that they were a much more plural and less ideologically monolithic group than many commentators would give them credit for. Many of the judges, admittedly, did not hesitate to reject the human rights arguments either brought forward by the defendants or their legal representatives. Others, however, embraced the various provisions stemming from international obligations to which Russia is a party (the International Covenant on Civil and Political Rights, UN Convention against Torture and Other Cruel, Inhuman or Degrading Treatment or Punishment, or the European Convention of Human Rights) and incorporated the human rights logic into adjudicating immigration and refugee law cases. Again, the way human rights were referred to by these judges was not straightforward: some *explicitly* acknowledged the relevance of specific human rights provisions to the case at hand (e.g. articles 2, 3 and 8 of the European Convention of Human Rights) by quoting and citing them directly in their judgments. Others preferred to remain within the remit of domestic laws and the Russian Constitution but *implicitly* relied on the principles of proportionality, human dignity, right to liberty and prohibition of torture – to the benefit of the defendant, and staying true to the spirit of human rights.

These concluding thoughts bring me back to the opening questions of this book. The picture of access to justice and realization of human rights for migrants and refugees in Russia is, perhaps, not as uniform or bleak as many commentators would portray it. This is not to say that migrants do not suffer from some of the structural ills of the Russian legal environment – institutional racism, xenophobia and populism fuelling the different anti-migrant sentiments (Abashin 2017; Agadjanian et al. 2017; Buckley 2018b; Schenk 2018). Of course they do. However, the approach of looking at their experiences in conjunction with the experiences of immigration, refugee and human rights lawyers, FMS officers and Russian domestic judges deciding their cases demonstrates that the everyday experiences of the law are more complex, quite nuanced and subtle.

Appendices

Appendix 1

List of interviewees

No.	Interviewee	Date	Place
1	Head of NGO	25 May 2014	Moscow
2	Professional advocate	6 June 2014	Moscow
3	Professional advocate	13 April 2014	Moscow
4	Migration researcher	6 April 2014	Moscow
5	Legal consultant	26 April 2014	Moscow
6	*Pro bono* lawyer for migrants	1 April 2014	Moscow
7	Labour rights researcher	16 May 2014	Moscow
8	Migrants' rights researcher	26 June 2014	Moscow
9	Legal consultant	15 May 2015	Moscow
10	Professional advocate	5 April 2014	Moscow
11	Professional advocate	14 April 2014	Moscow
12	Professional advocate	7 September 2014	Moscow
13	Human rights lawyer	16 April 2014	Moscow
14	Human rights lawyer	28 April 2014	Moscow
15	Professional advocate	18 June 2015	London
16	Social worker	23 April 2014	Moscow
17	Social worker	28 May 2014	Moscow
18	Social worker	27 May 2014	Moscow
19	Social worker	7 June 2014	Moscow
20	Social worker	18 June 2014	Moscow
21	Researcher	12 September 2014	Moscow
22	Federal Migration Service (FMS) representative	16 September 2014	Moscow
23	FMS representative	18 September 2014	Moscow
24	FMS representative	6 May 2014	Moscow
25	FMS representative	2 June 2014	Moscow
26	FMS representative	8 September 2014	Moscow
27	FMS representative	19 September 2014	Moscow
28	NGO employee	25 May 2014	Moscow

(*cont.*)

No.	Interviewee	Date	Place
29	NGO employee	6 June 2014	Moscow
30	NGO employee	5 September 2014	Moscow
31	Migrant, Uzbekistan, male	6 April 2014	Moscow
32	Migrant, Kyrgyzstan, female	12 April 2014	Moscow
33	Migrant, Kyrgyzstan, male	13 April 2014	Moscow
34	Migrant, Kyrgyzstan, female	15 April 2014	Moscow
35	Migrant, Kyrgyzstan, female	15 May 2014	Moscow
36	Migrant, Uzbekistan, male	17 April 2014	Moscow
37	Migrant, Uzbekistan, male	17 April 2014	Moscow
38	Migrant, Uzbekistan, male	17 April 2014	Moscow
39	Asylum seeker, Uzbekistan, male	26 June 2014	Moscow
40	Asylum seeker, Uzbekistan, male	24 May 2014	Moscow
41	Asylum seeker, Uzbekistan, male	19 June 2014	Moscow
42	Asylum seeker, Uzbekistan, male	23 September 2014	Moscow
43	Asylum seeker, Uzbekistan, female	23 September 2014	Moscow
44	Asylum seeker, Tajikistan, female	20 September 2014	Moscow
45	Asylum seeker, Uzbekistan, female	2 June 2014	Moscow
46	Refugee, Uzbekistan, male	18 September 2014	Moscow
47	Refugee, Uzbekistan, male	20 September 2014	Moscow
48	Refugee, Tajikistan, male	23 September 2014	Moscow
49	Asylum seeker, Syria, male	21 May 2014	Moscow
50	Asylum seeker, Syria, male	21 May 2014	Moscow

Appendix 2

Garabayev Group: List of Cases before the European Court of Human Rights, 2002–2018

No.	Application	Case	Judgment of	Final on	Abduction status
1	38411/02	*Garabayev*	7 June 2007	30 January 2008	
2	656/06	*Nasrulloyev*	11 October 2007	11 January 2008	
3	2947/06	*Ismoilov and Others*	24 April 2008	1 December 2008	
4	16074/07	*Shchebet*	12 June 2008	12 September 2008	
5	8320/04	*Ryabikin*	19 June 2008	19 September 2008	
6	42502/06	*Muminov*	11 December 2008	4 May 2009	Abducted
7	13476/04	*Khudyakova*	8 January 2009	8 April 2009	
8	42443/02	*Eminbeyli*	26 February 2009	26 May 2009	
9	38124/07	*Dzhurayev*	17 December 2009	28 June 2010	
10	24268/08	*Klein*	1 April 2010	4 October 2010	
11	52466/08	*Khodzayev*	12 May 2010	4 October 2010	
12	21055/09	*Khaydarov*	20 May 2010	4 October 2010	
13	52812/07	*Kamaliyevy*	3 June 2010	3 September 2010	Abducted
14	19316/09	*Galeyev*	3 June 2010	3 September 2010	
15	26876/08	*Kolesnik*	17 June 2010	22 November 2010	
16	14049/08	*Isakov Abdulazhon*	8 July 2010	22 November 2010	Abducted (para. 75 of the *Mukhitdinov* judgment)
17	1248/09	*Yuldashev*	8 July 2010	22 November 2010	
18	54219/08	*Karimov*	29 July 2010	21 February 2011	
19	19732/04	*Konontsev*	29 July 2010	29 October 2010	
20	17185/05	*Iskandarov*	23 September 2010	21 February 2011	Abducted
21	25404/09	*Gaforov*	21 October 2010	11 April 2011	
22	15303/09	*Sultanov*	4 November 2010	11 April 2011	
23	66317/09	*Elmuratov*	3 March 2011	15 September 2011	

(*cont.*)

No.	Application	Case	Judgment of	Final on	Abduction status
24	7265/10	*Yakubov*	8 November 2011	4 June 2012	Abducted (paras 10 and 75 of the *Mukhitdinov* judgment)
25	12106/09	*Ergashev*	20 December 2011	4 June 2012	
26	60045/10	*Kozhayev*	5 June 2012	22 October 2012	
27	55822/10	*Shakurov*	5 June 2012	22 October 2012	
28	52805/10	*Abidov*	12 June 2012	12 September 2012	
29	11209/10	*Rustamov*	3 July 2012	3 October 2012	
30	35692/11	*Alikhonov*	31 July 2012	31 October 2012	
31	17455/11	*Umirov*	19 September 2012	11 February 2013	
32	14743/11	*Abdulkhakov*	2 October 2012	11 February 2013	Abducted
33	49747/11	*Makhmudzhan Ergashev*	16 October 2012	11 February 2013	
34	27843/11	*Niyazov*	16 October 2012	16 January 2013	
35	50031/11	*Rakhmonov*	16 October 2012	11 February 2013	
36	30225/11	*Bakoyev*	5 February 2013	5 May 2013	
37	67286/10	*Zokhidov*	5 February 2013	8 July 2013	Abducted
38	39786/09	*Yefimova*	19 February 2013	8 July 2013	
39	67474/11	*Azimov*	18 April 2013	9 September 2013	Abducted
40	71386/10	*Savriddin Dzhurayev*	25 April 2013	9 September 2013	Abducted
41	69235/11	*K.*	23 May 2013	23 August 2013	
42	73455/11	*Sidikovy*	20 June 2013	4 November 2013	
43	31890/11	*Nizomkhon Dzhurayev*	3 October 2013	20 January 2014	Abducted
44	43165/10	*Ermakov*	7 November 2013	24 March 2014	Abducted
45	29604/12	*Kasymakhunov*	14 November 2013	24 March 2014	Abducted
46	77658/11	*Latipov*	12 December 2013	12 March 2014	Abducted
47	56662/09	*Oshlakov*	3 April 2014	3 July 2014	
48	39093/13	*Gayratbek Saliyev*	17 April 2014	8 September 2014	
49	20110/13	*Ismailov*	17 April 2014	8 September 2014	
50	22636/13+	*Nizamov and Others*	7 May 2014	8 September 2014	
51	62892/12	*Akram Karimov*	28 May 2014	13 October 2014	
52	34742/13	*Egamberdiyev*	26 June 2014	17 November 2014	
53	41970/11	*Shcherbina*	26 June 2014	17 November 2014	
54	50552/13	*Rakhimov*	10 July 2014	15 December 2014	

(*cont.*)

No.	Application	Case	Judgment of	Final on	Abduction status
55	42351/13+	*Kadirzhanov and Mamashev*	17 July 2014	15 December 2014	
56	5614/13	*Mamadaliyev*	24 July 2014	15 December 2014	
57	15590/14	*Turgunov*	22 October 2014	14 March 2016	
58	17239/13	*Mamazhonov*	23 October 2014	23 March 2015	Abducted
59	74759/13	*Fozil Nazarov*	11 December 2014	20 April 2015	
60	68900/13	*Eshonkulov*	15 January 2015	1 June 2015	
61	66373/13	*Khalikov*	26 February 2015	6 July 2015	
62	68894/13	*Khamrakulov*	16 April 2015	14 September 2015	
63	20999/14	*Mukhitdinov*	21 May 2015	19 October 2015	Abducted
64	44260/13	*Kim*	17 July 2014	17 October 2014	
65	8474/14	*Nabid Abdullayev*	15 October 2015	14 March 2016	
66	44095/14	*A.L. (X.W.)*	29 October 2015	29 January 2016	
67	17724/14	*Tadzhibayev*	1 December 2015	2 May 2016	
68	11916/15	*R.*	26 January 2016	6 June 2016	
69	58923/14	*Kholmurodov*	1 March 2016	4 July 2016	
70	14348/15	*U.N.*	26 July 2016	28 November 2016	
71	48917/15	*I.U.*	10 January 2017	10 January 2017	
72	42332/14	*Khamidkariyev*	26 January 2017	29 May 2017	
73	46721/15	*Allanazarova*	14 February 2017	3 July 2017	
74	52722/15	*S.K*	14 February 2017	14 May 2017	
75	2961/09	*Dumikyan*	13 March 2017	13 December 2016	
76	58182/14	*K.I*	7 November 2017	7 February 2018	
77	31189/15	*T.M. and Others*	7 November 2017	7 November 2017	
78	46637/09	*Butorin*	6 February 2018	6 February 2018	
79	46580/08	*Malimonenko*	20 March 2018	20 March 2018	
80	58221/10	*Koziyev*			Abducted to Tajikistan (para. 52 of the *Savriddin Dzhurayev* judgment)
81	12018/16	*U.A*	Lodged on 2 March 2016		
82	21535/16	*S.S.*	Lodged on 6 April 2016		
83	36321/16	*O.O.*	Lodged on 27 June 2016		Abducted

References

Aas, K. F. (2011). '"Crimmigrant" bodies and bona fide travelers: Surveillance, citizenship and global governance'. *Theoretical Criminology* **15**(3): 331–346.

Abashin, S. (2017). 'Migration policies in Russia: Laws and debates'. In *Migrant Workers in Russia: Global Challenges of the Shadow Economy in Societal Transformation*, eds A.-L. Heusala and K. Aitamurto. London, Routledge: 16–34.

Abrego, L. (2008). 'Legitimacy, social identity, and the mobilization of law: The effects of Assembly Bill 540 on undocumented students in California'. *Law and Social Inquiry* **33**(3): 709–734.

Afshar, A. (2005). 'Refugees in Russia: The Law on Refugees and its implementation'. *Journal of Refugee Studies* **18**(4): 468–491.

Agadjanian, V., C. Menjívar and N. Zotova (2017). 'Legality, racialization, and immigrants' experience of ethnoracial harassment in Russia'. *Social Problems* **64**(4): 558–576.

Aitieva, M. (2015). 'Materialities and moralities of remittances: The case of livestock and barn building'. In *Russia's Migration Regulatory Regime: Migration Policy, Laws, Enforcement and Effects*. London, SOAS, University of London.

Alba, R. and V. Nee (1997). 'Rethinking assimilation theory for a new era of immigration'. *International Migration Review* **31**(4): 826–874.

Aleinikoff, T. A., D. A. Martin, H. Motomura and M. Fullerton (2015). *Immigration and Citizenship: Process and Policy*. 8th edition. St. Paul, MN, West Tomson Reuters Publishers.

Aliverti, A. (2012). 'Making people criminal: The role of the criminal law in immigration enforcement'. *Theoretical Criminology* **16**(4): 417–434.

Amnesty International (2013). *Return to Torture: Extradition, Forcible Returns and Removals to Central Asia*. London, Amnesty International. Accessed from: www.amnesty.org/en/documents/EUR04/001/2013/en/.

(2015). *Secrets and Lies: Forced Confessions under Torture in Uzbekistan*. London, Amnesty International. Accessed from www.amnestyusa.org/.../eur_62_1086_2015_uzbekistantorture_fullreport.pdf.

(2016a). Asylum-seeker returned from Russia to Uzbekistan in blatant violation of international law. AI index number: EUR 62/4488/2016.

(2016b). *Fast-Track to Torture: Abductions and Forcible Returns from Russia to Uzbekistan*. London, Amnesty International. Accessed from: www.amnesty.org/download/Documents/EUR6237402016ENGLISH.PDF.

Anderson, J., J. Hollaus, A. Lindsay and C. Williamson (2014). 'The culture of disbelief: An ethnographic approach to understanding an under-theorised concept in the UK asylum system'. Refugee Studies Centre working paper 102.

Andrianova, V. (2018). 'The everyday experiences of Russian citizens in justice of the peace courts'. In *Sociology of Justice in Russia*, eds M. Kurkchiyan and A. Kubal. Cambridge, Cambridge University Press: 68–91.

Appelqvist, M. (2000). 'Refugee law and cause lawyering: A Swedish study of the legal profession'. *International Journal of Refugee Law* **12**(1): 71–89.

Aranda, E., C. Menjívar and K. M. Donato (2014). 'The spillover consequences of an enforcement-first U.S. immigration regime'. *American Behavioral Scientist* **58**(13): 1687–1695.

Bagenstos, S. R. (2009). *Law and the Contradictions of the Disability Rights Movement*. New Haven, CT, Yale University Press.

Bahovadinova, M. (2016). 'Tajikistan's bureaucratic management of exclusion: Responses to the Russian reentry ban database'. *Central Asian Affairs* **3**(3): 226–248.

Baldwin, J. (1998). *Early Novels and Stories* New York: Library of America.

Baron, J. B. (1993). 'Resistance to stories'. *Southern California Law Review* **67**: 255.

Baxi, U. (2011). 'Afterword: The struggle for sans-papiers human rights'. In *Are Human Rights for Migrants? Critical Reflections on the Status of Irregular Migrants in Europe and the United States*, eds M.-B. Dembour and T. Kelly. London, Routledge: 222–232.

BBC (2012). Prisoners will not get the vote, says David Cameron. Accessed from www.bbc.co.uk/news/uk-politics-20053244, 21 April 2018.

Bear, L. (2007). *Lines of the Nation: Indian Railway Workers, Bureaucracy, and the Intimate Historical Self*. New York, Columbia University Press.

Benedek, W. (2017). 'Russia and the European Court of Human Rights: Some general conclusions'. In *Russia and the European Court of Human Rights: The Strasbourg Effect*, eds L. Mälksoo and W. Benedek. Cambridge, Cambridge University Press: 385–399.

Birch, K. (2017). 'What exactly is neoliberalism?'. *The Conversation*, 2 November.

Bisharat, G. (1998). 'Attorneys for the people, attorneys for the land: The emergence of cause lawyering in the Israeli-occupied territories'. In *Cause Lawyering: Political Commitments and Professional Responsibilities*, eds A. Sarat and S. A. Scheingold. New York, Oxford University Press: 453–486.

Blok, A. and T. E. Jensen (2011). *Bruno Latour: Hybrid Thoughts in a Hybrid World*. London, Routledge.

Bocharov, T. and K. Titaev (2018). 'When business goes to court: Arbitrazh courts in Russia'. In *Sociology of Justice in Russia*, eds M. Kurkchiyan and A. Kubal. Cambridge, Cambridge University Press: 118–140.

Boon, A. (2004). 'Cause lawyers and the alternative ethical paradigm: Ideology and transgression'. *Legal Ethics* **7**(2): 250–268.

Booth, D. and D. Cammack (2013). *Governance for Development in Africa: Solving Collective Action Problems*. London, Zed Books.

Bosworth, M. and M. Guild (2008). 'Governing through migration control: Security and citizenship in Britain'. *British Journal of Criminology* **48**(6): 703–719.

Bosworth, M. and E. Kaufman (2011). 'Foreigners in a carceral age: Immigration and imprisonment in the United States'. *Stanford Law & Policy Review* **22**: 429.

Boukalas, C. (2013). 'Politics as legal action/lawyers as political actors'. *Social & Legal Studies* **22**(3): 395–420.

Boyes-Watson, C. (2013). *Crime and Justice: Learning Through Cases*. Lanham, MD, Rowman & Littlefield.

Brouwer, J., M. van der Woude and J. van der Leun (2018). '(Cr)immigrant framing in border areas: Decision-making processes of Dutch border police officers'. *Policing and Society* **28**(4): 448–463.

Buckley, C. and E. T. Hofmann (2012). 'Are remittances an effective mechanism for development? Evidence from Tajikistan, 1999–2007'. *Journal of Development Studies* **48**(8): 1121–1138.

Buckley, C., B. A. Ruble and E. T. Hofmann (2008). *Migration, Homeland and Belonging in Eurasia*. Washington, DC, Woodrow Wilson Center Press.

Buckley, M. (2018a). 'Policy and legislation on labour migrants'. In *The Politics of Unfree Labour in Russia: Human Trafficking and Labour Migration*. Cambridge, Cambridge University Press: 218–242.

(2018b). *The Politics of Unfree Labour in Russia: Human Trafficking and Labour Migration*. Cambridge, Cambridge University Press.

Burkov, A. (2017). 'The use of European human rights law in Russian courts'. In *Russia and the European Court of Human Rights: The Strasbourg Effect*, eds L. Mälksoo and W. Benedek. Cambridge, Cambridge University Press: 59–92.

Burnham, W., P. R. Maggs and G. M. Danilenko (2012). *Law and Legal System of the Russian Federation*. 5th edition. New York, Juris.

Burtina, E. (2018a). 'Court practice regarding the release of stateless persons from detention following the decision of the Russian Constitutional Court from 23 May 2017 in Mskhiladze case'. In *Stateless Persons in the Temporary detention Centers for Foreign Nationals of the Ministry of the Interior: Statistics, Legislation, Law Enforcement*, eds E. Burtina and O. Tseytlina. Moscow, Human Rights Centre Memorial: 43–56.

(2018b). 'Stateless persons in detention centres in Russia: Analysis of statistical data'. In *Stateless Persons in the Temporary Detention Centers for Foreign Nationals of the Ministry of the Interior: Statistics, Legislation, Law Enforcement*, eds E. Burtina and O. Tseytlina. Moscow, Human Rights Centre Memorial: 11–22.

Burtina, E. and O. Tseytlina, eds (2018). *Stateless Persons in the Temporary Detention Centres for Foreign Nationals of the Ministry of the Interior: Statistics, Legislation, Law Enforcement*. Moscow, Human Rights Centre Memorial.

Burtina, E., E. Korosteleva and V. Simonov (2015). *Russia as a Country of Asylum. Report on the Implementation of the 1951 Convention Relating to the Status of Refugees by the Russian Federation*. Moscow: Civic Assistance Committee. Accessed from: http://refugee.ru/en/news/russia-as-a-country-of-asylum, 3 June 2016 (English translation).

Campbell, J. R. (2017). *Bureaucracy, Law and Dystopia in the United Kingdom's Asylum System*. London, Routledge.

Caple James, E. (2004). 'The political economy of "trauma" in Haiti in the democratic era of insecurity'. *Culture, Medicine and Psychiatry* **28**(2): 127–149.

Castles, S. (2010). 'Understanding global migration: A social transformation perspective'. *Journal of Ethnic and Migration Studies* **36**(10): 1565–1586.

(2015). 'International human mobility: Key issues and challenges to social theory'. In *Social Transformation and Migration: National and Local Experiences in South Korea, Turkey, Mexico and Australia*, eds D. Ozkul. S. Castles and M. Cubas. Basingstoke, Palgrave Macmillan.

Castles, S., H. De Haas and M. J. Miller (2014). *The Age of Migration: International Population Movements in the Modern World.* Basingstoke, Palgrave Macmillan.

Chacón, J. M. (2009). 'Managing migration through crime'. *Columbia Law Review Sidebar* **109**: 135–148.

(2012). 'Overcriminalizing migration'. *Journal of Criminal Law and Criminology* **102** (3): 613–652.

(2018). 'Narrowing asylum grounds, family separations and supreme indifference at the U.S. border'. Border Criminologies Blog. Available at: www.law.ox.ac.uk/research-subject-groups/centre-criminology/centreborder-criminologies/blog/2018/07/narrowing-asylum (accessed 9 July 2018).

Chon, M. (1995). 'On the need for Asian American narratives in law: Ethnic specimens, native informants, storytelling and silences'. *UCLA Asian Pacific American Law Journal* **3**: 4–32.

Chupik, V. (2015). 'Laws as roots of corruption and xenophobia: Migrants' daily encounters with law and order authorities'. In Russia's Migration Regulatory Regime: Migration Policy, Laws, Enforcement and Effects workshop, SOAS, London, 19 June.

Cienski, J. (1994). 'Chilly reception for refugees in Russia'. *Refugees Magazine* **98**. Available at: www.unhcr.org/uk/publications/refugeemag/3b54109e4/refugees-magazine-issue-98-soviet-union-chilly-reception-refugees-russia.html (accessed 7 June 2018).

Cody, F. (2009). 'Inscribing subjects to citizenship: Petitions, literacy activism, and the performativity of signature in rural Tamil India'. *Cultural Anthropology* **24**(3): 347–380.

Cohen, R. (1995). *The Cambridge Survey of World Migration*, Cambridge, Cambridge University Press.

Comaroff, J. and J. Comaroff (2007). 'Law and disorder in the postcolony'. *Social Anthropology* **15**(2): 133–152.

Committee on Legal Affairs and Human Rights (2014). 'Urgent need to deal with new failures to co-operate with the European Court of Human Rights'. Strasbourg, Parliamentary Assembly Council of Europe. Available at: http://assembly.coe.int/nw/xml/XRef/Xref-DocDetails-EN.asp?fileid=20348 (accessed 26 May 2018).

Costello, C. (2016). *The Human Rights of Migrants in European Law*, Oxford, Oxford University Press.

Council of Europe – Committee of Ministers. (2017). 'H46-23 *Garabayev group* v. *Russian Federation* (Application No. 38411/02): Supervision of the execution of the European Court's judgments'. Available at: https://search.coe.int/cm/pages/result_details.aspx?objectid=09000016806e43fb (accessed 28 May 2018).

Coutin, S. B. (1998). 'From refugees to immigrants: The legalization strategies of Salvadoran immigrants and activists'. *International Migration Review* **32**(4): 901–925.

(2000). *Legalizing Moves: Salvadoran Immigrants' Struggle for US Residency.* Ann Arbor, MI, University of Michigan Press.

(2001). 'Cause lawyering in the shadow of the state: A US immigration example'. In *Cause Lawyering and the State in a Global Era*, eds A. Sarat and S. A. Scheingold. New York, Oxford University Press: 117–140.

(2002). 'Questionable transactions as grounds for legalization: Immigration, illegality, and law'. *Crime Law and Social Change* **37**(1): 19–36.

(2006). 'Cause lawyering and political advocacy: Moving law on behalf of Central American refugees'. In *Cause Lawyers and Social Movements.*, eds A. Sarat and S. A. Scheingold. Stanford, CA, Stanford University Press: 101–119.

Coutin, S. B., B. Maurer and B. Yngvesson (2002). 'In the mirror: The legitimation work of globalization'. *Law & Social Inquiry* **27**(4): 801–843.

Davé, B. (2014). 'Becoming "legal" through "illegal" procedures: The precarious status of migrant workers in Russia'. *Russian Analytical Digest* **159**: 2–6.

Davis, M. (1993). *Brutal Need.* New Haven, CT, Yale University Press.

de Certeau, M. (1984). *The Practice of Everyday Life.* London, University of California Press.

de Genova, N. P. (2002). 'Migrant "illegality" and deportability in everyday life'. *Annual Review of Anthropology* **31**: 419–447.

(2004). 'The legal production of Mexican/migrant "illegality"'. *Latino Studies* **2**(2): 160–185.

de Genova, N. P. and N. Peutz, eds (2010). *The Deportation Regime: Sovereignty, Space, and the Freedom of Movement.* Durham, Durham University Press.

de Haas, H. (2010). 'The internal dynamics of migration processes: A theoretical inquiry'. *Journal of Ethnic and Migration Studies* **36**(10): 1587–1617.

(2012). 'The migration and development pendulum: A critical view on research and policy'. *International Migration* **50**(3): 8–25.

Dedov, D. (2017). 'Dissenting Opinion of Judge Dedov: Z.A. and Others v Russia Judgment, Separate Opinion'. European Court of Human Rights. Judgment of 28 March 2017. Available at: http://hudoc.echr.coe.int/eng?i=001-172107 (accessed 28 May 2018): 26–28.

Delgado, R. (1989). 'Storytelling for oppositionists and others: A plea for narrative'. *Michigan Law Review* **87**(8): 2411–2441.

(1993). 'On telling stories in school: A reply to Farber and Sherry'. *Vanderbilt Law Review* **46**: 665.

(1996). *The Rodrigo Chronicles: Conversations about America and Race.* New York, New York University Press.

Dembour, M.-B. (2015). *When Humans Become Migrants: Study of the European Court of Human Rights with an Inter-American Counterpoint.* Oxford, Oxford University Press.

Dembour, M.-B. and T. Kelly (2011). *Are Human Rights for Migrants? Critical Reflections on the Status of Irregular Migrants in Europe and the United States.* London, Routledge.

Denisenko, M. and Y. Varshavskaya (2013). 'Migrants at the Russian labour market: Characteristics, status, mobility'. WP3/21 Search Working Paper. Moscow, Higher School of Economics. Available at: www.ub.edu/searchproject/wp-content/uploads/2013/07/WP_3_21.pdf (accessed 11 June 2018): 25.

Di Donato, F. (2011). 'Constructing legal narratives: Client-lawyers' stories'. In *Exploring Courtroom Discourse: The Language of Power and Control*, ed. L. Cheng. London, Routledge: 129–146.

Doolotkeldieva, A. (2008). 'Conducting interviews with labour migrants in Moscow'. *CESR* **7**(2): 31–34.

Espinoza, L. G. (1997). 'Legal narratives, therapeutic narratives: The invisibility and omnipresence of race and gender'. *Michigan Law Review* **95**(4): 901–937.

European Court of Human Rights (2018). *Annual Report 2017: European Court of Human Rights*. Strasbourg, Council of Europe. Available at: www.echr.coe.int/Documents/Annual_report_2017_ENG.pdf (accessed 1 June 2018).

European Court of Human Rights Registrar (2009). The pilot-judgment procedure. Information note issued by the Registrar. Available at: www.echr.coe.int/Documents/Pilot_judgment_procedure_ENG.pdf (accessed 28 May 2018).

Ewick, P. and S. Silbey (1995). 'Subversive stories and hegemonic tales: Toward a sociology of narrative'. *Law and Society Review* **29**(2): 197–226.

(2003). 'Narrating social structure: Stories of resistance to legal authority'. *American Journal of Sociology* **108**(6): 1328–1372.

Farber, D. A. and S. Sherry (1993). 'Telling stories out of school: An essay on legal narratives'. *Stanford Law Review* **45**(4): 807–855.

Federal Migration Service (2014). Статистические сведения по миграционной ситуации в Российской Федерации. (Statisticheskiye svedeniya po migratsionnoy situatsii v Rossiyskoy Federatsii/Statistical information on the migration situation in the Russian Federation). Available at: www.fms.gov.ru/about/statistics/data/ (accessed 19 August 2014).

Feenan, D. (2013). 'Exploring the "socio" of socio-legal studies'. In *Exploring the 'Socio' of Socio-Legal Studies*, ed. D. Feenan. London, Palgrave Macmillan: 3–19.

Feifer, G. (1964). *Justice in Moscow*. New York, Simon and Schuster.

Fielding, N. G. (2013). 'Lay people in court: The experience of defendants, eyewitnesses and victims'. *The British Journal of Sociology* **64**(2): 287–307.

Fomina E. (2015a). 'We were recognized as terrorists?'. *Novaya Gazeta*, 19 November. Available at: www.novayagazeta.ru/articles/2015/11/19/66441-171-nas-chto-za-terroristov-priznali-187 (accessed 2 March 2018).

(2015b). 'Today I'm so happy, we were released'. *Novaya Gazeta*, 23 November. Available at: www.novayagazeta.ru/articles/2015/11/23/66487-171-ya-segodnya-takaya-schastlivaya-nas-vypustili-187 (accessed 2 March 2018).

Foucault, M. (1977). *Discipline and Punish: The Birth of the Prison*. New York, Vintage Books.

(1982). 'The subject and power'. *Critical Inquiry* **8**: 777–795.

Freedland, J. (2018). The great divide of our times is not left v right, but true v false. *Guardian*. 20 April. Available at: www.theguardian.com/commentisfree/2018/apr/20/trump-us-syria-truth-tribal-robert-mueller-white-helmets-factse, accessed 16 November 2018.

Frohmann, B. (2008). 'Documentary ethics, ontology, and politics'. *Archival Science* **8**(3): 165–180.

Fu, H. and R. Cullen (2008). 'Weiquan (rights protection) lawyering in an authoritarian state: Building a culture of public-interest lawyering'. *The China Journal* **59**: 111–127.

Fura, E. and R. Maruste (2017). 'Russia's impact on the Strasbourg system, as seen by two former judges of the European Court of Human Rights'. In *Russia and the European Court of Human Rights: The Strasbourg Effect*, eds L. Mälksoo and W. Benedek. Cambridge, Cambridge University Press: 222–251.

Gambino, L. (2018). 'Trump policy of detaining children "may amount to torture", UN says – as it happened'. *Guardian*. 22 June. Available at: www.theguardian.com/us-news/live/2018/jun/22/trump-family-separation-crisis-immigration-border?page=

with:block-5b2d5ce2e4b0385b28421e90#block-5b2d5ce2e4b0385b28421e90 (accessed 2 July 2018).

Gannushkina, S. A. (2014). 'The most important changes in migration law of 2013 in Russia'. In Migration and Law seminar. Moscow, 24 May.

Geertz, C. (1975). *Interpretations of Culture*. Oxford, Oxford University Press.

(1983). *Local Knowledge: Further Essays in Interpretive Anthropology*. New York, Basic Books.

Gellner, E. (2008). *Nations and Nationalism*. New York, Cornell University Press.

Gibney, M. J. (2004). *The Ethics and Politics of Asylum: Liberal Democracy and the Response to Refugees*. Cambridge, Cambridge University Press.

Golash-Boza, T. (2010). 'The criminalization of undocumented migrants: Legalities and realities'. *Societies Without Borders* **5**(1): 81–90.

Golubok, S. (2018). The challenges of the defence attorney. In British Association for Slavonic and East European Studies Annual Conference. Cambridge, 13–15 April.

Greenberg, I. (2007). Central Asians chase jobs and endure exploitation. *New York Times*, 15 May.

Guardian (2016). 'UK must leave European convention on human rights, says Theresa May'. Available at: www.theguardian.com/politics/2016/apr/25/uk-must-leave-european-convention-on-human-rights-theresa-may-eu-referendum (accessed 18 April 2018).

Hagan, J. M. (1994). *Deciding to be Legal*. Philadelphia, PA, Temple University Press.

(1998). 'Networks, gender and immigrant incorporation: Resources and constraints'. *American Sociological Review* **63**(1): 55–67

Hajjar, L. (2001). 'From the fight for legal rights to the promotion of human rights: Israeli and Palestinian cause lawyers in the trenches of globalization'. In *Cause Lawyering and the State in a Global Era*, eds A. Sarat and S. A. Scheingold. New York, Oxford University Press: 68–95.

Hall, J. and M. Weicherding (2014). 'The "broken word": Central Asia's unreliable diplomatic assurances'. In *Shelter from the Storm? The Asylum, Refugee and Extradition Situation Facing Activists from the Former Soviet Union in the CIS and Europe*, ed. A. Hug. London, Foreign Policy Centre: 23–26.

Halliday, S. and B. Morgan (2013). 'I fought the law and the law won? Legal consciousness and the critical imagination'. *Current Legal Problems* **66**(1): 1–32.

Heathershaw, J. and D. W. Montgomery (2014). *The Myth of Post-Soviet Muslim Radicalization in the Central Asian Republics*. London, Chatham House. Available at: www.chathamhouse.org/publication/myth-post-soviet-muslim-radicalization-central-asian-republics, accessed 22 May 2018.

Heimer, C. A. (2006). 'Conceiving children: How documents support case versus biographical analyses'. In *Documents: Artifacts of Modern Knowledge*, ed. A. Riles. Ann Arbor, MI, University of Michigan Press: 95–126.

Hein, J. and R. R. Beger (2001a). 'Immigrants, culture and American courts: A typology of legal strategies and issues in cases involving Vietnamese and Hmong litigants'. *Criminal Justice Review* **26**(1): 38–61.

(2001b). 'Legal adaptation among Vietnamese refugees in the United States: How international migrants litigate civil grievances during the resettlement process'. *International Migration Review* **35**(2): 420–448.

Hendley, K. (2011). 'Varieties of legal dualism: Making sense of the role of law in contemporary Russia'. *Wisconsin International Law Journal* **29**(2): 233–262.

(2017). *Everyday Law in Russia.* Ithaca, NY, Cornell University Press.
Hetherington, K. (2008). 'Populist transparency: The documentation of reality in rural Paraguay'. *Journal of Legal Anthropology* **1**(1): 45–69.
Hilbink, T. M. (2004). 'You know the type: Categories of cause lawyering'. *Law & Social Inquiry* **29**(3): 657–698.
Hirschfeld Davis, J. (2018). 'Trump calls some unauthorized immigrants 'animals' in rant'. *New York Times.* 15 May. Available at: www.nytimes.com/2018/05/16/us/politics/trump-undocumented-immigrants-animals.html (accessed 1 June 2018).
Hobson, J. (2012). *Body as Evidence: Mediating Race, Globalizing Gender.* New York, SUNY Press.
Hollifield, J., P. L. Martin and P. Orrenius (2014). *Controlling Immigration: A Global Perspective.* Stanford, CA, Stanford University Press.
Hoshi, B. (2014). 'Immigration Act 2014: Removals and nationality provisions'. Free Movement. Updates and commentary on immigration and asylum law. Available at: www.freemovement.org.uk/immigration-act-2014-removals-and-nationality-provisions (accessed 18 August 2014).
Hull, M. S. (2003). 'The file: Agency, authority, and autography in an Islamabad bureaucracy'. *Language & Communication* **23**(3): 287–314.
(2012). 'Documents and bureaucracy'. *Annual Review of Anthropology* **41**: 251–267.
Human Rights Watch (2009). *Are you Happy to Cheat Us? Exploitation of Migration Construction Workers in Russia.* New York, Human Rights Watch.
(2013). Uzbekistan: Forced labor widespread in cotton harvest. Available at: www.hrw.org/news/2013/01/25/uzbekistan-forced-labor-widespread-cotton-harvest, accessed 22 May 2018.
(2017). Central Asia: Make improving rights a priority. End torture; respect basic freedoms. Available at: www.hrw.org/news/2017/01/12/central-asia-make-improving-rights-priority, accessed 22 May 2018.
(2018). *Human Rights World Report: Kyrgyzstan.* Washington, DC: Human Rights Watch. Available at: www.hrw.org/world-report/2018/country-chapters/kyrgyzstan, accessed on 11 July 2018.
Hunter, R. (2006). 'Narratives of domestic violence'. *Sydney Law Review* **28**(4): 733–776.
International Commission of Jurists (2017). *Transnational Injustices: National Security Transfers and International Law.* Geneva, International Commission of Jurists.
Ivakhnyuk, I. (2009). *The Russian Migration Policy and Its Impact on Human Development: The Historical Perspective.* Geneva, United Nations Development Programme.
Ivakhniuk, I. (2014). 'Eurasian migration system: Origins, vectors and trends'. In International Summer School: International Migration in the Post-Soviet Space – Reflections, Patterns and Implications. Koc University, Istanbul, 29 June–11 July.
(2015). 'Russian legislation on labour migration from 2007 to 2015: Trends and effects'. In Russia's Migration Regulatory Regime: Migration Policy, Laws, Enforcement and Effects workshop, SOAS, London, 19 June.
Kahn, J. (2001). 'Russian compliance with Articles Five and Six of the European Convention of Human Rights as a barometer of legal reform and human rights in Russia'. *University of Michigan Journal of Law Reform* **35**(3): 641–694.

(2002). *Federalism, Democratization, and the Rule of Law in Russia*. Oxford, Oxford University Press.

(2004). 'Russia's "dictatorship of law" and the European Court of Human Rights'. *Review of Central and East European Law* **29**(1): 1–14.

(2006). 'In Search for the rule of law in Russia'. *Georgetown Journal of International Law* **37**: 353–409.

(2008). 'Vladimir Putin and the rule of law in Russia'. *Georgia Journal of International and Comparative Law* **36**(3): 511–558.

(2010). 'Adversarial principles and the case file in Russian criminal procedure'. In *Russia and the Council of Europe: Ten Years After*, eds K. Malfliet and S. Parmentier. Basingstoke, Palgrave Macmillan: 107–133

(2018a). 'After 20 years: Russia and the European Convention on Human Rights'. Lecture given at the Russian and Eurasian Studies Centre, St Anthony's College, 12 February.

(2018b). 'The Richelieu effect: The Khodorkovsky case and political interference with justice'. In *Sociology of Justice in Russia*, eds M. Kurkchiyan and A. Kubal. Cambridge, Cambridge University Press: 231–258.

Kanstroom, D. (2000). 'Deportation, social control, and punishment: Some thoughts about why hard laws make bad cases'. *Harvard Law Review* **113**: 1890–1935.

Karatani, R. (2005). 'How history separated refugee and migrant regimes: In search of their institutional origins'. *International Journal of Refugee Law* **17**(3): 517–541.

Kay, D. and R. Miles (1988). 'Refugees or migrant workers? The case of the European volunteer workers in Britain (1946–1951)'. *Journal of Refugee Studies* **1**(3–4): 214–236.

Kelly, T. (2006). 'Documented lives: Fear and the uncertainties of law during the second Palestinian intifada'. *Journal of the Royal Anthropological Institute* **12**(1): 89–107.

Kelsall, T. (2008). 'Going with the grain in African development?' *Development Policy Review* **26**(6): 627–655.

Kondakov, A. (2017). 'Queer coalitions: An examination of political resistance to the Russian migration law'. *Europe-Asia Studies* **69**(8): 1222–1241.

Kononenko, V. and A. Moshes (2011). *Russia as a Network State: What Works in Russia When State Institutions Do Not?* Basingstoke, Palgrave Macmillan.

Krishnan, J. K. (2006). 'Lawyering for a cause and experiences from abroad'. *California Law Review* **94**(2): 575–615.

Kubal, A. (2009). 'Why semi-legal? Polish post-2004 EU enlargement migrants in the United Kingdom'. *Journal of Immigration, Asylum and Nationality Law* **23**(2): 148–164.

(2012). *Socio-Legal Integration: Polish Post-2004 EU Enlargement Migrants in the UK*. Abingdon, Ashgate/Routledge.

(2013). 'Conceptualizing semi-legality in migration research'. *Law & Society Review* **47**(3): 555–587.

(2014). 'Struggles against subjection: Implications of criminalization of migration for migrants' everyday lives in Europe'. *Crime Law and Social Change* **62**(2): 91–111.

(2016a). 'Refugees or migrant workers? A case study of undocumented Syrians in Russia – L.M. and Others v Russia (ECtHR 14 March 2016)'. *Journal of Immigration Asylum and Nationality Law* **30**(4): 265–282.

(2016b). 'Spiral effect of the law: Migrants' experiences of the state law in Russia – a comparative perspective'. *International Journal of Law in Context* **12**(4): 453–468.

(2017). 'Entry bar as surreptitious deportation? Zapret na v'ezd in Russian immigration law and practice: A comparative perspective'. *Law & Social Inquiry* **42**(3): 744–768.

(2018). 'In search of justice: Migrants' experiences of appeal in Moscow City Court'. In *Sociology of Justice in Russia*, eds M. Kurkchiyan and A. Kubal. Cambridge, Cambridge University Press: 92–117.

Kudaibergenova, D. T. and B. Shin (2018). 'Authors and authoritarianism in Central Asia: Failed agency and nationalising authoritarianism in Uzbekistan and Kazakhstan'. *Asian Studies Review* **42**(2): 304–322.

Kurkchiyan, M. (2003). 'The illegitimacy of law in post-Soviet societies'. In *Law and Informal Practices: The Post-Communist Experience*, eds D. J. Galligan and M. Kurkchiyan. Oxford, Oxford University Press: 25–47.

(2005). 'Researching Russian legal culture'. In *Theory and Method in Socio-Legal Research*, eds R. Banakar and M. Travers. London, Hart: 259–278.

(2009). 'Russian legal culture: An analysis of adaptive response to an institutional transplant'. *Law & Social Inquiry* **34**(2): 337–364.

(2018). 'The professionalisation of law in the context of the Russian legal tradition'. In *Sociology of Justice in Russia*, eds M. Kurkchiyan and A. Kubal. Cambridge, Cambridge University Press: 12–39.

Kurchiyan, M. and A. Kubal (2018a). 'Administerial justice: Concluding remarks on the Russian legal tradition'. In *Sociology of Justice in Russia*, eds M. Kurkchiyan and A. Kubal. Cambridge, Cambridge University Press: 259–277.

(2018b). 'Introduction: Exploring the diversity of experiences of justice in Russia'. In *Sociology of Justice in Russia*, eds M. Kurkchiyan and A. Kubal. Cambridge, Cambridge University Press: 1–11.

Laclau, E. and C. Mouffe (1985). *Hegemony and Socialist Strategy: Toward a Radical Democratic Politics*. London, Verso.

Latour, B. (2009). *The Making of Law: An Ethnography of the Conseil d'Etat*. London, Polity.

Lavrysen, L. and C. Poppelwell-Scevak (2018). 'Poll: Best and Worst ECtHR Judgment of 2017'. *Strasbourg Observers*. Available at: https://strasbourgobservers.com/2018/01/11/poll-best-and-worst-ecthr-judgment-of-2017 (accessed 23 April 2018).

Ledeneva, A. (1998). *Russia's Economy of Favours: Blat, Networking and Informal Exchange*. Cambridge, Cambridge University Press.

(2006). 'Behind the facade: "Telephone justice" in Putin's Russia'. In *Dictatorship or Reform? The Rule of Law in Russia*, eds M. McAulley, A. Ledeneva and H. Barnes. London, Foreign Policy Centre: 24–36.

(2008). 'Telephone justice in Russia'. *Post-Soviet Affairs* **24**(4): 324–350.

(2013). *Can Russia Modernize? Sistema, Power Networks and Informal Governance*. Cambridge, Cambridge University Press.

Legomsky, S. H. (2007). 'The new path of immigration law: Asymmetric incorporation of criminal justice norms'. *Washington & Lee Law Review* **64**(2): 469–528.

Levi, R. and M. Valverde (2008). 'Studying law by association: Bruno Latour goes to the Conseil d'etat'. *Law & Social Inquiry* **33**(3): 805–825.

Levit, N. (2010). 'Reshaping the narrative debate'. *Seattle University Law Review* **34**: 751.

Lezaun, J. (2017). 'Actor–network theory'. In *Social Theory Now*, eds C. Benzecry, M. Krause and I. A. Reed. Chicago, Chicago University Press: 305–336.

Light, M. (2010). 'Policing migration in Soviet and post-Soviet Moscow'. *Post-Soviet Affairs* **26**(4): 275–313.

(2012). 'What does it mean to control migration? Soviet mobility policies in comparative perspective'. *Law & Social Inquiry* **37**(2): 395–429.

(2016). *Fragile Migration Rights: Freedom of Movement in Post-Soviet Russia*. London, Routledge.

Loescher, G. (2001). 'The UNHCR and world politics: State interests vs. institutional autonomy'. *International Migration Review* **35**(1): 33–56.

Long, K. (2013). 'When refugees stopped being migrants: Movement, labour and humanitarian protection'. *Migration Studies* **1**: 4–26.

Luban, D. (1988). *Lawyers and Justice: An Ethical Study*. Princeton, NJ, Princeton University Press.

Maier, A. (2014). *Tajik Migrants with Re-Entry Bans to the Russian Federation*. Dushanbe, International Organization for Migration (IOM) – Mission in the Republic of Tajikistan. Available at: https://auca.kg/uploads/Migration_Database/Publications/Tajik_Migrants_Report_15Jan.pdf (accessed 19 June 2018).

Malakhov, V. S. (2014). 'Russia as a new immigration country: Policy response and public debate'. *Europe-Asia Studies* **66**(7): 1062–1079.

Mälksoo, L. (2014). 'Concluding observations: Russia and European human-rights law – margins of the margin of appreciation'. In *Russia and European Human-Rights Law: The Rise of the Civilizational Argument*, ed. L. Mälksoo. Leiden, Martinus Nijhoff Publishers: 217–227.

Mälksoo, L. and W. Benedek, eds (2017). *Russia and the European Court of Human Rights: The Strasbourg Effect*. Cambridge, Cambridge University Press.

Mamouri, A. (2015). 'Explainer: What is Hizb ut-Tahrir?'. *The Conversation* Available at: http://theconversation.com/explainer-what-is-hizb-ut-tahrir-37963 (accessed 1 June 2018).

Marochkin, S. (2017). 'ECtHR and the Russian Constitutional Court: Duet or duel?' In *Russia and the European Court of Human Rights: The Strasbourg Effect*, eds L. Mälksoo and W. Benedek. Cambridge, Cambridge University Press: 93–124.

Massaro, T. M. (1989). 'Empathy, legal storytelling, and the rule of law: New words, old wounds?' *Michigan Law Review* **87**(8): 2099–2127.

Matsuda, M. J. (1989). 'Public response to racist speech: Considering the victim's story'. *Michigan Law Review* **87**(8): 2320–2381.

Matusevich, Y. (2018) 'Russia's catch-22 asylum system'. *Refugees Deeply*. Available at: www.newsdeeply.com/refugees/community/2018/01/29/russias-catch-22-asylum-system (accessed 2 June 2018).

McAulley, M., A. Ledeneva and H. Barnes (2006). *Dictatorship or Reform? The Rule of Law in Russia*. London, Foreign Policy Centre.

McCall, L. (2005). 'The complexity of intersectionality'. *Signs* **30**(3): 1771–1800.

(2018). 'Decision-making in the Russian criminal justice system: Investigators, procurators, judges and human trafficking cases'. In *Sociology of Justice in Russia*, eds M. Kurkchiyan and A. Kubal. Cambridge, Cambridge University Press: 205–230.

McEvoy, K. (2017). 'Lawyering, professionalism & struggle in conflict & transition'. Annual Socio-Legal Lecture, University of Oxford, 4 May.

Menjívar, C. (2000). *Fragmented Ties: Salvadoran Immigrant Networks in America*. Berkeley, CA, University of California Press.

(2006). 'Liminal legality: Salvadoran and Guatemalan immigrants' lives in the United States'. *American Journal of Sociology* **111**(4): 999–1037.

(2014a). 'Immigration law beyond borders: Externalizing and internalizing border controls in an era of securitization'. *Annual Review of Law and Social Science* **10**: 353–369.

(2014b). 'The "poli-migra": Multilayered legislation, enforcement practices, and what we can learn about and from today's approaches'. *American Behavioral Scientist* **58**(13): 1805–1819.

Menjívar, C. and L. J. Abrego (2012). 'Legal violence: Immigration law and the lives of Central American immigrants'. *American Journal of Sociology* **117**(5): 1380–1421.

Menkel-Meadow, C. (1998). 'The causes of cause lawyering: Toward an understanding of the motivation and commitment of social justice lawyers'. In *Cause Lawyering: Political Commitments and Professional Responsibilities*, eds A. Sarat and S. A. Scheingold. New York, Oxford University Press: 31–68.

(2002). 'When litigation is not the only way: Consensus building and mediation as public interest lawyering'. *Washington University Journal of Law & Policy* **10**: 37.

Messina, C. and O. Shamshur (1997). 'Regional conference to address the problems of refugees, displaced persons, other forms of involuntary displacement and returnees in the countries of the Commonwealth of Independent States and relevant neighboring states'. *The International Migration Review* **31**(2): 461–467.

Morawetz, N. (1998). 'Rethinking retroactive deportation laws and the due process clause'. *New York University Law Review* **73**: 97–161.

Munger, F. W. (2015). 'Trafficking in law: Cause lawyer, bureaucratic state and rights of human trafficking victims in Thailand'. *Asian Studies Review* **39**(1): 69–87.

Natapoff, A. (2005). 'Speechless: The silencing of criminal defendants'. *New York University Law Review* **80**: 1449–1504.

Nelken, D. (2004). 'Comparing legal cultures'. In *The Blackwell Companion to Law and Society*, ed. A. Sarat. London, Blackwell.

Nikiforova, E. and O. Brednikova (2018). 'On labor migration to Russia: Central Asian migrants and migrant families in the matrix of Russia's bordering policies'. *Political Geography* **66**: 142–150.

O'Barr, W. M. and J. M. Conley (1985). 'Litigant satisfaction versus legal adequacy in small claims court narratives'. *Law and Society Review* **19**(4): 661–702.

Open Society Institute (2006). *Ethnic Profiling in the Moscow Metro*. New York, Open Society Institute.

Ortiz Maddali, A. (2011). 'Padilla v Kentucky: A new chapter in Supreme Court jurisprudence on whether deportation constitutes punishment for lawful permanent residents?' *American University Law Review* **61**(1): 1–58.

Pastukhov, V. (2002). 'Law under administrative pressure in post-Soviet Russia'. *East European Constitutional Review* **11**(3): 66–74.

Pels, D., K. Hetherington and F. Vandenberghe (2002). 'The status of the object'. *Theory, Culture & Society* **19**(5–6): 1–21.

Perelman, J. (2005). 'The way ahead-access-to-justice, public interest lawyering, and the right to legal aid in South Africa: The Nkuzi case'. *Stanford Journal of International Law* **41**: 357.

Permanent Mission of the Russian Federation to the United Nations (2015). 'Statement by the Representative of the Russian Federation at the 13th Coordination Meeting on International Migration', 12 February. Available at: http://russiaun.ru/en/news/ga_intmgr (accessed 1 June 2018).

Pilkington, H. (1998). *Migration, Displacement, and Identity in Post-Soviet Russia*. London, Routledge.

Polyanina, M. (2015). 'The labour rights of migrant workers in Russia'. In Russia's Migration Regulatory Regime: Migration Policy, Laws, Enforcement and Effects workshop, SOAS, London, 19 June.

Pomorski, S. (1998). 'Reflections on the first criminal code of post-Communist Russia'. *American Journal of Comparative Law* **46**: 375–393.

Porter, A. (1998). 'Norris, Schmidt, Green, Harris, Higginbotham, and Associates: The sociolegal import of Philadelphia cause lawyers'. In *Cause Lawyering: Political Commitments and Professional Responsibilities*, eds A. Sarat and S. A. Scheingold. New York, Oxford University Press: 151–180.

Portes, A. and R. Bach (1985). *Latin Journey: Cuban and Mexican Immigrants in the United States*. Berkeley, CA, University of California Press.

Portes, A. and M. Zhou (1993). *The New Second Generation: Segmented Assimilation and Its Variants*. Berkeley, CA, University of California Press.

Pound, R. (1910). 'Law in books and law in action'. *American Law Review* **44**: 12–36.

Preclik, P. (2014). 'Culture re-introduced: Contestation of human rights in contemporary Russia'. In *Russia and European Human-Rights Law: The Rise of the Civilizational Argument*, eds L. Mälksoo. Leiden, Martinus Nijhoff Publishers: 31–89.

Press Unit ECtHR (2017). 'Prisoners' right to vote'. Factsheet of the European Court of Human Rights. Available at: www.echr.coe.int/Documents/FS_Prisoners_vote_ENG.pdf (accessed 5 April 2018): 1–6.

(2018). 'Interim measures'. Factsheet of the European Court of Human Rights. Available at: www.echr.coe.int/Documents/FS_Interim_measures_ENG.pdf (accessed 5 April 2018).

Putin, V. (2005). 'Introductory remarks at Security Council Meeting on immigration policy on 17 March 2005'. Available at: http://en.kremlin.ru/events/president/transcripts/22861 (accessed 11 June 2018).

Rainsford, S. (2015). 'Syrian migrant family in limbo at Moscow's Sheremetyevo airport'. *BBC News*. Available at: www.bbc.co.uk/news/world-europe-34657582 (accessed 1 March 2018).

Rasanayagam, J. (2014). 'The politics of culture and the space for Islam: Soviet and post-Soviet imaginaries in Uzbekistan'. *Central Asian Survey* **33**(1): 1–14.

Reed, A. (2006). 'Documents unfolding'. In *Documents: Artifacts of Modern Knowledge*, ed. A. Riles. Ann Arbor, MI, University of Michigan Press: 158–177.

Reeves, M. (2013). 'Clean fake: Authenticating documents and persons in migrant Moscow'. *American Ethnologist* **40**(3): 508–524.

(2015). 'Living from the nerves: Deportability, indeterminacy, and the "feel of law" in migrant Moscow'. *Social Analysis* **59**(4): 119–136.

(2016). 'The black list: On infrastructural indeterminacy and its reverberations'. In *Infrastructures and Social Complexity: A Companion*, eds P. Harvey, C. P. Jensen and A. A. Morita. Oxford, Routledge: 296–308.

Rhodes, L. A. (2004). *Total Confinement: Madness and Reason in the Maximum Security Prison*. Berkeley, CA, University of California Press.

Riazantsev, S. V. (2007). *Trudovaya migratsiya v stranakh SNG i Baltt: tendentsii, posledstviya, regulirovaniye* [Labor migration in the CIS and Baltic States: Trends, consequences, regulation]. Moscow, Formula Prava (in Russian).

Riles, A. (1999). 'Wigmore's treasure box: Comparative law in the era of information'. *Harvard International Law Journal* **40**(1): 221–284.

(2000). *The Network Inside Out*. Ann Arbor, MI, University of Michigan Press.

Riva, S. (2018). 'Encounters of US state violence at the border: Separation, confinement, and punishment of Central American asylum-seeking nuclear families'. Border Criminologies Blog. Available at: www.law.ox.ac.uk/research-subject-groups/centre-criminology/centreborder-criminologies/blog/2018/05/encounters-us (accessed 9 July 2018).

Roberts, D. (2017). 'Donald Trump and the rise of tribal epistemology'. *Vox*. Available at: www.vox.com/policy-and-politics/2017/3/22/14762030/donald-trump-tribal-epistemology (accessed 11 June 2018).

Romero, V. (2010). 'Decriminializing border crossings'. *Fordham Urban Law Review* **38**: 273–302.

Rosstat – Federal State Statistics Service (2018). *Social and Economic Situation of Russia*. Moscow, Rosstat [Federal'na sluzhba gosudarstvennoy statistiki]. Available at: www.gks.ru/wps/wcm/connect/rosstat_main/rosstat/ru/statistics/publications/catalog/doc_1140086922125 (accessed 1 June 2018).

Round, J. and I. Kuznetsova (2016). 'Necropolitics and the migrant as a political subject of disgust: The precarious everyday of Russia's labour migrants'. *Critical Sociology*. DOI: 10.1177/0896920516645934.

Ruget, V. and B. Usmanalieva (2008). 'Citizenship, migration and loyalty towards the state: A case study of the Kyrgyzstani migrants working in Russia and Kazakhstan'. *Central Asian Survey* **27**(2): 129–141.

(2010). 'How much is citizenship worth? The case of Kyrgyzstani migrants in Kazakhstan and Russia'. *Citizenship Studies* **14**(4): 445–459.

Sakwa, R. (2009). *The Quality of Freedom: Khodorkovsky, Putin, and the Yukos Affair*. Oxford, Oxford University Press.

(2010). 'The dual state in Russia'. *Post-Soviet Affairs* **26**(3): 185–206.

Salcido, O. and C. Menjívar (2012). 'Gendered paths to legal citizenship: The case of Latin-American immigrants in Phoenix, Arizona'. *Law & Society Review* **46**(2): 335–368.

Sarat, A. (1998). 'Between (the presence of) violence and (the possibility of) justice: Lawyering against capital punishment'. In *Cause Lawyering: Political Commitments and Professional Responsibilities*, eds A. Sarat and S. A. Scheingold. New York, Oxford University Press: 317–346.

Sarat, A. and T. R. Kearns (1995). *Law in Everyday Life*. Ann Arbor, MI, University of Michigan Press.

Sarat, A. and S. A. Scheingold (1998a). 'Cause lawyering and the reproduction of professional authority: An introduction'. In *Cause Lawyering: Political*

Commitments and Professional Responsibilities, eds A. Sarat and S. A. Scheingold. New York, Oxford University Press: 3–28.

eds (1998b). *Cause Lawyering: Political Commitments and Professional Responsibilities*. New York, Oxford University Press.

eds (2001a). *Cause Lawyering and the State in a Global Era*. New York, Oxford University Press.

(2001b). 'State transformation, globalisation, and the possibilities of cause lawyering: An introduction'. In *Cause Lawyering and the State in a Global Era*, eds A. Sarat and S. A. Scheingold. New York, Oxford University Press: 3–31.

(2006). *Cause Lawyers and Social Movements*. Stanford, CA, Stanford University Press.

Sarat, A., L. Douglas and M. M. Umphrey, eds (2011a). *Law as Punishment/Law as Regulation*. Stanford, CA, Stanford University Press.

Sarat, A., L. Douglas and M. M. Umphrey (2011b). 'On the blurred boundary between regulation and punishment'. In *Law as Punishment/Law as Regulation*, eds A. Sarat, L. Douglas and M. M. Umphrey. Stanford, CA, Stanford University Press: 2–17.

Sarkorova, A. (2015). 'Zarina Yunusova: "I will never forgive what was done to me"'. *BBC Russian Service Dushanbe*. Translated by 'The Russian Reader'. Available at: https://therussianreader.com/tag/umarali-nazarov (accessed 9 July 2018).

Sayeed, S. (2014). 'Appeals provisions of the Immigration Act 2014'. Free Movement. Updates and commentary on immigration and asylum law. Available at: www.freemovement.org.uk/appeals-provisions-of-the-immigration-act-2014 (accessed 19 August 2014).

Scheffer, T. (2007). 'File work, legal care, and professional habitus: An ethnographic reflection on different styles of advocacy'. *International Journal of the Legal Profession* **14**(1): 57–80.

Scheingold, S. (2001). 'Cause lawyering and democracy in transnational perspective'. In *Cause Lawyering and the State in a Global Era*, eds A. Sarat and S. A. Scheingold. New York, Oxford University Press: 382–405.

Scheingold, S. and A. Bloom (1998). 'Transgressive cause lawyering: Practice sites and the politicization of the professional'. *International Journal of the Legal Profession* **5**(2–3): 209–253.

Scheingold, S. and A. Sarat (2004). *Something to Believe In: Politics, Professionalism and Cause Lawyering*. Stanford, CA, Stanford University Press.

Schenk, C. (2018). *Why Control Immigration? Strategic Uses of Migration Management in Russia*. Toronto, University of Toronto Press.

Scheppele, K. L. (1989). 'Foreword: Telling stories'. *Michigan Law Review* **87**(8): 2073–2098.

Schuck, P. (1984). 'The transformation of American immigration law'. *Columbia Law Review* **84**(1): 25–27.

Scott, J. (1985). *Weapons of the Weak*. New Haven, CT, Yale University Press.

Serov, V. (2003), *Entsiklopedicheskiy slovar' krylatykh slov i vyrazheniy*. Moscow, Lokid Press. Available at: https://dic.academic.ru/dic.nsf/dic_wingwords/141/%D0%91%D0%B5%D0%B7 (accessed 16 October 2017).

Shamir, R. and S. Chinski (1998). 'Destruction of houses and construction of a cause: Lawyers and Bedouins in Israeli courts'. In *Cause Lawyering: Political*

Commitments and Professional Responsibilities, eds A. Sarat and S. A. Scheingold. New York, Oxford University Press: 227–260.

Shevel, O. (2011a). *Migration, Refugee Policy, and State Building in Postcommunist Europe*. New York, Cambridge University Press.

(2011b). 'The Russian Federation'. In *Migration, Refugee Policy, and State Building in Postcommunist Europe*. Cambridge, Cambridge University Press: 73–133.

Siegelbaum, L. H. and L. P. Moch (2014). *Broad is my Native Land: Repertoires and Regimes of Migration in Russia's Twentieth Century*. Ithaca, NY, Cornell University Press.

Sigona, N. (2012). '"I've got too much baggage": The impact of legal status on the social worlds of irregular migrants'. *Social Anthropology/Anthropologie Sociale* **20**(1): 50–65.

Silbey, S. (2010). 'J. Locke, op. cit.: Invocations of law on snowy streets'. *Journal of Comparative Law* **5**(2): 66.

Silvestri, A. and O. Tchernishova (1998). 'The legal framework regulating asylum in the Russian Federation'. *International Journal of Refugee Law* **10**(1–2): 184–198.

Simmel, G. (1994). 'Bridge and door'. *Theory, Culture & Society* **11**(1): 5–10.

Smith, G. B. (1996). *Reforming the Russian Legal System*. Cambridge, Cambridge University Press.

Solomon, P. (2005). 'Informal practices in Russian governance: Courts and law enforcement'. In Europe - Our Common Home? ICEEES VII World Congress, Berlin, 29–31 October.

Starzhenetskii, V. (2014). 'Assessing human rights in Russia: Not to miss the forest for the trees – a response to Preclik, Schönfeld and Hallinan'. In *Russia and European Human-Rights Law: The Rise of the Civilizational Argument*, ed. L. Mälksoo. Leiden, Martinus Nijhoff Publishers: 207–215.

Steiker, C. (1997). 'Punishment and procedure: Punishment theory and the criminal-civil procedural divide'. *Georgetown Law Journal* **85**(4): 775–819.

Sterett, S. (1998). 'Caring about individual cases: Immigration lawyering in Britain'. In *Cause Lawyering: Political Commitments and Professional Responsibilities*, eds A. Sarat and S. A. Scheingold. New York, Oxford University Press: 31–68.

Stumpf, J. (2006). 'The crimmigration crisis: Immigrants, crime, and sovereign power'. *American University Law Review* **56**(2): 367–419.

Tam, W. (2010). 'Political transition and the rise of cause lawyering: The case of Hong Kong'. *Law & Social Inquiry* **35**(3): 663–687.

Taylor, G. H. (2007). 'Derrick Bell's narratives as parables'. *New York University Review of Law and Social Change* **31**: 255–271.

Ticktin, M. (2006). 'Where ethics and politics meet'. *American Ethnologist* **33**(1): 33–49.

Transparency International (2007). *Global Corruption Report 2007: Corruption in Judicial Systems*. New York, Cambridge University Press.

Travers, M. (1999). *British Immigration Courts: A Study of Law and Politics*. Bristol, The Policy Press.

Trenina, D. (2014). 'Extradition and expulsion of persons from Russia to countries of Central Asia'. In *Shelter from the Storm? The Asylum, Refugee and Extradition Situation Facing Activists from the Former Soviet Union in the CIS and Europe*, ed. A. Hug. London, Foreign Policy Centre: 17–22.

Trenina, D. and K. Zharinov (2017). 'From Russia to torture: Lack of or deficient remedies against prohibited treatment in extradition and other types of removal proceedings'. In *Closing the Door: The Challenge Facing Activists from the Former Soviet Union Seeking Asylum or Refuge*, ed. A. Hug. London, Foreign Policy Centre: 38–42.

Trochev, A. (2012). 'Suing Russia at Home'. *Problems of Post-Communism* **59**(5): 18–34.

Troitskiy, K. (2017). '39 persons granted refugee status in 2016: Russian anti-records and why Malta is stronger than Russia?' [39 priznannykh bezhentsev v 2016 godu. Rossiyskiye antirekordy i pochemu Mal'ta sil'neye Rossii]. Civic Assistance Committee. Available at: https://refugee.ru/publications/39-priznannyh-bezhentsev-v-2016-godu-rossijskie-antirekordy-i-pochemu-malta-silnee-rossii (accessed 1 June 2018).

(2018). 'The degradation of the institution of asylum in Russia and the new anti-record of migration services: Statistics for 2017 and brief analysis' [Degradatsiya instituta ubezhishcha v Rossii i novyye antirekordy migratsionnykh sluzhb: statistika za 2017 god i yeye kratkaya analitika]. Civic Assistance Committee. Available at: https://refugee.ru/publications/degradatsiya-instituta-ubezhishha-v-rossii (accessed 20 June 2018).

Trubek, L. and E. M. Kransberger (1998). 'Critical lawyers: Social justice and the structures of private practice'. In *Cause Lawyering: Political Commitments and Professional Responsibilities*, eds A. Sarat and S. A. Scheingold. New York, Oxford University Press: 201–226.

Tseytlina, O. (2018). 'The problem of restricting the freedom of foreign citizens and stateless persons in the light of the decisions of the European Court of Human Rights and the Constitutional Court of the Russian Federation'. In *Stateless Persons in the Temporary Detention Centers for Foreign Nationals of the Ministry of the Interior: Statistics, Legislation, Law Enforcement*, eds E. Burtina and O. Tseytlina. Moscow, Human Rights Centre Memorial: 23–43.

Tuitt, P. (2005). 'Legal practice and modes of dying: Bruno Latour, technology and the critical legal instance'. *Law and Critique* **16**(1): 113–129.

United Nations Population Divison (UNPD) (2017). 'International migration stock 2017'. Available at: www.un.org/en/development/desa/population/migration/data/estimates2/estimates17.shtml (accessed on 6 November 2018).

United Nations High Commissioner for Refugees (UNHCR) (no date). 'UNHCR's mandate for refugees, stateless persons and IDPs.' In *UNHCR Emergency Handbook*. Geneva: UNHCR. Available at: https://emergency.unhcr.org/entry/113370/unhcrs-mandate-for-refugees-stateless-persons-and-idps (accessed 1 November 2018).

United Nations Human Rights Council (UNHRC) (2008). 'Promotion and protection of all human rights, civil, political, economic, social and cultural rights, including the right to development: Report of the Special Rapporteur on the Human Rights of Migrants. Addendum mission to the United States of America. J. Bustamante'. United Nations Human Rights Council.

Urinboyev, R. (2016). 'Migration and transnational informality in post-Soviet societies: Ethnographic study of po rukam ("handshake") experiences of Uzbek migrant workers in Moscow'. In *Migrant Workers in Russia*, eds A.-L. Heusala and K. Aitamurto. London, Routledge.

Vakulenko, E. and R. Leukhin (2017). 'Wage discrimination against foreign workers in Russia'. *Russian Journal of Economics* **3**(1): 83–100.

van der Woude, M. (2016). 'Starting to decipher Dutch border practices'. Border Criminologies Blog. Available at: www.law.ox.ac.uk/research-subject-groups/centre-criminology/centreborder-criminologies/blog/2016/02/starting-decipher (accessed 12 June 2018).

Van Hear, N. (2004). 'I went as far as my money would take me: Conflict, forced migration and class'. COMPAS Working Paper Series WP-04-06.

Van Hear, N., R. Brubaker and T. Bessa (2009). 'Managing mobility for human development: The growing salience of mixed migration'. Human Development Research Paper 2009/20.

van Oorschot, I. (2014). 'Seeing the case clearly: File-work, material mediation, and visualizing practices in a Dutch criminal court'. *Symbolic Interaction* **37**(4): 439–457.

van Oorschot, I. and W. Schinkel (2015). 'The legal case file as border object: On self-reference and other-reference in criminal law'. *Journal of Law and Society* **42**(4): 499–527.

Vismann, C. (2008). *Files: Law and Media Technology*. Stanford, CA, Stanford University Press.

Woolgar, S. (2002). 'After word? On some dynamics of duality interrogation'. *Theory, Culture & Society* **19**(5–6): 261–270.

World Bank (2016). 'Personal remittances, received (% of GDP)'. In *World Bank Staff Estimates Based on IMF Balance of Payments Data, and World Bank and OECD GDP Estimates*. New York, World Bank. Available at: https://data.worldbank.org/indicator/BX.TRF.PWKR.DT.GD.ZS?end=2016&start=1970 (accessed 14 June 2018).

Yeo, C. (2014). 'Serious and irreversible harm and deportation appeals'. Free Movement. Updates and commentary on immigration and asylum law. Available at: www.freemovement.org.uk/serious-and-irreversible-harm-and-deportation-appeals (accessed 18 August 2014).

Yudina, T. N. (2005). 'Labour migration into Russia: The response of state and society'. *Current Sociology* **53**(4): 583–606.

Yusupova, G. and E. Ponarin (2016). 'Social remittances in religion'. *Problems of Post-Communism* **65**: 188–200.

Index